THE FIRST HENRY FORD

The MIT Press   Cambridge, Massachusetts, and London, England

Anne Jardim

THE FIRST HENRY FORD:
A STUDY IN PERSONALITY AND
BUSINESS LEADERSHIP

ISBN 0 262 10008 8 (hardcover)

Library of Congress catalog card number: 74–122259

CONTENTS

Industrial management as an object of research is especially sensitive to interpretations based upon particular views of man and society. As a consequence, there can be as many histories of industrialization, and theories of industrial development, as there are serious investigators. Each brings a perspective uniquely suited to how he sees history—as a flow of forces to which man responds passively, or as a set of opportunities to be defined and shaped by gifted men.

Dr. Anne Jardim in her study of Henry Ford, the founder of the Ford Motor Company, selects the man as her object of study. That she selected one of the great innovators in industrial management and consumerism is perfectly clear. That she selected a man whose talents and personal conflicts coexisted is also clear to anyone familiar with the events in Henry Ford's life and work. He has had a number of biographers among historians and work associates who leave no doubt that Henry Ford embodied more than one human being's share of strength and weakness, love and hate, sophistication and naïveté. Dr. Jardim shows very convincingly that Ford's strengths centered in his attachment to inanimate objects like the automobile and the assembly line, while his weaknesses were in his attachments to people. And, when Ford could no longer separate the world of products and techniques on the one hand and people on the other, he and his company began the long decline which put its survival into doubt.

Dr. Jardim while clarifying Ford's strengths and weaknesses as a leader, his tendency to polarize what he could love and hate, and the way he ultimately distorted reality, goes well beyond narrative biography into analysis and explanation. She poses the question "why" and in doing so mobilizes the methods and theories of psychoanalysis as applied to biography. The particular question she examines is why Ford changed *after* his great success as an industrialist. Dr. Jardim rejects the notion that there must be two psychologies, one to explain success and the other failure. In rejecting the two theories approach, Dr. Jardim then traces how Ford's work patterns and character structure during his productive and innovative years served defensive as well as adaptive functions in his personality. Ford had no fewer personal conflicts during his productive years than in the years of his decline. It is just that he managed the conflicts differently during these two periods of his career. Dr. Jardim interprets Ford's innovations leading to the success of the Model T in part as one man's unique version of the search for the father. Why Ford sought restitution and restoration of the father through the automobile cannot be explained. But the psychological significance of this search and the symbolic connections between work and the object world can be interpreted and Dr. Jardim does just that.

The end result of her interpretation is to cast into a new light the nature of innovation. Her contribution in this regard is very important, particularly in an age where people are willing to discard and devalue the "great man" theory of leadership and innovation. One of the reasons for this disenchantment with the "great man" theory is the fear of the harm that genius can do—harm that sometimes outweighs the benefits to society. Unless one is willing to be naive about the human being, we have to accept the dual nature of man—how he can love and hate, build and destroy. We are then faced with the problem of the transformation of motives, of their refinement and adaptation. The psychological study of great men, such as Henry Ford, provides the material out of which understanding can come.

It is fair to ask what ends this understanding serves. In its broadest conception, psychological biography can contribute to a redefinition of rationality. Psychoanalysis, despite the misunderstandings about it, takes the side of the ego and concerns itself with human rationality. This conception stands as a challenge to the mechanistic rationality of economic theory, or classical management theory and, on the other side, as a challenge to the various secular religions based upon the free expression of impulse. In its concern for rationality, psychoanalysis centers the problem in man, rather than exclusively in society. Dr. Jardim traces the struggle for rationality in Henry Ford under conditions where he had to live with the way life continually fell short of his dreams and wishes. The end result of this study is to present one great industrialist as a human being whose personal battle with the conflicting forces in his nature had a direct bearing on how he affected society.

Dr. Jardim conducted this study under the auspices of the Research Program in Applied Psychoanalysis, which I direct, at the Harvard Business School. The financial support came from the Division of Research of the Harvard Business School and we are grateful to Dean Emeritus George Pierce Baker and the former Director of Research, Professor Bertrand Fox for their interest.

The primary research for this study was undertaken at the Ford Archives in Dearborn, Michigan. Mr. H. E. Edmunds, the Director of the Archives, and Mr. Winthrop Sears, the Assistant Director were very helpful in making available to Dr. Jardim the materials on file in the Archives. We are grateful for their cooperation.

Finally, a special word of gratitude is in order to the Group for Applied Psychoanalysis in Cambridge, Massachusetts and to Professors Bruce Mazlish, C. Roland Christensen, and the late Dr. Joseph J. Michaels, all of whom were extremely helpful in guiding Dr. Jardim's research.

Abraham Zaleznik

Cahners-Rabb Professor of Social Psychology of Management
Harvard University
Affiliate Member
Boston Psychoanalytic Society and Institute

Cambridge, Massachusetts
March 1970

In the year 1892 a horse and carriage could cover the distance from Salem to Lynn in Massachusetts in just under two hours. On a bicycle, a vigorous young man might hope in fair weather to make the journey in considerably less than one. But . . . what if the bicycle were powered by an engine? Or even better the horse cut loose from the carriage and a motor installed to propel the wheels? "Distance would be halved. Towns would become near together. More people would intermingle. It would profoundly influence the course of civilization itself."[1]

To Hiram Percy Maxim as he pedaled along the lonely road to Lynn late one summer's night dreaming of means other than his tired legs to move him, a revolution in transportation seemed at hand.

Maxim was then in his early twenties, and he was employed as superintendent of the American Projectile Company at Lynn. His father had invented the Maxim gun, and Maxim's vocation, as he recorded in his reminiscences, was simply making projectiles. His avocation soon became one that uncounted others were feverishly pursuing: the development of the horseless carriage. He wrote in 1937:

As I look back, I am amazed that so many of us began work so nearly at the same time, and without the slightest notion that others were working on the problem. In 1892 when I began my work on a mechanical road vehicle, I suppose there were fifty persons in the United States working on the same idea.

Why did so many different and widely separated persons have the same thoughts at about the same time? In my case the idea came from looking down and contemplating the mechanism of my legs and the bicycle cranks while riding along a lonely road in the middle of the night. I suppose not another one of us pioneers had his original inspiration come to him as mine came to me. Probably every one of us acquired his original conception from an entirely different set of circumstances resulting from accidental conditions.

It has always been my belief that we all began to work on a gasoline-engine-propelled vehicle at about the same time because it had become apparent that civilization was ready for the mechanical vehicle. It was natural that this idea should strike many of us at about the same time. It has been the habit to give the gasoline engine all the credit for bringing the automobile as we term the mechanical road vehicle today. In my opinion this is a wrong explanation. We have had the steam engine for over a century. We could have built steam vehicles in 1880, or indeed in 1870. But we did not. We waited until 1895.

The reason why we did not build mechanical road vehicles before this, in my opinion, was because the bicycle had not yet come in numbers and had not directed men's minds to the possibilities of independent, long-distance travel over the ordinary highway.

We thought the railroad was good enough. The bicycle created a new demand which it was beyond the ability of the railroad to supply. Then it came about that the bicycle could not satisfy the demand which it had created. A mechanically propelled vehicle was wanted instead of a foot-propelled one, and we now know that the automobile was the answer.[2]

But if a mechanically propelled vehicle was wanted and the automobile was the answer, it was by no means clear to the experimenters of the 1890s how the vehicle should be assembled or what method of propulsion they should use. As late as 1902 there were 106 builders of steam cars and 40 electric manufacturers, as against 99 builders using the gasoline-driven internal combustion engine.[3] "Three groups there were," wrote McManus and Beasley, "each located at the point of a triangle and sniping along the boundaries of its three sides. In one corner, the steam manufacturers; in another, the exponents of electricity; in the third the gasoline disciples."[4] In this heady atmosphere of technological uncertainty it appeared that any man with mechanical aptitude could build a car. The main thing was to get it to run—on the road—and until this was done there was little to be gained from academic disputes over which means of propulsion was the best.

For Maxim, the decision to use a gasoline engine was

reached almost lightheartedly. He neither knew whether this was the engine he wanted nor indeed was there any way in which he could achieve certainty: he had still to discover how to vaporize and ignite the fuel. His first experiments were severely practical. In a brass cartridge case two and one-half inches in diameter and twelve inches deep he let fall a single drop of gasoline; he plugged the case with a wooden stopper, shook it to mix the gas with air, unplugged it, and tossed a lighted match into the open end.

The explosion when it came was terrifying: flame shot from the cartridge case and the match hurtled towards the ceiling. "It was evident," Maxim wrote, "that there was about a thousand times more kick in a drop of gasoline than I had pictured in my wildest flights of imagination."[5]

Working in a world without carburetors, spark plugs, or magnetos, Maxim painfully taught himself how to build and operate a gasoline-driven engine. That done he then had to devise a vehicle which would carry it, and he settled at first for a tricycle on which he nearly lost his life on his first attempt to drive it downhill. But, on the strength of this unpredictable vehicle, he was employed by the Pope Manufacturing Company at Hartford, Connecticut, in 1895.

The Pope Company was at that time the largest and best-equipped bicycle manufacturer in the country, and in employing Maxim they were attempting to keep in step with the development of the automobile. Yet, despite this, and advanced as their production methods were, these leaders in the field of horseless transportation had little conception of the real function their product served or of the direction in which the market was moving. The success of the bicycle, Maxim was initially told by a Pope manager, "was due to the physical exercise involved in it. If a motor were put on, it would eliminate the one thing that made the bicycle popular."[6]

The company in these circumstances attempted to touch as many bases as it could. Maxim was set to work on both gasoline and electrically driven vehicles. Gradually he became committed to the gasoline motor, but it was a commitment that came to be shared less and less by the company's management.

The electric car, because of its cleanliness and smooth, quiet operation, strongly appealed to George H. Day, vice-president of the Pope Company. By 1898 Maxim was being urged to build a gasoline car that was "positively not . . . complicated and . . . as nearly like the electric in operating method as was humanly possible."[7]

The sight of a machine's gears swimming in thick, black oil had repelled Mr. Day, and his first ride in an automobile had shaken him to the point of speechlessness.[8] George H. Day, Maxim wrote later, "was struggling to allocate in the general scheme of things a place for a vehicle such as this throbbing, noisy, complicated, greasy accumulation of mechanical odds and ends."[9]

In the six years before 1901, Maxim developed a series of improved gasoline cars, while the management of the Pope Manufacturing Company moved more and more firmly behind the electrics. And, in a phrase of perhaps special poignancy, in doing so they backed the wrong horse.

Maxim's reminiscences stand out as the most vivid description of the enormous task faced by the pioneer automobile builders. "Everything had to be created," he wrote. "There were no suitable bearings, suitable wheels, tires, batteries, battery-handling equipment, battery-charging equipment, gasoline engines, carburetors, spark plugs, brakes, or steering gears. Every detail of a motor vehicle had to be laboriously thought out and then worked out."[10] Despite this, in Maxim's case the job was easier than that confronting many other pioneers. Maxim was backed by the resources of a great company which in the course of developing the bicycle had branched out into metallurgical research and quantity methods of precision manufacture. The machining of bevel gear units at the Pope Manufacturing Company, for example, could be carried to tolerances of 1/2000 of an inch;[11] in contrast, Henry Ford as late as 1903 had to be content with tolerances of 1/64 of an inch.[12]

As if the problems of design, tooling, and materials were not enough, added to them were the complexities of financing, manufacturing, and selling a product whose novelty was so great that in an attempt to disguise it a whipsocket was placed in the dash.[13] And where even this proved insufficient to allay the foreboding with which the cars were regarded, people seriously considered following the example of Uriah Smith of Battle Creek, Michigan, who fixed to the dashboard, like a hunter's trophy, the harnessed head, neck, and shoulders of a wooden horse.[14]

The apathy and often outright antipathy of much of the public drew sustenance from every weakness of the early cars, and the noisy, uncomfortable, unreliable gasoline cars reaped the largest share of opprobrium. People seemed unable to separate the horse from transportation, and in a classic example of the fruitlessness of circular reasoning, the car builders themselves contributed to this condition. Their attempts at disguise went much further than the whipsocket. The design of the horseless carriage hewed so close to that of the horse and carriage that the early automobiles had four buggy wheels, a buggy dash, and buggy springs ". . . the 1898 automobile was nothing but a complete self-propelled buggy—just because people wanted buggies and because builders knew how to make them."[15]

The problems this created were insuperable: steel-tired wheels were hopelessly unsatisfactory; the engine placed beneath and to the rear to preserve the time-honored lines of the horse and carriage was inaccessible to repair, and repair was endlessly, monotonously necessary. The builders, striving to achieve two mutually incompatible ends at once, were producing "buggies" which were radical breaches of existing custom, and at the same time were desperately seeking to win the public's acceptance by invoking the trappings of a tradition which so impaired the cars' performance as to lead to rejection and ridicule.

Until form began to follow function, the infant industry was at an impasse, the builder was a crackpot, and the car was a menace on the roads. Every approaching horse demanded a full stop and the delicate negotiation of animal past machine. The procedure called for a dash from the car to the horse's head to prevent him turning sharply round, grasping the bridle—if at all possible, by men on either side—and leading the horse slowly past the car, talking to him all the while in as soothing a tone as could be mustered under the circumstances.[16]

Legislation compounded the difficulties. An ordinance passed in 1899 in San Rafael, California, required cars to come to a stop three hundred feet from a moving horse. It is left to conjecture how a horse was ever overtaken on the road. In 1900 the state of Vermont required motorists to employ a "person of mature age" to walk one-eighth of a mile ahead of the car carrying a red flag to warn of the vehicle's approach. Many cities enforced a speed limit of eight miles an hour, while in the country farmers bitterly denounced the "devil wagons."[17] And as if to add financial injury to public insult, the *Detroit Journal* could report as late as August 1899 that carriage manufacturers were doing better than ever. Superintendents of two carriage factories admitted to a reporter that they had given thought to the manufacture of automobiles, but they seemed reluctant to take the matter seriously. It was apparent that as yet they did not fear the competition of the horseless carriage.[18]

Taken together, technological uncertainty (was it, at its most basic, to be steam, gasoline, or electricity?), confusion as to the need, if any, that the automobile was meant to fill, and the at best indifferent attitude of the public all conspired in the late 1890s to give the most optimistic pioneer builder little ground for enthusiasm. Some of them in fact were on the verge of abandoning their early vision.

In Springfield, Massachusetts, the Duryea brothers had completed their first car in 1893, formed a company, and in 1896 had built a new model that remained in design and performance the most advanced American automobile until it was eventually superseded by the cars of 1902. But the Duryeas left the company nearly bankrupt in 1898, having earlier made the error of refusing an offer for the British manufacturing rights, the income from which would have given them the capital they needed to carry on into mass production.[19]

In Kokomo, Indiana, Elwood Haynes had begun building experimental cars early in 1893, and in 1895 the Haynes-Apperson Company was formed with Apperson contributing a machine shop to the venture. Yet by 1899 when the company placed its first order with the Hyatt Roller Bearing Company, it had still not managed to progress beyond "a dirty little factory . . . (with) most of the work . . . being done on a dirt floor."[20]

To men like these, Maxim's labors at the Pope Manufacturing Company, though arduous, would almost certainly have seemed shot through with a security which they never knew. "This art is at present in a crude state," wrote Charles B. King, one of the earliest Detroit pioneers, in 1896, "and is mainly in the hands of the inventor, who has not yet been encouraged by capital."[21] King himself hunted unsuccessfully for backers to form a company, finally abandoned the idea and began building marine engines. He had been one of the most ingenious of the early innovators, but as the question increasingly became where did one go from here—a question that bridged the gap between a prototype and production—he, like the Duryeas, left the stage to others.

By the late 1890s this question gained new urgency from the vital need for capital investment in the industry. Sources of capital were almost nonexistent. Yet to do the businessmen justice there was little contemporary evidence of what the future held. The bicycle had been the great fad of the 1890s. Why should the automobile prove different? If it did capture the public's fancy, and the "if" loomed large, the market would nonetheless be restricted by price since only the very expensive automobiles gave any real promise of reliability. Technological advances as well as capital would be needed to bring down production costs, and until these occurred the market clearly lay only with the very rich. In their own turn, the limits of such a market inhibited the investor and effectively precluded the break-throughs in equipment and material that adequate financing might have made possible. And as if these very real obstacles were not enough for the builders to contend with, newspaper articles fanned the public's skepticism, deriding "the fad of the automobile" and laying open to their readers the parasitical nature of its followers. A typical news story read:

The gilded youth of Detroit suffer from a dreadful malady, a disease which perhaps pursues them even in the horseless carriage. Our language yields no equivalent for the French word "ennui." The electric motor for a time drives away this black trouble which holds in its clutches that smart class of society freed from the necessity of earning their daily bread. The price of the little machine, as much as a laboring man's house and lot, is necessarily a deterrent on the aspirations of the penniless young man. Strolling about town, meeting owners of machines, one is ushered first into a mansion on a leading avenue, and finds himself surrounded by works of art, tapestries, gorgeous furniture; then again, automobile devotees are discovered in splendid offices with white tile floors and decorative finishings in white and gold. Here, lolling on a magnificent sofa of mahogany, with the oriental luxury of great pillows stitched in bullion, the rich young man tells how and why he bought his automobile.[22]

With such a background, the more rhapsodic the forecasts of the future which came from the pioneer builders, the greater must have been the businessman's sense of alarm. "I had so much more capital than all the others in the game that I thought I had better stay out and keep it," one investor later admitted to an early industry analyst.[23]

The automobile was a rich man's toy, a passing craze, the general feeling ran. It seemed even more dangerously speculative than the bicycle, and among the men with money to invest there were many who had cause to regret the enthusiasm evoked by this earlier attempt at horseless transportation. By 1900 the bicycle industry was burdened by excess manufacturing capacity created in response to the boom years. One observer wrote in 1896 that scattered over the country from New England to California "were manufacturing towns which had sprung into new life and prosperity after years of slow decay, through the advent of this new industry."[24] As the craze faded, many plants in as many small towns were frantically searching for products to which they could convert their facilities. The boom had burst, fortunes had been lost, and the potential offered by the dawning automobile industry seemed clear to only a few.

The men working with the cars were the ones who sensed that the bicycle, far from being a fad, was in fact the beginning of a sequence which their own labor was carrying further.[25] Many of the pioneers experimented endlessly with motor bicycles: caught fast in a dream like Maxim's on the road to Lynn were the bicycle's sprocket wheel and chain drive, wire wheels with tangent spokes, and seamless steel tubular frames. All found a place in the early cars.

The pity was that the men with money saw it all so much less clearly and capital as a consequence bypassed the struggling builders of the gasoline car. Only one man, R. E. Olds, managed to secure adequate financial backing and with it the means of putting his cars on the road; and for Olds personally this initial success proved a bitter subsequent disappointment.

Beginning in 1886 with steam, Olds moved to gasoline and produced his first gasoline-driven car in 1895.[26] He had at the outset been fortunate in finding a financial backer, S. L. Smith, a Detroit copper millionaire, who bought stock in a company formed by Olds in 1892 to manufacture gasoline engines for farm and marine use.

In 1897 a separate company was formed to develop Olds's gasoline prototype and the singlemindedness of the board of directors is recorded in the minutes of the first meeting: Olds was instructed to "build one carriage in as nearly perfect a manner as possible."[27] He produced a "buggy" with tiller steering which nonetheless ran satisfactorily, and in 1899 the Olds Motor Works was incorporated to build the car, acquiring in the process the assets of the two earlier companies. S. L. Smith, apparently motivated more by the desire to provide business careers for his two sons than by any visionary assessment of the industry's potential, became the dominant shareholder with 19,960 of the 20,000 shares originally issued and paid in.[28] Olds himself held only ten shares, but the company had the money available to start quantity production—or so it seemed at the time.

By 1903, however, Olds was out, following a policy disagreement with the Smith sons.[29] That Olds was right in the dispute, which concerned mass production and the company's marketing strategy, Henry Ford was later to prove. But the more relevant issue at this point was the builder's predicament: without capital he could hardly get his cars off the ground, and this was literally true not only in Haynes's case; with capital, the builder ran the risk of control by men who failed to share his vision. To the Smiths the car was a product on which to make a high unit profit; to Olds as to Maxim, another visionary builder, it was the future that mattered. "Distances would be halved. . . ."

By the close of 1900 the Olds Motor Works was in financial straits. In its one and a half years of operation the company had sold 400 cars, far outdistancing any other manufacturer but making in the process an $80,000 loss.[30]

Priced at $1250, the Olds car was manufactured in a large

modern plant which was the first of its kind; it included a foundry, forge and machine shops, and finishing and testing departments, all made possible by the investment of S. L. Smith.[31] The car itself included many advanced features: a pneumatic clutch, cushion tires, and a not too reliable electric push-button starter. Yet for all this the model was a failure. It was too complicated and too expensive for the mass market and too simple and too cheap for the rich.

As late as 1904 a letter to the editor of the automobile magazine, *Horseless Age,* was still hammering home the message of simplicity and cheapness that in 1900 the Olds Company had missed:

A thousand dollars may sound well as the selling price of a machine, but $500 apiece for ten machines is a far sweeter song to the financial ear of the wise builder. There is an easy success awaiting the men who first produce a cheap, good, plain machine without frills, brass railings, or monkey traps, and that is guiltless of seventeen coats of paint when four are all that practical use calls for.[32]

At the same time, there was the "other" market, addicted to vastly expensive hand-built cars which in this way achieved a measure of reliability. Such cars, predominantly of French, German, or English manufacture, were frighteningly complicated, and it was taken for granted that none but a trained chauffeur could cope with them. This market too the company had missed.

Its lively presence as late as 1903 was attested to by Benjamin Briscoe, who visited New York in an attempt to find backing for the Maxwell-Briscoe. "All the men with money and automobile enthusiasm," he said, were owners of high-priced foreign cars.

I can recall now [Briscoe wrote later], that when showing the car to a wealthy and prominent New Yorker, whom I had "bothered" into letting us take him out for a demonstration, he marvelled that the car would run at all because, as he said, his car had all sorts of gadgets on the dash, all of which his chauffeur told him were necessary: the Maxwell-Briscoe had nothing there except one of those force-feed drop oilers. We told him that if we had known how he felt we would have hung some old alarm clocks on the dash, they being just about as useful as many of the contraptions his $10,000 car was lumbered up with.[33]

Harried by financial losses, the Olds Company had to reach a decision: Which market was it to choose? Nominally Olds was operating head of the company but in fact he was in continuous disagreement with his backers. The attempt at compromise which the 1900 model appeared to represent had proved a failure. The Smith sons were determined to concentrate production on high-priced quality cars. It was a policy that Olds felt less and less able to support.[34]

Adding urgency to the quarrel in the Olds Company was the rising popularity of the electrics. In 1897 the Electric Vehicle Company had been formed by a group of Eastern financiers, many of whom had earlier been involved in the promotion of electric-traction streetcar companies and had made considerable fortunes in the process. This group included Thomas Fortune Ryan, Anthony Brady, P. A. B. Widener, William C. Whitney, and, some time later, Samuel Insull. Their company acquired the Pope firm at Hartford where Maxim had fought a losing battle for the gasoline car, and by 1899, evidently hoping to wring further dividends from the demand for public transportation, the company began operating several hundred electric taxicabs on the streets of New York and planned expansion to Chicago, Boston, Philadelphia, and other cities.[35]

Through Colonel Pope, head of the now subsidiary Pope firm, the Electric Vehicle Company gained control of a patent that had been issued to George B. Selden in November 1895 and that purported to cover "the application of the compression gas engine to road or horseless carriage use." In this way, a company designed for and designated by the electric car acquired a means of holding the rest of the industry—the struggling gasoline builders—to ransom.[36] Nonetheless, by 1900 only two suits had been brought by the Electric Vehicle Company against gasoline builders, and the potential threat went largely ignored. Of much greater concern were the inroads being made by electrics into the market on which the gasoline builders were basing their future.

In the Olds Company the controversy over the market continued into the early months of 1901. "Finally," Olds said later,

after a long sleepless night I decided to discard all my former plans and to build a little one-cylinder runabout, for I was convinced that if success came it must be through a more simple machine.

It was my idea to build a machine which would weigh about 500 pounds and would sell for about $500. The result was the curved dash "Oldsmobile," weighing 700 pounds and selling at $650. My whole idea in building it was to have the operation so simple that anyone could run it and the construction such that it could be repaired by any local shop.[37]

Here Olds was of course reminiscing long after the fact. In reality the progression from decision to the curved-dash Oldsmobile priced at $650 went nothing as smoothly as he implied, and by early March of 1901 only one prototype runabout had been built.[38]

Then on March 9, 1901, the company's factory was totally destroyed by fire. All that was saved was Olds's prototype. "The fire beyond question was the best move ever made by management," the elder Smith wrote subsequently, "it put an end to the experimenting and chasing after strange electric gods."[39] In fact, the fire did far more than decide the vexed question of gasoline or electricity which the 1900 market had seemed to pose and which the company had half-heartedly approached with the Stanhope, an electric model of its own. The fire emphatically settled for the time being the policy dispute over the gasoline market itself.

With nothing left but the inexpensive runabout, the higher-priced model disappeared overnight from the company's list.[40] New drawings were made directly from the runabout and a new pattern of manufacturing adopted. That it held the clue to the expansion of an industry shackled by a lack of capital passed almost unnoticed for the moment, so necessary and inevitable did the fire make it seem.

This new pattern was subcontracting, hardly new in itself but now employed on a scale unprecedented since the Civil War. Until it was put into effect in 1901, the Olds experience prior to the fire had set the ground rules for the industry's expansion. Other builders too believed that they needed foundries, forge and machine shops, and substantial backing to pay for them, before they could even begin to think seriously of quantity manufacture. Where financial support was not forthcoming a new company reconciled itself to the production of cars at the rate of less than one a month: in August 1899 a newspaper report of the formation of the Detroit Automobile Company, the first venture in which Henry Ford was concerned, announced that the management "expected that one or two automobiles will be ready by October."[41]

Olds was now to turn the tide. Engines, transmissions, radiators, bodies, wheels, tires, springs, cushions, lamps, and other accessories had all to be contracted for. To start with, Olds placed an order for 2000 engines with the Leland and Faulconer Company, precision manufacturers of gasoline motors for marine use.[42] Henry Leland was nearly sixty when the Olds order came; he was the first builder to enter the industry not only with a thorough knowledge of the gasoline engine but with an extensive background of manufacture to close tolerances. The engine he built to Olds's design developed 3.7 horsepower as against 3.0 for the Olds prototype, and, a Leland associate reported, "this superiority was due entirely to closer machining."[43] The extra power enhanced the performance of the runabout, and manufacture to Leland's standards gave it an appreciable measure of reliability at a time when the industry had still a long way to go.

Leland's achievement comes into focus when one considers that as late as 1907 manufacturers were still being attacked for their slapdash methods. The October issue of the magazine *Motor World* described in ominous detail a situation in which interest in doing the work was being sacrificed to interest in completing it. Small attention was paid to the alignment of bearings, adjustments were hastily made or overlooked entirely; nuts turned down "hand tight" and left for the wrench which was perpetually busy elsewhere; piping and wiring strung up with an eye to convenience in the beginning rather than convenience in service; bolt holes "drifted" into line; bearings left slack or shimmied out instead of being shaped to a seat. Hardly surprisingly, such cars racked themselves to pieces, and the high maintenance costs of many low-priced cars became chargeable less to their cheap construction than to their hasty production.[44]

Leland's methods protected the engine from many of these deficiencies, and an editorial in the *Automobile and Motor Review* of August 1902 was perhaps intended as a tribute to his work. "Up to possibly a twelvemonth ago," it read, "most of the successful designs on the market had been developed by the simple process of adding metal to any part that broke too often."[45] Leland in the meantime continued to refine Olds's design, and by introducing larger valves and an improved timing system he was able to increase the power of the one-cylinder motor from 3.7 horsepower which Olds accepted to a massive 10.25 which Olds refused. Leland later used this more powerful engine in the first cars built by the Cadillac Automobile Company which he helped to organize in August 1902.[46]

The Olds order for transmissions went to John and Horace Dodge. These brothers had opened a machine shop in Detroit in 1899 after having earlier been involved at

Windsor, Ontario in the manufacture of a ball-bearing bicycle which they had themselves perfected. In 1901 when the Olds order came they employed just twelve men.[47] By the spring of 1903 they were building engines and transmissions for the Ford Motor Company's first cars and employing 150 men for this purpose in a shop said to be one of the best in the Middle West.[48] They were, as well, in a sufficiently strong position by then to assume the role of financial backers; the Ford Motor Company was launched largely on the basis of suppliers' credits, and those of the Dodge Brothers played the largest part.

Radiators for the runabout were ordered from the Briscoe Manufacturing Company. Benjamin Briscoe was then a manufacturer of sheet metal goods and stampings, but by 1901 he had reached a state of near bankruptcy. He was saved by a loan of $100,000 from J. P. Morgan which he had personally negotiated—to his own ecstatic astonishment—after being unable to raise the money from anyone in Detroit. Everyone there, he said, "seemed scared to death."[49] With the money from Morgan, Briscoe was able to enlarge and improve his plant and business recovered. Then came the Olds order:

Mr. R. E. Olds accompanied by Mr. J. D. Maxwell came to my office [Briscoe wrote later], bringing with them a sample of what they said was a "cooler" for the Olds runabout. I did not at that time recognize it as part of an automobile. It looked to me like some antiquated band instrument. It was, however, the very first cooler (as then called) that they had made for the Olds curved-dash runabout.

I made samples and soon afterwards secured an order for 4400 together with an equal number of tanks, sets of fenders, and other sheet-metal parts in addition. . . . Starting with this order from the Olds Motor Works, our business grew by leaps and bounds, so that within two or three years we were employing more than 1200 hands and making a very substantial profit. In fact, the business grew to be the largest producer in the world of the kinds of automobile parts it manufactured.[50]

Bodies for the little car were ordered from the C. R. Wilson Carriage Company, which as the Wilson Body Company was later to supply bodies for the first Fords. Five hundred sets of wire wheels at a time were ordered from the Weston-Mott Company, formerly a bicycle manufacturer in Utica, New York.

Arthur Pound, the official historian of General Motors, later estimated that a full roster of Olds pioneers, suppliers as well as employees, who were to fill prominent positions in the industry would include at least 150 names.[51]

While in no way depreciating Olds's commitment to the cheap car, the fire to an almost unbelievable extent seems to have contributed to making Detroit the center of the automotive industry. In the large-scale subcontracting of component parts which followed it the foundations of the industry were laid. The subcontractors were for a short but crucial time to come to be suppliers of nearly every part which went into the finished cars while at the same time they carried the capital risk which other investors had shunned.[52]

Produced in this piecemeal fashion the Olds runabout swept to early success. At $650 there was no other car on the market to match it. By the end of 1901, 425 had been sold, and 1902 promised to be a boom year. An order for 1000 runabouts, then the largest ever made at one time, was placed at the New York automobile show in October 1901 after Roy D. Chapin successfully drove a runabout from Detroit to New York in seven and a half days over execrable roads.[53] Production for the year, in fact, rose to 2500 cars.

Assembly was carried on temporarily at Lansing while the Olds factory in Detroit was rebuilt, but even when it came into operation the parts builders continued to grow for the company's sales of the runabout showed little sign of leveling off. Four thousand runabouts were sold in 1903, 5000 in 1904, and 6500 in 1905.[54] All sales were for cash, reflecting initially as much the company's financial position as the continuing caution, and sometimes hostility, of the banks.

That this caution was still shared by a great many others emerges from the company's early advertising. It was aimed at convincing the public that the car was cheaper and more durable than the horse. Detailed figures were produced to prove that the horse was more expensive in the long run, and illustrations often showed the runabout easily over-taking some beaten animal laboring up a steep hill. But as rising sales of the car took the edge off public skepticism, the Oldsmobile was increasingly sold on its own merits: it was, later advertisements proclaimed, "the ideal vehicle for shopping and calling—equally suitable for a pleasant afternoon drive or an extended tour. It is built to run and *does* it."[55]

Olds's achievement was by any standard phenomenal; he had successfully built the first car for the mass market, it was cheap, and it was reliable; the car had won wide ac-ceptance, Olds was selling as many as he could build. The widespread prejudice against the automobile was beginning to crumble under the impact of these factors, for as more and more people saw more and more runabouts on more and more streets, the complacency that attended the pane-gyrics in support of the horse was becoming increasingly difficult to sustain. Added to this was the enormous expan-sion of machine shops and parts manufacturers in Detroit and elsewhere which had taken place after the company's subcontracting had taken effect; and equally important was the new confidence that the men who managed them could now place in the young industry. Even to the conservative bankers, the Olds Company's dividend record of 105 per-cent in less than three years must have given grounds for new evaluations. Not surprisingly, Henry Ford's largest backer in 1903 was a banker.

It is with something akin to regret that one is forced to set down that the Olds record ends right here. Olds left the

Olds Motor Works in 1903, and although he soon established his own organization, the Reo Company, his cars never achieved the popularity of the curved-dash runabout. Olds was forty-one when he resigned. He had made a million dollars. He was not prepared to stay on and fight the Smiths for the cheap car, the battle for which had been resumed as soon as the company overcame the dislocation caused by the fire. Roy D. Chapin's biographer says unequivocally that the Smiths were insistent that the rich man's market should be exploited.[56] Chapin himself managed the company through the successful years to 1906 and then he resigned, at odds with the Smiths over their decision to abandon the curved-dash runabout. He took with him three other executives and together they organized what eventually became the Hudson Motor Company.[57]

In defense of the Smiths, Arthur Pound has written that they foresaw the competition in the low-priced field from the rising Ford enterprise.[58] But since at the time of Olds's resignation in 1903 the Ford Motor Company was struggling simply to stay afloat, this is to credit the Smiths with a prescience other events were never to confirm. By 1908, with the curved-dash runabout only a memory, the company was able to sell only 1055 of its four- and six-cylinder cars and for it to continue operations $1 million in additional capital had to be advanced by the elder Smith.[59] When the company was finally sold in the same year, General Motors was said to have paid "a million dollars for some road signs."[60]

In view of the expansion of the industry as a whole, the Olds Company's backward progress seems in retrospect almost inexcusable, yet the Smiths could have pointed to a variety of positive reasons to support their decision to produce for the high-priced market—positive at any rate when set alongside the negative rationalization later put forward by Pound.

In 1903 cars selling at $1375 or under represented approximately two-thirds of total production, and this reflected the popularity of the curved-dash runabout. At a price of $650, it had found 4000 buyers while no other car was then produced in quantity. By 1906, however, the position had changed considerably: cars in the price range $2275 to $4775 represented 45 percent of total production, and by 1907, in a complete reversal of the 1903 position, cars costing less than $1375 formed only one-third of total sales. Given these figures, it was far from easy to foresee in 1905 that demand in the high-priced range would rapidly decline; few would have believed that by 1916 these cars would hold less than 2 percent of the total market.[61]

In addition to the message of the numbers a clear advantage was believed to lie with the company which made nearly all of the parts for its cars. In some unarticulated way these cars were "better" and in general, the higher the price of the car, the more fully had its manufacture been carried out by the company whose name it bore. In 1904 the Maxwell-Briscoe Company took pains to advertise that the Maxwell plant was not an assembly plant, but one where every part of the Maxwell automobile was actually made under the direct supervision of the designer, Mr. J. D. Maxwell.[62] A year and a half earlier the Thomas B. Jeffery Company of Kenosha, Wisconsin, makers of the Rambler, felt it to their advantage to claim that "excepting only the body, tires, and spark coil, every part of the Rambler touring car is made in our own factory."[63]

With the pronounced trend toward the expensive car to back them up, the Smiths, on considering the facilities of their own plant, may well have thought the expensive market too good to miss. Following the fire the factory had been rebuilt on a much larger scale, and by 1904 the company was again making its own castings and manufacturing its engines and transmissions. A description of the factory layout in 1904 in fact quickly erases any impression that the job being done was still largely one of assembly:

Rows upon rows of lathes and special machinery are humming and buzzing away, bewildering the onlooker with their number. A great expanse of floor space stretches away before the visitor, along which are arrayed these ingenious devices, each with its own peculiar work to do. Some bore out the cylinders, each machine making two cylinders at a time; some finish the connecting rods and shafts; in fact every step in the process of turning out the finished machinery of a modern car is carried out by a group of these beautiful machines. . . . In the assembling room the same orderly process is to be observed. The engines move along from one group of men to another until they are ready for the car, thoroughly tested and proved worthy of use. The finishing and enamelling of the bodies, the upholstering of seats and cushions, etc. are carried on in a separate, large part of the plant.[64]

With the trend clear toward the expensive automobile and with their plant equipped to sustain a claim of a "better" car for the extra money, the Smiths, it might well have seemed to any sensible observer at the time, made the "right" decision. Yet the "right" decision was increasingly coming to depend upon the answer to a fundamental question: Why should people want cars?

Many years later Alfred P. Sloan, Jr., chairman of General Motors, was to quote the definition of William S. Knudsen, then president of the company: "Everybody," said Knudsen, explaining the demand for the automobile, "wants to go from A to B sitting down."[65] In the early 1900s, however, this was a wish the car could hardly be said to meet. Drivers were as often lying under a stalled vehicles as sitting triumphantly behind the wheel; they were as often struggling to shift a car caught fast in mud as bowling along a paved road punctually arriving for appointments. To the early buyers the gift that the car brought with it was hardly the comfort of the more sophisticated years of the industry's development; rather, it was a new and dramatic vision of controlling the progress of time: "Everywhere that the pikes ran, travellers gained a new idea of the importance of time."[66] And the more reliable the car, the firmer was a man's grasp over the hours which made his day: the farmer could choose, he could defer a trip to town confident that he could make two in the following week should he need to. Indeed the demand came overwhelmingly from prosperous farmers and from land agents, traveling salesmen, doctors—everyone in fact whose business or profession carried him on long journeys in any kind of weather.

The type of car they wanted was lightly built and for this reason moderately priced, but above all it had to be durable. These features by 1902 were increasingly emphasized in editorials, articles, and letters in the correspondence columns of the automobile magazines, for the Olds runabout had proved to be the exception rather than the rule.

On the worst roads which it is possible for an automobile to negotiate [read one early editorial], which will show the better results, a heavy machine or a light one? The tendency of construction generally in this country seems to indicate a strong preponderance of sentiment for the former horn of the dilemma (but) unless it can be depended upon to break down but one-half or one-third as often, the heavy machine is inferior from a purely economic point of view to the light one. Moreover, on roads at their very worst the big machine is, other things being equal, more likely to be hopelessly stalled than the small one, its sheer weight and bulk being against it.[67]

Significantly, the writer stressed that his line of reasoning was necessarily a little theoretical, since most light machines were intended only for light work and were built accordingly.

Such cars had little chance of meeting the conditions set by a buyer bent on defeating time and distance. Yet they were bought in increasing numbers and incongruously put to work on country roads which were little more than two separate tracks worn six inches or a foot into the earth by the heavy wheels of horse-drawn wagons and which in wet weather were near-impassible swamps of clay and mud.[68]

At the other end of the price range the heavy, expensive automobile had proved equally unsuitable. In May 1903 in a letter to the editor of *Horseless Age,* one of the greatest of the early pioneers, Charles Duryea, pleaded for a car designed to suit American conditions:

The masses who will eventually use automobiles will use them not for the fun of it, but for the service rendered. . . . If these facts are admitted then manufacturers should design accordingly and not retard the growth of the industry by copying [foreign] forms unsuited to American needs, even though apparently demanded by a few snobs who wish to show off the fact that they have been abroad and acquired a motor vehicle taste.[69]

The answer to the question of why people should want automobiles was thus becoming more and more explicit. By August 1906, the year in which the first really popular successor to the Olds runabout was finally produced by the Ford Motor Company, the magazine *Motor Age* went still further: it spelled out in detail the bonanza that the Model T was to strike a full two years later. Written at a time when the expensive car was in full ascendant, the editorial showed remarkable foresight:

The simple car is the car of the future as only a few years will show and the maker who will begin on the policy of extreme simplicity will have his reward in an ever-increasing business and possibly small but satisfactory and steady profits. . . . The present-day design of the motor car does not tend toward extreme simplicity. . . . The simple car will not only be the car for the masses but will be easier to make, more satisfactory to sell and more sensible for the ordinary man to use. [The average man] wants a simple car—the simplest that can be made—and such a car will prove so popular, as to bring sufficient credit and remuneration to its maker. A golden opportunity awaits some bold manufacturer of a simple car.[70]

To Henry Ford, on the threshold of his rise to fortune, this editorial would doubtless have made more sense than all the sales figures and all the trends projected for the industry. It was Ford alone who was now to prove the scattered prophets worthy of honor and the prestigious experts wrong. In the fall of 1906, the same year in which the curved-dash runabout was abandoned by the Olds Motor Works, the Ford Motor Company introduced the Model N. The car was a well-designed four-cylinder, "distinctly the most important mechanical traction event of 1906," and it sold for just $500.[71] Within a few months the price was raised to $600 but despite this, in the financial year ending September 30, 1907, the Ford Motor company sold 8243 cars, the great majority of them the Model N and its slightly more expensive versions, the R and S. Only a small number of the costly Model K, a $2800 car built at the behest of Ford's original partner, Alexander Malcomson, were taken off the company's hands.[72] In the previous year, with two models on the market, the Model F selling at $1000 and the Model B at $2000, the company had sold 1599 cars.[73]

Ford had struck the mother lode. Later he was to say that he had been very lucky in his competitors, that they had left him almost alone in the market below $1000.[74] But this serves simply to emphasize the intensity with which he grasped the vision that so many had seen and then let slip. Ford's competitors, the established manufacturers, did in fact leave him alone. Convinced that he was wrong, they continued to build for the wealthy and discounted his initial success as a flash in the pan which would lead no further.

Those who felt that Ford was right lacked the resources to compete with him. They were the carriage builders and farm equipment manufacturers of the Middle West, and they sprang overnight into a market in which the Ford Motor Company was rapidly laying the foundations of its future dominance. In June 1907, *Horseless Age* reported:

The largest producer of harvesting machines in the world has come into the market with a power vehicle especially intended for use by farmers; two carriage and buggy builders having large factories in Chicago are now producing low-priced motor runabouts and surreys, with running gear and bodies of the horse-drawn type; another in an Indiana city, operating three plants, and a Cincinatti concern engaged in the extensive production of road vehicles for all sorts of utilitarian purposes have entered the same field of late.[75]

These, and at least 16 other builders, the report pointed out, were all located in the five central states of Ohio, Illinois, Indiana, Iowa, and Missouri, with access to a rural market of thousands. The report concluded by casting doubt on the ability of the automobile manufacturers, who had once had the low-priced runabout business almost entirely in their own hands, to deal with this new development.

Ford alone excepted, the doubts were justified. Even had they wished it, many manufacturers would have found it difficult to adapt their plants to the production of the lighter four-cylinder car.[76] What was involved was not only a redesigned engine but at a minimum new axles and transmissions as well. Then there would be heavy expenses for new equipment and losses on existing inventory, which for some ambitious companies included large quantities of parts manufactured for chassis produced at a rate of up to three different models a year.[77]

For all of these reasons the builders whose skills, experience, and existing organizations afforded them the means of outflanking not only Ford but the johnny-come-lately buggy-builders as well, were all effectively written out of the market. The buggy-builders themselves were soon unable to consolidate their early penetration of the low-priced field. Within a year of *Horseless Age*'s glowing forecast, the buggy was under fire for its unsatisfactory design and construction. While the rural car owner was unwilling to spend more than $1000 for a car, and in fact the limit was often much lower, he did want reliability and at the same time "a car of first class appearance."[78] The jerry-built buggies, "with running-gear and bodies of the horse-drawn type," met neither of these conditions: design had been sacrificed to tradition and performance to an exploitation of price. The skill and experience which joined reliability to cheapness were Henry Ford's; he came straight down the middle of the low-priced field with a car that left the buggy-builders floundering on the one hand and the established manufacturers frozen into a contracting market on the other.

Of all the men who had begun to build the cheap car, he was the only one with the determination to persist. Henry Ford, one of the earliest marketing studies of the industry reported,* saw several things clearly. First, $500 was a large sum of money to a vast number of people. Second, a car must be built to sell: "Other manufacturers as prosperity came their way thought that the whole world grew more prosperous with them . . . they built automobiles for themselves instead of for the public."[79] Third, the need existed for a highly efficient, single-model chassis: Ford designed so simple and efficient a car that there was no need to incur the expense of further design changes, and his personal decision to avoid a multiplicity of models removed one of the main causes of manufacturing failure. Fourth, he saw that maximum value for price required quantity production and a heavy investment in machinery, in itself made feasible by the single-model car. While the report credited Ford with "the most striking success in the history of American production," it nonetheless hastened to point out that he had exploited a sellers' market and that he had done so by default of his competitors.

But such riders serve really to obscure the issue. Why was it Ford of all the other early builders who trusted so explicitly in the future of the cheap car that he could ruthlessly discard those who did not share it, stake everything he had on his conviction and bend every energy to the design

* 1914

and production of a car that would prove him right? Had it not been Ford who did this it would doubtless have been someone else. Social and industrial progress had made the coming of the mass car inevitable. But it was not someone else. It was Henry Ford.

By 1914–1915 from the humblest of beginnings the Ford Motor Company had become the largest automobile manufacturer in the world.[80] The huge plant that Ford built at Highland Park was the most modern, the best equipped. As such it was the subject of serious study both in the United States and abroad. The record-breaking level of production which the company achieved with the Model N—8423 cars in the first year of its introduction—had by then been so far surpassed as to make it seem primitive. In 1915 alone the Ford Motor Company would build 472,350 Model Ts. Ford himself would be acclaimed as a mechanical genius, and after the introduction of the $5 day, as a philanthropist and near miracle worker.

The issue of why it was Ford who not only saw the need for the mass car, but met it, cannot be discussed in isolation from Ford's subsequent career. Having succeeded so triumphantly he was to entrench himself in a position of such rigidity that he effectively destroyed the great company he had built. Once the Model T's success was established the Ford Motor Company slid, at first almost imperceptibly and then with increasing speed, into a morass of despotic, one-man rule, and the repercussions of the organizational collapse were evident in every area of company functioning.

The explanation for both Ford's early success and later failure is rooted in the manner of man that he was. The most crucial contributing factor to the company's decline was Ford's adamant refusal to break with the Model T, even as earlier his single-minded concern with the car had been the source of the company's greatest strength. From its birth in 1908 to its death in 1927, no fundamental change in the Model T was permitted, and a list of improvements in automobile design pioneered by the Ford Motor Company comes to a dead halt in 1908, a year that saw the cylinder block and crankcase cast integrally; stamped crankcase pans; front and rear transverse springs and the three-point suspension introduced; a flywheel-type magneto developed to provide a reliable source of electric power, and the lesser innovation of the left-hand drive. The list resumes in 1923 with a "welded steel wire spoke wheel" and in 1927 with such innovations as a "steel cored steering wheel."[81]

Throughout the years Ford turned a deaf ear to suggestions for improvement in the Model T, and as early as 1912 when he returned from his first visit to Europe he forcibly demonstrated the immovable character of his fixation. During his absence his closest and most trusted subordinates, Wills, Sorensen, and Martin, had developed a new model. In design it was lower and 12 to 15 inches longer than the Model T. While it represented a departure from Ford's concept of a "universal chassis," it nonetheless embodied real advances, carried out in a spirit of wishing to surprise and please the head of the company. Ford tore the car to pieces. An eyewitness account reads:

He had his hands in his pockets and he walked around that car three or four times, looking at it very closely. It was a four-door job, and the top was down. Finally he got to the left-hand side of that car that was facing me, and he takes his hands out, gets hold of the door, and bang! He ripped the door right off! God! how the man done it, I don't know! He jumped in there, and bang goes the other door. Bang goes the windshield. He jumps over the back seat and starts pounding on the top. He rips the top with the heel of his shoe. He wrecked the car as much as he could.[82]

After this incident, Wills, one of Ford's earliest and most gifted collaborators, was moved out of engineering and design into purchasing. Although Ford could still command the services of talented engineers, it was *his* ideas on design which were now paramount. In 1918–1919 Joseph

Galamb, the designer who replaced Wills, attempted to re-design a faulty radius rod on the Model T; according to E. J. Farkas, the designer whose turn it then was to step into the forefront, "Joe Galamb went off the scene after that."[83]

As far as Sorensen was concerned the incident apparently served to confirm an earlier pattern of behavior which he was to use more adroitly in the future. Of his rise to vast power within the company he later said:

Throughout the years, casualties at the top of the Ford organization were enormous. No one retained Henry Ford's confidence longer than I. None, not even his son Edsel, had or exercised greater authority. . . . One advantage I had over others was that from my pattern-making days on I could sense Henry Ford's ideas and develop them. I didn't try to change them. . . . When designers were given Mr. Ford's ideas to execute the usual result was incorporation of some of their ideas too. But it was part of my pattern-making training to follow through with what was given me.[84]

In effect, men held Ford's favor for only so long as they did as they were told, and Ford's almost exclusive preoccupation with the car meant that for executives in the areas of design and development tenure was at best precarious; Sorensen's forty years with Ford were almost as much a consequence of his job as manager of production as they were of his blind acceptance of Ford's demands. Joseph Galamb, looking at the issue from the standpoint of his own responsibility, denounced Sorensen's willingness to play yes-man to Ford. When finally the Model A succeeded the Model T, Ford insisted that the dashboard and the body should be built as separate units, a design that later had to be revised because of serious leaks in wet weather. Sorensen, Galamb said, backed him up: "Sorensen went along with Mr. Ford rather than doing what was right. He did that lots of times. That's why he got along with Mr. Ford for so many years. He did everything Mr. Ford wanted. He wouldn't stand up for his own ideas."[85]

The question of design, however, was clearly something that Sorensen could usefully trade for Ford's continuing approval. He bore no responsibility for design nor was he prepared voluntarily to seek or accept it in any form of cooperative endeavor. If later it happened that Ford's initial design was incorrect, "Mr. Ford," Galamb noted, "would never apologize. . . . He would just pass it off and say nothing."[86]

Ford's use of his designers and engineers, when they did stay with the company, effectively stifled their innovative ability. He set rigid conditions and often seemed deliberately bent on making them impossible to meet. Farkas in his reminiscences described an incident toward the end of the First World War:

Mr. Ford came in with the idea of this robot bomber. . . . [He] told us we couldn't put a carburetor on it. We had to go back into the days when motors were run without a carburetor. . . . It was just an impossible job and I think that's the way we left it. We never checked it with a carburetor to see what we could do with it. That was taboo, Mr. Ford wouldn't let us put it in.[87]

In the early 1930s, with the Model T's successor, the A, already slipping badly on the market, Edsel Ford tried to interest his father in a six-cylinder engine which would have allowed the company to compete more effectively with Chevrolet. In 1932 Farkas was assigned the task of developing the engine but, he said later, "Mr. Ford tied so many strings on a six-cylinder job that we couldn't quite lick it." After insisting that the design incorporate a larger than customary crank, Ford "put restrictions on the oiling system: no pressure. A big crank like that sure needed the pressure."[88] Work on the engine was soon abandoned and the first Ford six-cylinder engine was not produced until 1939.

On the evidence, by 1912–1915, with the success of the Model T assured, Ford's style as a leader of men had begun to change from the easier, more flexible approach which had been characteristic of him when the development of the car wholly absorbed him.

Then his men had regarded Ford as "a great godfather and benefactor." In a room twelve feet by fifteen equipped with a milling machine, a drill press, and a lathe, Ford had worked tirelessly on the Model T's engine and chassis. His were the ideas that Joseph Galamb translated into blackboard drawings and that Sorensen, simply on hearing them discussed, would give form to in a rough casting. And yet the important innovations in the Model T had not come only from Ford. The magneto was largely the contribution of Ed Huff, an early Ford associate.[90] The carburetor had been developed by George Holley, earlier a builder of motorcycles, and Ford's demand for a light, strong car was met by Wills and John Wandersee. Wills became interested in vanadium steel, a new light alloy for which J. Kent Smith, a consulting metallurgical engineer in Pittsburgh, was largely responsible, and Wandersee developed heat treatments that gave the steel a tensile strength nearly three times greater than that of ordinary steel.

Ford himself suggested the planetary transmission and the movable cylinder head. "People thought," said Galamb, "that you couldn't build an engine with a moveable cylinder head which wasn't going to leak. [It] was Mr. Ford's idea."[91] Within a few years other manufacturers were following Ford's example.

With his determination to build a cheap car that was light, strong, and powerful as the controlling strategy, Ford had brought out the best in his men. "All of us at the Ford Motor Company," said Wandersee, "tried to equal or better any material or part for less money. We worked on it and worked on it."[92] They were a long way from the exclusive preoccupation of each with his own survival which was later to become so marked a characteristic of the Ford organization.

From this conflicting background the figure that emerges

seems blurred at best. From the man with a vision that others feared to share, from the creative innovator bent on building "a car for the multitude,"[93] Ford became the tyrant of the Rouge, the vast plant along the river in Dearborn. That somehow he became a different man was sensed in different ways by many of his biographers; even so uncritical an observer as Allan Benson opened his 1923 biography with the dramatic statement, "The Henry Ford of 1914 is gone."[94]

The Reverend Samuel Marquis, an Episcopalian clergyman who joined the company in 1915 to run the Sociological Department [in effect personnel and labor relations] and who left at bitter odds with Ford in 1921, later published a perceptive account of Ford as he knew him.

For many years Mr. Ford shunned the public gaze, refused to see reporters, modestly begged to be kept out of print; and then suddenly faced about, hired a publicity agent, jumped into the front page of every newspaper in the country, bought and paid for space in which he advertised what were supposed to be his own ideas . . . and later bought a weekly publication and began to run "his own page."[95]

The period in which Ford "suddenly faced about" begins with the $5 day and the Peace Ship; it continues with a senatorial nomination and thoughts of running for the presidency; it develops further with a vicious and prolonged anti-Semitic campaign; then came battles with the Unions, Wall Street, and the New Deal—with the holders of any authority that seemed to threaten his. Woven through all of this is the issue of why it was Ford and not some other early builder who came to control the market, and then having done so, why he led his company to the verge of chaos. There is a progression from success to failure whose origins are rooted in the personality of Henry Ford.

In the chapters that follow, an attempt will be made to trace this progession by looking first at Ford's fixation on the car, second at the nature of its adaptation to reality, and third at the consequences once "success" was achieved. At the outset it is perhaps sufficient to say that in the manner of man that he was, in the reasons for it, and in the ways in which these factors combined to affect the development of the Ford Motor Company there lies a consistent pattern of motivation and action, not a sudden change. Opened to analysis this pattern permits definition of a style of leadership which although unique in its individual emphasis may nonetheless shed light on the behavior of other men.

"Mr. Ford," W. J. Cameron liked to say, "had a twenty-five track mind and there were trains going out and coming in on all tracks at all times."[1] Here Cameron was attempting to account for the diverse interests and the singular opinions that at one time or another Ford saw fit to uphold. How else, runs the implication, does one make sense of Ford's excursions into international politics, racial bigotry, newspaper publishing, fertilizer manufacture, old-fashioned dancing, antique collecting, and the professions of medicine and education?

One of the less friendly of Ford's biographers described Cameron as Ford's "verbal alter ego," and this was in essence a job description. After the closing in 1927 of Ford's newspaper, the *Dearborn Independent*, Cameron's sole job, apart from a weekly broadcast on the "Ford Sunday Evening Hour," was to interpret Henry Ford to the public. The function he served was in no way designated by the company— he carried no official title—nor was it acknowledged by Cameron himself: "The Ford Motor Company," he insisted, "has no public relations department and employs no public relations counsel or 'spokesman.' "[2]

But the need for his services was real. With the introduction of the $5 day in 1914, Henry Ford burst upon the public stage, and, as Cameron said later, "he spoke in telegrams and epigrams . . . they had to be translated."[3] Significantly enough, the telegrams and epigrams had little to do with the world of machines and they bore no mark of prior thought or real commitment. Fred L. Black, one of Cameron's associates on the *Dearborn Independent*, said:

Mr. Ford expressed very positive opinions about things without thinking very much about it. . . . If some newspaperman would ask him some question on a subject he hadn't thought very much about, he'd express a snap judgment. It practically became Cameron's function to weed that out of the interview. I've heard Cameron say, "Well, I wouldn't say anything about that. I don't know what he

2

FIXATION AND THE TWENTY-FIVE TRACK MIND

meant myself. It would be dangerous to express his thoughts about something or other unless we understood him."[4]

Sometimes Ford managed to elude his protectors and the flippancy came through bare of any deeper meaning which might otherwise have been imposed. His belief in reincarnation, he told reporters, was based on simple observation: "When the automobile was new and one of them came down the road, a chicken would run straight for home—and usually be killed. But today when a car comes along, a chicken will run for the nearest side of the road. That chicken has been hit in the ass in a previous life."[5]

At a time when rumors abounded that he would run for the presidency he gave his opinion on the state of society: "All that is the matter with this world is injustice," he said. "Establish justice and everything will be all right." Pressed for what should be done to remove injustice, he offered his own solution: "Increase the salaries of the supreme court judges. Pay them more money. They don't get enough. Put their salaries up where they should be."[6]

The point at issue here has been made by one of Ford's earliest biographers. There were hundreds of men prominent in the business world of no greater learning than Ford, Dean Marquis wrote, "but on matters with which they are not familiar they have the gift of silence and a correspondingly low visibility."[7] Despite Cameron's descriptive phrases and best efforts, Henry Ford's public forays after 1914 bear little resemblance to the actions of a man possessed of wide interests, who capably and methodically pursued them. Rather they bear the stamp of a man grasping at straws.

Indeed, the twenty-five track mind comes more and more to look like a single track of the narrowest gauge, intercepted by spurs leading nowhere, and laid in an inexorable line from the farm and the farmer to the farmer's car.

Why, at its simplest, should it have been Henry Ford who so unerringly sensed the future of the automobile? There were so many others who saw it too and who lacked the determination or the desire to put their vision to work. In this the pioneer Olds was not alone. William C. Durant, the founder of General Motors, foresaw the million-car years to come, even as the entire industry was struggling to manufacture 65,000 cars in 1908.[8] In Kenosha, Wisconsin, Thomas B. Jeffery began building the Rambler in 1901. He integrated his plant and was among the first builders to adopt a single-model strategy.[9] But while other men saw the market, the method, and the policy, why was it Ford alone who put them together?

He began haltingly enough in the 1890s. In 1879 at the age of sixteen he left his father's farm for Detroit's machine shops, but after only three years in the city he returned home. He worked only irregularly on the farm after this, spending the bulk of his time operating and servicing steam engines for neighboring farmers and others throughout southern Michigan.[10] In the early 1880s—the date cannot be fixed—he built a "farm locomotive" using for a chassis the frame of an old mowing machine which his father had discarded. Essentially a tractor powered by steam, the locomotive ran for forty feet and then stopped for lack of pressure; it never ran again.

Later Ford said that it was during this period that he changed from steam to the gasoline engine, but neither his wife nor his sister could afterwards remember that an engine was ever built as a result.[11] He seems in fact to have been slowly teaching himself basic principles rather than pushing any fixed idea. Many years later in the first of the autobiographical volumes written in collaboration with Samuel Crowther, he said:

It was life on the farm that drove me into devising ways and means to better transportation. I was born on July 30, 1863, on a farm at Dearborn, Michigan, and my earliest recollection is that, considering the results, there was too much work on the place. . . . There was too much hard hand labor on our own and all other farms of the time.

People had been talking about carriages without horses for

many years back—in fact, ever since the steam engine was invented—but the idea of the carriage did not seem so practical to me as the idea of an engine to do the harder farm work, and of all the work on the farm ploughing was the hardest.

To lift farm drudgery off flesh and blood and lay it on steel and motors has been my most constant ambition. It was circumstances that took me first into the actual manufacture of road cars. I found eventually that people were more interested in something that would travel on the road than in something that would do the work on the farms. In fact, I doubt that the light farm tractor could have been introduced on the farm had not the farmer had his eyes opened slowly but surely to the automobile.[12]

These statements were made long after the event, and as an explanation for Ford's failure to pursue his early concern with a farm tractor they seem plausible enough. Yet his progress was so much a matter of fits and starts in the immediate years to follow that there seem grounds to hold that his early disappointment over the tractor was a more serious setback than he ever later admitted.

In September 1891, accompanied by his wife of three years, Ford abandoned the farm his father had given to him when he married, and returned to Detroit to work as an engineer with the Edison Illuminating Company. His salary was forty-five dollars a month. "I took it," he said later, "because that was more money than the farm was bringing me and I had decided to get away from farm life anyway. The timber had all been cut."[13]

The two years which followed are sparsely and confusingly documented. Ford said that he immediately set to work and by 1892 had built his first car.[14] But this was not so; his first automobile was completed in the summer of 1896, and in the meantime Ford seems to have spent his time on the job picking up information where he could and experimenting haphazardly, with little of the urgency that he was later to develop.

Nevins and Hill, in the first volume of their history of the

Ford Motor Company, have cited the evidence of Charles B. King, the earliest of the Detroit pioneer builders, to the effect that Ford's first gasoline engine was completed late in 1895, and King is corroborated to some extent by Oliver Barthel who was in King's employ at the time. Barthel said that he showed Ford an article in the *American Machinest* of November 7, 1895, which gave instructions on how to build an engine from odd bits and pieces of machinery. Ford, he said, decided to build one.[15]

King wrote later that when he was at work on his first car using the facilities of the Lauer machine shop, "Henry Ford was then an engineer in the Edison Illuminating Company. . . . He looked after the repair of the engines and this brought him to Lauer's shop where my work was in progress. Ford realized the possibilities of the automobile then and started at once to work building his first car in the little brick shop at the rear of 58 Bagley Avenue."[16]

The address sets a limit to predating work on the car, for the Fords moved to Bagley Avenue in December 1893. But the accuracy of King's memory grows doubtful when he goes on to say that Ford's funds were so low at the time that he started to teach night classes in metalworking at the Detroit YMCA. While Ford did do so, the classes were held in the winter of 1892–1893, at least one year earlier than King's first statement would indicate.[17]

The discrepancy, in fact, seems to arise in the attempt to fix an approximate date for Ford's first efforts at building a car as distinct from a gasoline engine. That Ford worked with a series of engines, unclear as to the final purpose to which they would be put, supports the belief that when he moved to Detroit it was *not* with a car in mind but with a much vaguer notion of developing gasoline engines for use on the farm. The evidence of King and Barthel attests only to Ford's continuing interest in engines: King's memory is unreliable as to when work on the first car began, and the Barthel reference is indicative only of Ford's lack of familiarity with the engines whose plans Barthel showed him.

The wish to tie an automobile to the engines has led Nevins and Hill to the assumption that Ford went to Detroit in 1891 bent on building a "horseless carriage": he had earlier repaired a gasoline engine at a bottling plant in Detroit, became convinced it could be applied to a road vehicle, and said so to his wife who later remembered it.[18] This is then cited in support of their conclusion that Ford *must* have been working on the car during the first years of the 1890s. "It is difficult to believe," they wrote, "that a man of Ford's skill, experience, and energy should have repaired an Otto [an early gasoline engine] in 1885 and studied various other models including the one which prompted him to come to Detroit and yet more than four years after his arrival have done nothing in the area of experiment which was professedly his reason for leaving the country."[19]

And yet this is precisely what seems to have happened; in these early years Ford's concern lay with the engine and hardly at all with the automobile.

In the course of writing their first volume, Nevins and Hill appear not to have had available to them the reminiscences of Frederick Strauss which clearly indicate that Ford was working on engines rather than attempting to develop a car. Strauss first met Ford when as boys they worked together at a Detroit machine shop in 1879 and the acquaintance was resumed when Ford returned to Detroit. "In 1893, when I was working down at the Wain [machine] shop," Strauss said later,

Henry had all kinds of time and he used to come down to see me. He had a little shop of his own back of the Edison Company. . . . They had old motors down there and the Electric Company used that as a storage place. Henry used that as a hangout. He was never hardly in the power station.

While I was working at Wain, I used to go up there and hang out too. There were other fellows who would come and sit in there. . . . He had this idea of making a little gasoline engine out of scrap. . . . It was a one-cylinder engine. I built the whole thing but he gave the instructions.

We didn't work every night. We would just joke away. Sometimes we would work and sometimes not. It took about six weeks to get this little engine built.

On Saturday nights we had quite a crowd. Henry had some kind of a "magnet." He could draw people to him, that was a funny thing about him.

We had an awful time with the ignition. . . . There was a kind of a little make and break spark. There was no battery or anything. It was something like a cigar lighter. . . . It wasn't a flint because I can remember that we took the head of a nail and soldered that onto a little spring. Later on we found that that would burn. Somehow or other we got hold of a little piece of platinum and we soldered that on . . . and it didn't corrode. I think the cylinder was brass made out of a piece of pipe, a steam pipe of some kind.[20]

The engine ran satisfactorily and Ford sold it to a boat owner for installation in his boat. In 1896 Ford helped Strauss set up a small machine shop. He invested $30 for two months rent on the building and $94.82 of a total of $268.50 spent on equipment. Two more gasoline engines were built, one for a neighbor of Ford's in Dearborn and the other to power yet another boat.[21] In the meantime, Strauss and men in other shops in Detroit machined parts for what was to become Ford's first car. It was put together in a workshop behind Ford's home without their knowledge and with Ford working almost entirely alone.

The saga of Ford's first years in Detroit in the 1890s is thus one in which the gasoline engine is central. From it the automobile gradually evolved, and while Ford took longer than the other pioneers to build a car which would run on the road, his preoccupation with the engine was to give him his greatest advantage. His first car weighed less than 700 pounds, and except for the Duryeas' it was faster than other cars of the time, which not only weighed up to 2000 pounds but ran on ignition systems so inferior that the driver was almost always enveloped in clouds of oily smoke.[22]

Toward the end of 1898 Ford completed a second and better car, and within a year several prominent Detroit businessmen agreed to back him. They formed the Detroit Automobile Company with a capitalization of $150,000 of which $15,000 was in cash. Ten days after the company's incorporation on August 5, 1899, Ford resigned from the Edison Company to work full time as a builder of cars.

The shareholders in the new automobile company included some of the wealthiest men in Detroit, and in W. C. McMillan they could lay claim to a close relationship with the most powerful family in Michigan. William C. Maybury, another shareholder, was at the time mayor of Detroit. His family had long had close ties with Ford's, and by 1897 Maybury had already helped Ford financially and had procured machine tools for his use.[23]

The shareholders clearly anticipated that upon incorporation the company would put Ford's second car into production. A year earlier in August 1898 one of them had written Maybury with this assumption implicit:

With all the failures there have been in experimenting with gasoline, I still think it would be a good idea to examine into the others and compare them with Mr. Ford's, and see wherein his excels and to what extent. I believe it would be money well invested. It might save us a heap of money hereafter, or it might give us such faith and confidence that we would go ahead and push the business and make ten times as much as what it cost us.[24]

Yet, on July 24, 1899, when Henry Ford signed a contract of employment with the Detroit Automobile Company to work as mechanical superintendent "performing such duties as may be assigned him," the "second car" moved into the background.

A three-year lease was signed on a building which, Strauss said later, was "just perfect for our shop." Equipment was bought and machinists hired. Within three weeks the shop was ready and the new directors anxious to begin. But, said Strauss,

Henry wasn't ready. He didn't have an automobile design.

To get the shop going, Henry gave me some sketches to turn up some axle shaftings. I started machining these axle shaftings to show them we were doing something. It was just to get it going but they didn't belong to anything. We never used them for the automobile. It was just a stall until Henry got a little longer into it.

There was a woods back there and Henry said that he and Bille Boyer were going back in the woods where it was quiet. They were going to design an automobile.

The first thing I knew I never heard or saw any more of Bille Boyer. . . . Nobody took Boyer's place. Henry then had the business all to himself. He never put much time in the shop. He was going all the time. He might come in every day for about an hour or two. . . . Every time he would come in he would bring a little sketch. . . .[25]

With no reasons given for the abandonment of the "second car" the company's production was restricted to a heavy delivery wagon, and Ford's design was a flat failure: the vehicle was slow, heavy, and unreliable. The machinists got so far ahead of Ford's sketches that parts mounted up in the shop, initially to the satisfaction of the directors but soon to contribute to a growing sense of unease as out of the mountain of parts came only two completed and unsatisfactory vehicles.[26]

Ford's agreement with the company had given him no part as a shareholder; he worked for a salary of $150 a month, yet he had agreed "to give his whole time and attention and devote his best energies" to the company's business.[27] Either he could not or would not use the promising "second car" which had formed the basis for the company's incorporation. Instead, he set himself the near impossible task of building a heavy vehicle when all of his previous experience lay with a light design. "The directors weren't satisfied," said Strauss. "One of them wanted to throw in the sponge. Everything was going too slow for him. They had a directors' meeting but Henry said that he wasn't going to do any more on these two cars until they gave him a better settlement. . . . Henry had told me that they were going to have a meeting. He said 'if they ask for me, you tell them that I had to go out of town.' "[28]

When asked for Ford, Strauss dutifully gave the message and the directors in the absence of their mechanical superintendent evidently agreed to disband. Formal notice of dissolution was not filed until January 1901, but in the meantime operations were reduced to experimental work in a much smaller shop in the same building.

On the day following the meeting Strauss was ordered by the directors to destroy the car bodies previously built and to call in a junk dealer and sell everything else. He later recalled that they

brought the bodies down and put them into the boiler room, and we took a sledge hammer and busted all these beautiful bodies. Then we burned them under the boiler. The machine parts were sold to a junk man. . . . There was a lot of steel castings and bronze gear-wheels. Everything was sold out and we started in new in the new shop. I didn't hear from Henry for a few days, maybe a week. I just did what I got orders to do. All at once Henry came in one morning. He took a little corner of the shop and he started to hire Ed Huff for electrician, Harold Wills as the draughtsman and he also hired a pattern-maker. . . . They started to make a little car.[29]

Ford had weathered the storm and had in fact managed to keep a handful of the original backers interested enough to pay the bills. But when they discovered that the "little car" was nothing more than a front for Ford's continuing experiments, that he was in fact not attempting to perfect it but was at work on two bigger experimental cars, the situation again came to a head. Murphy, the wealthiest remaining backer, discovered what Ford was doing and, Strauss said: "he got disgusted and they had a break-up. Murphy told me to go on and to pay no attention to Henry at all. Then the pattern-maker was laid off, and that was the end of Henry and Wills and Huff. I didn't see them any more."[30]

Ford later described the directors of the Detroit Automobile Company as "a group of men of speculative turn of mind" who were determined to exploit him. They gave no support to his one desire to make a better car for the public. "The main idea," he wrote, "seemed to be to get the money. And being without authority other than my engineering position gave me, I found that the new company was not a vehicle for realizing my ideas but merely a money-making concern—that did not make much money."[31]

This is a judgment as harsh as it is inaccurate. The Detroit Automobile Company lost $86,000 during the brief period of its existence, and at its dissolution there was still nothing ready for the market.[32] The facts were that the company was formed expressly to build a car for sale. Ford's behavior, his biographers have called it "perfectionism," in reality betrayed an ambivalence that was to stay with him for several years to come. It was a device which protected him from an outright commitment to building the cars as he had undertaken to do, and at the same time it freed him from control by other men despite his nominal acceptance of their direction. He moved into commitment and subordinacy and as quickly moved back. He had built his first car almost entirely alone; others had built or machined parts for him, but he had put it together. And he had done so in such secrecy that Frederick Strauss, who could properly be called Ford's partner in the machine shop they established, did not know that Ford was at work on a car. Ford had never told him.[33] Two months after his first car was completed, Ford sold it despite the hard work he had put into it. But this after all was but a single car, built by an amateur, and it could be sold on this basis. It represented no real commitment. The "second car" which might have put the Detroit Automobile Company on its feet never went into production, and while the shareholders held on, Ford designed failure after failure.

In the months following the final disagreement in the Detroit Automobile Company, Ford began work on a racer, using the two unfinished cars which must have formed the bulk of the company's assets at its dissolution. By April 1901 he had again succeeded in interesting W. H. Murphy, the director of the defunct company who had earlier opposed him, since Mrs. Ford's diary records that on April 25th, "Henry and Mr. Murphy went out with Automobile."[34] In May he was sufficiently solvent to employ Oliver Barthel, King's former assistant, to work part time with Huff and Wills to develop the racer.[35]

The point has often been made by Ford's biographers that the venture into racing was the outcome of Ford's need, first, to find backers—a successful racing car would lead to wide public acceptance of a commercial model and capital to manufacture would thus be more easily forthcoming; second, to surmount the problems of design—a successful racer had to withstand the strain of an engine running flat out and generally to attain a much higher level of performance than the average car.[36] The myth was fostered by Ford himself. "The public," he wrote, "thought nothing of a car unless it made speed—unless it beat other racing cars."[37]

But the facts are different. Ford had backing. He had been better financed than any other builder, R. E. Olds alone excepted. It was Ford's fault alone that his company had never gone into production. The design of his second car was as good as the Olds curved-dash runabout, of which Olds was to build 425 in 1901 and 2500 in 1902 without once having to prove the car's merits on the track. In fact no racer was to achieve wide public acceptance.

For Henry Ford, racing seems to have been yet another way out. Once again he could play the amateur without the risk of real failure; and when he sold the cars, as he would, they were discards, not symbols of his own commitment—a commitment which would be inevitable once his cars were put on the market in numbers.

In October 1901 Ford's racer defeated Winton at a Grosse Pointe track, and at the end of November his early backers again agreed to finance him. The ever-hopeful Murphy and four former shareholders in the Detroit Automobile Company organized the Henry Ford Company, with Ford a shareholder for the first time. Each man held 1000 shares of $10 each, and $30,500 was advanced in cash by the five former shareholders.

The company, according to Barthel, who now joined Ford full time, was to manufacture a small car. But Ford had the racing fever: "He did not seem inclined to settle down to a small car production plan. He talked mostly about wanting to build a larger and faster racing car. This, together with some dissatisfaction as to the amount of interest he was to share in the company led to considerable dissension between himself and Mr. Murphy, who represented the group."[38]

On Ford's instructions Barthel began drawings for still another racing car with a four-cylinder, in-line vertical engine, and in the meantime Ford took up racing as a business with increasing seriousness. In January 1902 he wrote to his wife's brother about his intention to race the French champion, Henri Fournier:

My Dear Brother,

If I can bring Mr. Fournier in line there is a barrel of money in this business. It was his proposition and I don't see why he won't fall in line if he don't I will chalenge him until I am black in the face. As for managing my end of the racing business I would rather have you than anyone else that I know of. My company will kick about me following racing but they will get the advertising and I expect to make $ where I can't make ¢s at manufacturing. we are writing to Mr. Fournier.

Henry[39]

The advertising that the company received was apparently insufficient. Murphy discovered the purpose of Barthel's nightly labors and this, added to the lack of progress on the small car, precipitated the final break. Ford left the company on March 10, 1902.[40] He was given $900, Barthel's unfinished drawings, and the company agreed to discontinue the use of his name. Asked by Ford to join him in completing the racer in return for a ten percent interest in any subsequent Ford venture, Barthel refused; and Ford moved to new premises, working with Wills's assistance to finish the racing car. Within weeks he had new backing, this time from the bicycling champion, Tom Cooper, who with another famous cyclist, Barney Oldfield, had decided to move into motor racing.[41]

Cooper financed Ford's work on two racing cars, the red-painted "Arrow" and the yellow "999." In mid-October 1902, with Oldfield driving, the "999" defeated Alexander Winton and two other nationally known drivers at Grosse Pointe. But in line with precedent, the partnership had already broken up. "Henry sold his machine to Cooper two weeks ago," Mrs. Ford wrote to her brother on October 27, 1902, "thinks himself lucky to be rid of him. He caught him in a number of sneaky tricks. He (Tom) was looking out for Cooper and Cooper only. . . . I am glad we are rid of him. . . . He thinks too much of low-down women to suit me."[42] But Oldfield's version of the break differs considerably in its emphasis. It seemed to be Henry Ford rather than Cooper who looked out for himself and himself only:

The red car [Oldfield wrote later] was finished first and taken out to the old Grosse Pointe one mile track for its first trial, which was a flat failure. The engine was as hot as mother's cook stove and it looked like Cooper and Ford had not only wasted their money but a lot of time and energy. The fact of the matter was Ford finally got disgusted with the machines and turned the red one over to a fellow in Detroit whose main business was a piano tuner. Ford would not tell Cooper where the red machine was. He was so disgusted that he wanted to wash his hands of the whole affair and therefore agreed to sell Cooper the two cars for the actual cash value he had put in (not charging for his or Mr. Wills' time). In addition Cooper was to assume all outstanding indebtedness and was to pay for the machinery that was then in the shop, namely a drill press, lathe, and emery wheel. Hence Cooper was practically forced to buy Ford out before Ford would produce the red car and help finish the yellow car.[43]

Lighting the way for his biographers, Ford himself was later to attribute the venture into racing entirely to pressures over which he had no control. "I never really thought much of racing," he wrote, "but following the bicycle idea the manufacturers had the notion that winning a race on a track told the public something about the merits of an automobile—although I can hardly imagine any test that would tell less."[44] And so a later rationalization was called in to explain the earlier inability to come to terms with the work he had undertaken.

Even as Ford broke with Cooper, however, still another backer appeared on the scene and he brought with him the first faint shadow of what in a few months was finally to become the Ford Motor Company. He was Alexander Malcomson, a well-to-do Detroit coal merchant, who in August 1902 signed an agreement with Henry Ford to establish an automobile company. John W. Anderson, the lawyer who drafted the agreement, later testified that

Mr. Ford . . . had designed a motor car, an engine along rather novel lines; and Mr. Malcomson who was then driving a Winton car, and was interested in automobiles, had become interested in Mr. Ford's idea, and thought it was a good one, and was willing to back his faith by advancing money to supply materials and pay the labor necessary to create a car based upon the designs which Mr. Ford had made.[45]

The agreement required Ford "to devote his time to the construction of a Commercial Automobile for exhibition purposes"; the partnership would continue until the car was built and capital raised to form a manufacturing company. The partners would hold a majority of the shares in such a company and these would be divided equally between them. Malcomson, it was stipulated, would "have charge of the financial and commercial departments and

. . . Henry Ford . . . of the mechanical and factory departments of the business."

Malcomson agreed to contribute $500 to the partnership and "such further sums of money as may be needful and necessary to complete and equip said sample Commercial Automobile."[46]

Malcomson soon assigned responsibility for the financial details of the partnership to James Couzens, the managing clerk of his coal business. On October 30, 1902, Malcomson wrote Ford from Cleveland:

Mr. Couzens tells me Mr. Wills is getting around and I am glad to hear it. Hope you will get everything running in good shape at the shop, so that the work can be pushed with all possible speed. Our salvation for next season will be in getting the machine out quickly and placing it on the market early. It is pleasing that you have been so successful thus far in getting the right kind of help. Mr. Couzens and I called at the shop last week and found quite a change, it is taking on quite a business aspect. Anything you may need while I am away will be attended to by Mr. Couzens. He understands the situation thoroughly.[47]

The "right kind of help" for Ford included Harold Wills and Frederick Strauss. In an effort to induce Oliver Barthel to stay with him, Ford had earlier made a vain offer of a 10 percent stock interest in any future Ford enterprise. Now, to keep Strauss, he offered to assign to him the earnings of $2000 worth of stock for a period of two years after incorporation of an automobile company, the stock to become Strauss's property if he remained with the company during the two-year period. According to Strauss, a similar offer was made to Harold Wills.[48] But Strauss did not take up the offer nor did he stay with Ford for the required length of time; he lasted for only three months, from October to December 1902, when, with only an engine and transmission completed, work stopped temporarily due to a shortage of funds. "I couldn't wait," Strauss said later, "I had to go and get a job."[49]

What is remarkable about these offers is that they were made by the Henry Ford, who years later would write that he left the Detroit Automobile Company "determined never again to put himself under orders."[50] But he had done so in the Henry Ford Company, and now the Malcomson agreement made it clear that at best he would hold a minority interest in any company formed, and even this he was willing to share. At this point, in fact, Ford's inability to stay with a car long enough to put it into production was closely paralled by his indecision on the issue of control. It was only when finally he froze his design that the need for control of his company became dominant. Mass production and the need for control were as intimately related as the ambivalence and perfectionism of the past.

But this lay far ahead of him. The immediate problem, taken much more seriously by Malcomson than by Ford, was incorporation. Not until June 16, 1903, was the search for capital brought to an end and the company registered.[51]

The new venture was capitalized at $150,000 with $100,000 issued and $28,000 in cash. One thousand shares of $100 par value were issued, and Malcomson and Ford, with 255 shares each, together held control with 51 percent of the issue. Malcomson put in no new capital, and Ford in return for his shares turned over what equipment and patents he owned. The new shareholders bore little resemblance to the glittering array of Detroit businessmen who had first backed Ford.

Almost alone Malcomson had put the company on its feet. John S. Gray, who put in $10,500 in cash, was Malcomson's uncle. John W. Anderson and Horace H. Rackham were Malcomson's lawyers; Anderson paid in $5000 in cash and Rackham $3500, giving a note for $1500. Charles H. Bennett had been referred to Ford by a cousin of Malcomson's; he bought 50 shares and gave notes for the entire amount, $2500 of it being guaranteed by Malcomson. Vernon C. Fry, Malcomson's cousin, bought 50 shares, paying $3000 in cash and giving a note for $2000. Charles J. Woodall, Malcomson's bookkeeper, gave a four-month note for $1000 for 10 shares. Albert Strelow, Malcomson's contractor, paid in $5000 for 50 shares four weeks after incorporation. James Couzens, who was Malcomson's managing clerk at the coal company and was soon to take over the administration of the Ford Motor Company, bought 25 shares, paying $1000 in cash and giving a four-month note for $1500. The only shareholders who did not in some way owe their investment to a close relationship with Malcomson were John and Horace Dodge. But Malcomson had already discussed a manufacturing contract with them, and each brother bought 50 shares, with John Dodge giving a three-month note for $5000 and Horace a four-month note for the same amount.

The Dodges contracted to make 650 engines, chassis, and transmissions to Ford's designs and received $10,000 in cash to begin manufacture.[52] Other contracts were let for bodies, cushions, wheels, and tires. The new company had no manufacturing facilities, it was to be entirely an assembly operation.

By the middle of August, wrote Ford's first "official" biographer, eight to ten cars had been assembled, "but none had been shipped because Ford felt they were not yet as good as he could make them."[53]

The biographer of John W. Anderson, in the same vein, referred to Ford's stoppage of all shipments as a consequence of customer complaints.[54] It was James Couzens in his capacity as business manager who insisted that the cars should be put on the road. "Ford's sudden abandonment of his former do-nothing policy defies rational explanation," wrote Professor Quaife, Anderson's biographer. "As good a guess as any would be that he was now subject to the influence of such aggressive men of action as Couzens and John and Horace Dodge."[55]

Indeed Couzens's influence on Ford seems to have been

incalculable. He was by all accounts a hard, driving man, and took control of every aspect of the company's business apart from engineering and assembly which were Ford's responsibility. "Couzens was handling all the books . . . the sales and purchasing—everything," John Wandersee, one of the earliest employees, said later.[56] And John W. Anderson in a 1926 interview said that Couzens understood the financial operations of the business better than anyone in the company.[57]

To Ford, looking back from the vantage point of many years later, "the business went along almost as by magic."[58] And for this Couzens was almost solely responsible. Ford was still unable to freeze a design—between 1903 and 1907 there were seven models produced—but the assembly method of operation meant that substantial contracts had to be let months in advance and with Couzens driving him to it, Ford was compelled either to have his design changes ready or to defer them to a subsequent model.

In Strauss's account of the circumstances under which he stopped working for Ford, he referred to the months of delay before the Ford Motor Company was finally organized: "Henry wanted this company to make the complete automobile, to manufacture the whole automobile. Couzens was very much against it."[59] And this rings true. Control over manufacturing operations would have given Ford the means of building but not selling, of constantly changing and of assiduously avoiding the market, and possibly the cycle begun in the Detroit Automobile Company would have been repeated for the third time. Now, with deadlines to meet and hardheaded businessmen to contend with, he restricted his talent to model lines rather than to the individual car and despite the legends which have formed, his later obsession with volume and cheapness was at this point still far from clear.

In the 1920s John W. Anderson testified that in 1903 Ford had said to him: "The way to make automobiles is to make one automobile like another automobile, to make them all alike, to make them come through the factory just alike—just like one pin is like another pin, when it comes from a pin factory, or one match is like another match when it comes from a match factory."[60] This statement has frequently been cited as an indication of Ford's early commitment to the mass car, but again the facts are different. The inconsistency has been accurately summed up by Roger Burlingame, a recent Ford biographer. He is cited here at length for his description of the problem rather than for any attempt at explanation:

The Ford-can-do-no-wrong biographers [he wrote] insist upon the twin impulses of quantity and cheapness as a profound driving force that appeared with their hero's earliest consciousness and from which he never deviated. The debunkers point out many cases in which Ford completely departed from this line, such as when he forgot everything in his supposed passion for racing; when he designed and built several expensive models before his Model T arrived, and when he stood on the very threshold of success, he seems to have been willing to sell out for cash. Both of these proponents are partly right and both are quite obviously, from the records available to us, partly wrong.

It is hard to deny that Henry Ford was ridden by two obsessions: mechanical perfection and the common man. Sometimes one of these dominated the other. It is probable that in the years before Model T he was continuously searching for some sort of balance between the concentrations. Perhaps there were fleeting instants when the effort seemed too much for him . . . there is little doubt that in 1904 the technical obsession dominated the mass car in Ford's mind.

In 1905 we see an interesting demonstration of the two obsessions seeking some kind of common level. In that year Ford tested the Model C, a two-cylinder four seater, at $950.[61]

Burlingame's "technical obsession" is of course the old "perfectionism," Ford's inability to freeze design, which nonetheless was modified from 1903 to 1905 by the circumstances under which the cars were produced. If Burlingame's statement is carried to its logical conclusion, it then follows that with the enormous success of the Model T in later years, the "technical obsession" must be seen as giving way to the mass obsession—but this would leave unexplained Ford's inability to check mass desertion to the Chevrolet, by changing the car in ways which would have preserved its usefulness and attraction to the "common man."

The fundamental issue is never raised, yet Burlingame is among the most perceptive of Ford's biographers. Given his statement of the two "obsessions" the issue of why they should exist is never questioned: Why, for instance, should the "technical obsession" be in the ascendant in 1904? Why should 1905 appear to be a compromise year? Why should the shift to the "mass obsession" begin to appear in late 1905, with plans for the first Ford car to be produced in volume?

In going through the chronology of 1905 it might be noted that 1695 cars were produced in the year ending July 31, thirteen cars fewer than in the company's first year of operations. It might be noted too that in May 1905 Henry Ford called in newspaper reporters to announce what must have seemed to be grandiose plans. He declared that he meant to reach the masses with 10,000 cars selling at $500 each: "It will take some time to figure out what we can do," he said, adding a little incongruously, "we do not care to say much until we know what the result will be."[62] In November 1905 one might find that plans were announced for the Model N, a fifteen-horsepower four-cylinder Ford runabout designed to sell at a price between $400 and $500;[63] and that in the same month Henry Ford took a long first step toward control of the company's manufacturing operations with the formation of the Ford Manufacturing Company, a concern quite separate from the Ford Motor Company, in which Ford with 2550 of the 5000 shares issued was in majority control for the first time.

The only other event of the year which might appear worthy of record would be the death of Ford's father on

March 8, 1905. But, in fact, William Ford's death fixes a point in time for the emergence of a very different man, and it is only apparently coincidental that the real growth of the Ford Motor Company should begin with the year 1905.

William Ford, at least as his son remembered him and gave biographers, reporters, friends, and business associates to understand, had always opposed Henry Ford's bent for machinery. William Ford wished his son to be a farmer, wrote Benson, to whom Ford talked freely in the early 1920s, and although

Henry did not like farmwork, he worked hard at it. But his heart was always in his mechanical pursuits, which his father detested because he realized that they were leading the lad away from the country . . . [Henry] worked with his tools always against the wishes of his father. . . . For a time the struggle went on between the father's will and the son's determination. One day, when the boy was 16 the struggle ended. The mother had died three years before, the old home did not seem the same, and the call of the city silenced everything in the boy's heart. Without saying a word to anyone, he walked nine miles to Detroit, rented a room in which to sleep, and sought employment in a machine shop.[64]

To Arnold and Faurote who published in 1915 the definitive account of the company's production system, *Ford Methods and Ford Shops*, Henry Ford reiterated his father's disapproval in a face-to-face interview.[65] These are only two examples of an attitude which will subsequently be dealt with much more fully. They have been introduced here to bring into focus a dominant myth in Ford's life, myth because the facts which they claim to portray are simply not so. Ford said they were, but the evidence of his father's encouragement and interest in him is overwhelming.

A new man emerged in the months following the elder Ford's death and it would seem implausible at the very least to attribute this "new" Ford to anything other than psychological change. When one considers the 1890s—the preoccupation with engines, the late start on the car built almost alone, the inability to settle down to manufacture, the failure of the first two companies, the breakout into "racing fever" and the still uneven progress after 1903—the strong figure which begins to emerge late in 1905 is on the face of it almost incredible. Yet emerge it did, sure and purposeful, in pursuit of the car for the American everyman.

The Model N entered the scene as the original cast of shareholders was about to disband. In the industry at large, despite some firmly held convictions to the contrary, every market trend indicated a movement toward the heavy, expensive car. The Olds curved-dash runabout, the biggest seller to that point, was about to be discarded by the Smiths in favor of more costly cars.

Within the Ford Motor Company a dispute over product policy which reflected the tensions in the industry grew increasingly bitter. In 1905 the company had produced two different models, the four-cylinder "B" at $2500 and the two-cylinder "F," unchanged from the previous year, at $1000; and fewer cars had been sold than in any year since incorporation. Later, in explanation of the fall in sales, Ford wrote:

Some said it was because we had not brought out new models. I thought it was because our cars were too expensive—they did not appeal to the 95 per cent. I changed the policy in the next year having first acquired stock control. For 1906–1907 we entirely left off making touring cars and made three models of runabouts and roadsters, none of which differed materially from the other in manufacturing process or in component parts but were somewhat different in appearance. The big thing was that the cheapest car sold for $600 and the most expensive for only $750, and right here came the complete demonstration of what price meant. We sold 8423 cars—nearly five times as many as in our biggest previous year.[66]

This change in policy brought with it Alexander Malcomson's resignation from the board. Malcomson, like the Smiths at the Olds Motor Works, was convinced that the future lay with the high-priced car and Ford's now-focused convictions were wholly at odds with the direction in which

Malcomson believed the company should move. Supporting him, Malcomson had Fry, Woodall, and Bennett; against him, Ford and Couzens, whose concern with sales gave a practical edge to his position.

In a maneuver which completely outflanked the Malcomson faction Ford organized the Ford Manufacturing Company in November 1905 and excluded Malcomson and Fry from participation. Malcomson threatened to sue and he would have had strong grounds since the new company was to be given the manufacturing contracts for the Model N, previously held by the Dodge Brothers for all Ford cars, and would in fact represent expansion of the Motor Company's operations. But at this crucial point Malcomson announced his own intention to form a rival automobile company, the Aerocar, and the other Ford directors, who so far had maintained an uneasy neutrality in the dispute, on December 6, 1905, unanimously demanded his resignation from the board. In a strongly worded letter dated December 15, 1905, Malcomson refused to resign:

My connection with the company . . . and with its success has been too long and too close to allow me to sever my official relations with it without weighty reason. . . . It is true that I am interested in another corporation about to engage in the automobile business but you may be assured that that interest will not diminish my interest in the Ford Motor Company, nor will it interfere with the proper performance of my duties to the Ford Company. . . . But (and this is a matter you seem to overlook in assuming that my interests are adverse to those of the company) I am the owner of more than a quarter of the stock of the Ford Motor Company which now is, and under proper management will continue to be, a valuable property. Such occurrences as the recent precipitate action of the Board in doubling the Manager's salary [this referred to Couzens] despite protest and without waiting for a full Board meeting, are not calculated to induce the belief that my withdrawal would result in a management more careful of the stockholders' interests. It is true that there may be reasonable differences of opinion over matters of expense, and instances of increased expense are important only as showing a general tendency to sacrifice the interests of the general body of stockholders to those of some individuals. The most striking instance of this tendency in the management of the Ford Motor Company is the organization of the Ford Manufacturing Company, comprised and controlled by the holders of the majority both of stock and directorships of the Motor Company, and designed, as I am reliably informed, to sell its products to the Motor Company—presumably not without profit. In this new Company the minority stockholders were not invited to join. . . . I consider this scheme to be as unwise as it is unfair and I propose to exercise whatever power my official position in the Motor Company may give, as well as—if it becomes necessary—my rights as a stockholder, to prevent the accomplishment of the result for which the plan was designed. . . .[67]

But Malcomson went no further. He was effectively excluded from managerial control and faced with the prospect that the Motor Company's profits would be absorbed in the prices charged by the Manufacturing Company for the engines and transmissions it supplied; he sold his shares to Henry Ford on July 12, 1906, for $175,000. Woodall, Fry, and Bennett sold theirs to both Ford and Couzens shortly after, and with 58½ percent of the shares issued, Ford had finally won stock control.[68]

In the meantime, the company backed Ford's new-found certainty to the limit. On January 1, 1906, the first advertisements for the Model N appeared, and in the light of the company's total production for the previous year, an unexceptional 1599 cars, they were sensational:

This is why we can build the Ford 4-cylinder Runabout for less than $500 [the advertisements proclaimed]. We are making—
40,000 cylinders
10,000 engines
40,000 wheels
20,000 axles
10,000 bodies
10,000 of every part that goes into the car—think of it! Such quantities were never heard of before. . . .

Henry Ford's idea is to build a high-grade, practical automobile, one that will do any reasonable service, that can be maintained at a reasonable expense, and at as near $450 as it is possible to make it, thus raising the automobile out of the list of luxuries, and bringing it to the point where the average American citizen may own and enjoy his automobile.[69]

A few days later the *Detroit Journal* carried a story on the "Local Auto Manufacturer, who stakes his Reputation on a $500 Auto." Ford had already built two prototypes of the Model N, it was reported, and they were to be shipped to New York within a week for the annual motor show; twenty-thousand N's were to be built during the year and the company had already received orders for half this number. Ford was quoted directly: "I believe that I have solved the problem of cheap as well as simple automobile construction," he said. "Advancement in auto building has passed the experimental stage and the general public is interested only in the knowledge that a serviceable machine can be constructed for a price within reach of many. I am convinced that the $500 auto is destined to revolutionize automobile construction and I consider my new model the crowning achievement of my life."[70]

The demand for the Model N confirmed Ford's convictions and in order to meet it the Manufacturing Company was forced constantly to improve its methods of production. "Model N was the first job on which the company introduced the idea of sequence of operations," one employee said subsequently. "They worked out at that time the closest possible sequence—so close that there was no chance of parts even falling off the bench. . . . Before that there were lathes in one place, drill presses in another . . . and we moved the materials around from place to place."[71]

For Henry Ford the commitment had finally been made and with it came, perhaps inevitably, a renewed interest in the farm tractor. In the fall of 1905, the year in which he went to work for the Ford Motor Company, C. E. Sorensen helped to establish an experimental tractor shop in a barn a short distance from the Ford plant.[72] Joseph Galamb, the designer who was to play a large part in planning the Model T, later recalled that it was sometime in 1906 that he first became aware that Ford was interested in tractors. "Mr. Ford came to me and said, 'Joe, we have to build a light tractor that we can use out on the farm where the wheat is growing, and we need a binder. We have to build a tractor in three days.' "[73]

With Sorensen's help Galamb finished the tractor within a week. It was the first of a long series of experiments which culminated in mass production only during the First World War when an urgent order from the British Government had to be met. When the Model T was finally abandoned in 1927, the tractor went with it.

But this was far in the future and the Henry Ford of 1906 still had a long way to go. Momentarily he faltered and in 1907 produced a fifty-horsepower six-cylinder car, the Model K, which had earlier been designed at Malcomson's insistence. Sold at $2800 the car was a disaster and had to be forced onto the company's dealers: for every ten of the cheap cars ordered the dealer had to accept a Model K.[74] But within the same year work on the Model T had begun.

In January or February, Galamb said later, Ford selected him to begin work on his designs. "Mr. Ford," Galamb said, "first sketched out on the blackboard his ideas of the design he wanted. He would come in at seven or eight o'clock at night to see how we were getting along. . . . There was a rocking chair in the room in which he used to sit for hours and hours at a time discussing and following the development of the design."[75]

Slowly the car rose from the drawing boards and into it Ford put every detail of his experience. "The Model T," he wrote in 1923, "had practically no features which were not contained in some one or other of the previous models. . . . There was no guessing as to whether or not it would be a successful model. It had to be. There was no way it could escape being so, for it had not been made in a day."[76]

The car was introduced on October 1, 1908, and it won wide public acceptance. Interviewed in 1926, Galamb detailed its advantages over other contemporary models: Ford's insistence on lightness and strength had led to the extensive use of vanadium steel in the crankshaft, spindle, and other parts where wear and strain were heavy; because this alloy steel was far more durable than the poorly treated steels in use at the time, less of it needed to be used. The planetary transmission, which was essentially Ford's design, eliminated one of the worst defects of the early cars.

In the earlier days of the automobile industry [Galamb said], people did not know how to shift gears. The materials in the gears were very soft and as a result the gears were often stripped, clutches were heavy and sticky and shifting difficult. Things were still in a primitive stage and the public wanted a transmission which could be handled easily and without danger of damage to the mechanism. This made the planetary transmission very important at that time.

The three-point suspension of the motor prevented distortion of the motor base, and in the light of the poor roads of the time it gave an advantage to the Model T that other manufacturers soon adopted. After initially ridiculing it, they adopted the detachable cylinder head as well. With this innovation, Galamb said, Ford was easily six years ahead of the industry.

And there were still other advantages: at a time when ignition systems were notably poor, Ford insisted that a flywheel magneto should be used to supply current. "We first tried to make it in one piece," Galamb said, "but this proved impractical and at Mr. Ford's suggestion we made up the sixteen magnets separately, charged them, and then built up the whole circle . . . it has been subject to very few modifications since."[77]

This then was the car which in 1909 took the market by

storm. Of it, the man who earlier had fought so hard against giving success a chance, who had undermined two companies because he could not freeze a design, who had hopped and skipped across market segments, said:

It is strange how, just as soon as an article becomes successful somebody starts to think that it would be more successful if only it were different. There is a tendency to keep monkeying with styles and to spoil a good thing by changing it. The salesmen were insistent on increasing the line. They listened to the five per cent, the special customers who could say what they wanted and forgot all about the 95 per cent. . . .
In 1909 I announced one morning without any previous warning, that in the future we were going to build only one model, that the model was going to be Model T and that the chassis would be exactly the same for all cars.[78]

In the five years that followed, Ford cut the price of the basic car, from $900 in 1909 to $440 in 1914, and the average monthly total of unfilled orders swelled from 2172 to 59,239.[79]

The car was strikingly successful in the vast agrarian market. As early as March 1908 a *Motor World* editorial reported the rapid development of the farmer market, "particularly in the broad area which the New Yorker dismisses as the 'middle west.' "[80] And a year later, Thomas B. Jeffery, builder of the Rambler, cited sales to farmers in the Southwest in support of his assertion that the Midwest would soon tax the capacities of all the builders then equipped for production.[81] "No small portion of the money of the country appears to be in the hands of the prosperous farmers," declared a *Motor World* editorial and the price cuts which became Ford's equivalent of an annual model change were the impetus to demand down the line to the poorest farmer.[82] "Those who insist," read a prescient, if bitter, editorial in 1908,

on doing business with the kid-glove and check-book set or not at all, may see no possibilities in the well-recognized prosperity of the agricultural communities. To them the thought of dealing with so rude and uncouth a class . . . [is] more or less impossible, due to certain antiquated impressions and prejudices which actual contact with the Western farmer would quickly remove. But for the manufacturers who can adapt themselves to conditions and markets, without sacrificing any tenets of sound business, the assured prosperity of the farmer is a call to action.[83]

The tocsin sounded for Henry Ford as for no one else, the Model T might have been built for the farmer. Where the back roads and swamps of the farm states were the undoing of other cars, they made the Model T. Severely functional in its appearance, the car could lurch through mud, ford streams, and plough through snow, attributes which found the greatest favor on the farms. By 1914 when a comprehensive survey of the automobile market was made by the Curtis Publishing Company, the extent to which Ford had penetrated, and depended on, the rural market was overwhelmingly clear; time and again in their interviews the researchers came up against the commitment of the farm trade to Ford.[84] The researchers estimated that perhaps 10 percent of the country's farmers had already bought cars, leaving a market of 2.5 million who could afford to buy but had not yet done so, and this was the demand which Ford met with increasing success as the years passed.[85]

The Model T was sold on service—it was rugged and reliable and could easily be fixed by men accustomed to handling machinery; it was sold on price—at $440 in 1914 a gap of nearly $500 existed between the Model T and its nearest reliable competitor;[86] and it was sold for cash on the barrelhead by the company. If they needed it, Ford dealers were compelled to arrange their own financing, and since the largest market segment prepared to pay cash was the farm belt, this was the market which was most intensively cultivated.[87] The Model T, more than any other, was the farmer's car.

In the first years of the Model T's success, Henry Ford did many things: he bought land and he went into farming extensively; he concentrated on the tractor as never before, and for a short time letters coming into Dearborn from unknown farmer correspondents asking about tractor developments received his personal attention; and what this represents must be judged against the thousands of letters in the Ford Archives to which the only reply made was, "Mr. Ford is out of town . . ." A typical letter, which gives an impression of Ford's interest went to a farmer in Fowler, Kansas, in October 1909:

Dear Mr. Waldron:

The points brought out in your letter . . . to Mr. Henry Ford are in exact accordance with Mr. Ford's ideas and the very principles you mention are being brought out in the sample tractors which he is now building.

He is building a tractor of from fifty to sixty horsepower that will easily handle four 14-inch plows and also has a pulley from which farm machinery can be easily driven.

He has been using a tractor on his farm for two years that was constructed by using a four-cylinder automobile engine and some wheels purchased from an agricultural implement company with an old automobile radiator, steering gear, etc. This machine developed about twenty horsepower and easily did the work of four or five horses. It would handle a double gang plow very nicely, pull an eight inch feed cut grain binder at a speed of five miles an hour, and other work on the farm in about a like proportion. But the tractor that he is now building will be far and away superior to the sample which he has been using and will probably be out as a commercial proposition some time next season.

From the fact that Mr. Ford has experimented for two years makes it an assured fact that the tractors which he will put out next season will be a success and he should be pleased to hear from you sometime early next spring at which time he will be able to send you photographs and possibly more information regarding the machine.[88]

In contrast with Ford's lively interest in the problems of the farmers who wrote to him is Galamb's description of the conditions under which the experimental tractors were built. The promised photograph could never have been sent, for none of the tractors was to have its design frozen until after the outbreak of the First World War. In the meantime, Galamb said: "Mr. Ford asked me to keep everything away from the Ford Motor Company. He said the tractor was his own personal business and he didn't want anyone else butting in. That was why he had that little shop . . . to keep it away from Couzens and the others."[89]

As the endless experimenting continued Ford would occasionally break into print with the promise of innovations even more important than the tractor: an "auto crop-harvester," for instance, which was "a combination of plow, harrow, seeder and roller in one machine, so arranged that the plow will lead and the other parts follow."[90] But like the early tractors it was never put into production.

It would be difficult not to draw parallels with the development of the first cars. Then, too, Ford talked freely about engines and built them just as freely, for boats and work on a Dearborn farm. But the car itself he built in near secrecy, and then he could not freeze the design. The repetition of this pattern in the years following the introduction of the Model T, when the car's success was quickly becoming evident, suggests that for Henry Ford something had gone very wrong. And it would remain a suggestion but for the fact that between 1908 and 1916 he three times considered selling his interest in the Ford Motor Company. And this, in its own turn would seem unexceptional but for the violent drive for absolute control over every aspect of the company's life which was to dominate him in later years.

In 1908 and 1909 when the first offers were considered, Ford, said Couzens later, "really wanted to sell. He was sick in body and disturbed in mind."[91]

The first offer came from Benjamin Briscoe and W. C. Durant. According to Briscoe, he had approached Durant with a proposal to organize a corporation to include Buick, Ford, the Reo Company, and Maxwell-Briscoe; he had already talked to R. E. Olds, who was willing to discuss the proposal further.

After several meetings with Couzens it was agreed that each company would present its financial statements at a meeting to be held in New York where an audit would establish the basis for an exchange of preferred stock for each company's assets, with the common stock to be divided on a separate basis. At the New York meeting, Briscoe said, Couzens stated that he and Ford had changed their minds and rather than take preferred stock they wanted $3 million in cash; only if the audit showed the Ford assets in excess of this would they be willing to take preferred stock for the balance. Olds then spoke up, Briscoe recalled. "Well," said he, "if the Ford Company is to get $3 million in cash, my company must get it also."[92] Briscoe and Durant were unable to raise $6 million and the deal fell through.

Two years later Durant resumed talks with Couzens. In 1926, interviewed in the course of a suit brought by the former Ford shareholders against the Commissioner of Internal Revenue, Durant said that in 1910 Ford and Couzens were in New York. Couzens came to his office and told him that Ford was a sick man and suffering from nervous dyspepsia; for that reason Couzens had gone to see Durant alone but he was authorized to sell the Ford Motor Company for $8 million. Couzens himself was not prepared to sell: he told Durant that he wished to retain a one-fourth interest in the company. On this basis Durant took the proposal to his associate bankers but they turned it down.[93]

Sometime later the indefatigable Briscoe made another offer for the company:

Based on information that had come to me concerning the Ford Company, it occurred to me that the time might be propitious for approaching them again. . . . I accordingly sent a friend of mine, Mr. George F. McCullough . . . to see Messrs Ford and Couzens and endeavor to obtain an option on the Ford Company. Mr. McCullough did get a letter from them, virtually an option as I recall it now. They agreed to sell at $8 million, but would give no definite option until they saw "the color of his money."[94]

But once again the problem of raising funds proved insuperable and the agreement lapsed. "I dare say," Briscoe commented in 1921, "that Messrs Ford and Couzens have never known until now that I had any connection with McCullough negotiation and option."[95]

What is of special interest is Henry Ford's professed willingness not only to share control of the company as consideration of the first Briscoe-Durant offer indicates, but as time passed his evident wish to get out of the automobile industry entirely; and yet he set the terms so high that they could not be met. By 1916 his indecisiveness was to take even clearer form in a series of discussions which he entered into with Thomas W. Lamont of the House of Morgan. Lamont wrote to Ford after a stay in Detroit:

When you said to me that you would like to have me think about some plan that would embody the "best ideas of Ford and Morgan" you gave me a great deal to think about. . . .
You have in mind, and are working upon a wonderful development for the benefit of the farmers of America and in fact of the world. You wish to be able to carry out in splendid fashion your fine ideas along this line. You have some question in your own mind as to your ability to do this and, at the same time, to carry the full responsibility of the present motor car business. There must, it seems to me, come to you moments of almost deep oppression [sic] for the responsibility that you have to carry day by day. I do not wonder, therefore, that your mind comes back, as it seemed to do when you talked with me, to this problem, and to the question which I will make a beginning to paragraph,
Fourth: Can I form any alliance under which I can still maintain intact the present sort of management, which has proved so successful and energetic in the Ford motor business, so that I can, at the same time, develop my tractor idea, so that I can at the same time share with others the heavy responsibilities which I have to bear?[96]

Lamont's letter put the issues clearly: to sell or not to sell—to build tractors or not build tractors. And despite Ford's soon-to-be-articulated loathing of bankers, it was the House of Morgan, the very embodiment of a predatory Wall Street, which was called on for help.

The question raised is that of the unmistakable self-doubt which seems to have been Ford's constant companion in the years that followed the Model T. What did the car's success mean to Ford that he should follow it with a movement back in time to the tractor with which he had first begun—and yet find himself bound by an inhibition which is implicit in the continuous experimenting, the search for advice, the wish to give up responsibility?

The tractor finally went into production in 1917 under pressures which are not dissimilar to those which Couzens brought to bear on Ford in 1903; the similarity lies in the atmosphere of crisis which compelled Ford to freeze a design. He could finally say "this is it"—but not for himself, for someone else.

The British Government in 1917 was desperately seeking a means to increase its supplies of food. German submarines had decimated the merchant ships upon which the British traditionally depended and the tractors available in the country were both inadequate and expensive.

The approach to Ford carried Ministerial sanction. The company's British representative cabled:

The need for food production in England is imperative and large quantity of tractors must be available at earliest possible date for purpose breaking up existing grass and ploughing for Fall wheat. Am requested by high authorities to appeal to Mr. Ford for help. Would you be willing to send Sorensen and others with drawings of everything necessary, loaning them to British Government so that parts can be manufactured over here and assembled in Government factories under Sorensen's guidance? Can assure you positively this suggestion is made in national interest and if carried out will be done by the Government for the people with no manufacturing or capitalist interest invested and no profit being made by any interests whatever. The matter is very urgent. Impossible to ship anything adequate from America because many thousand tractors must be provided. *Ford tractors considered best and only suitable design.* Consequently national necessity entirely dependent Mr. Ford's design . . . urge favorable consideration and immediate decision because every day is of vital importance.[97]

But the British Government soon found it impossible to secure facilities to manufacture the tractor, and the work was undertaken at Dearborn. Ford wrote later:

The tractor works was not ready to go into production . . . [but] we ran up an emergency extension to our plant . . . equipped it with machinery that was ordered by telegraph and mostly came by express, and in less than sixty days the first tractors were on the docks in New York in the hands of the British authorities. . . . The entire shipment of five thousand tractors went through within three months and that is why the tractors were being used in England long before they were really known in the United States.[98]

The experimenting continued for the U.S. market on a machine that the British had found the "best and only suitable design," and it is with this as a background that the Model T resumes the center of the stage.

The theme which emerges is one of finality: Ford's work was done; the Model T had been built, the perfect car had reached the people. But with this came an unmistakable period of not knowing what he could now turn to. In some way the car was not enough, and yet it was all that he had. The halfhearted attempts to give it up were erased by the drive to confirm himself—by bringing the car to the people in ever-increasing numbers.

It is as if the numbers served to justify what he had done. They made his achievement more real and at the same time they ministered to a deeper injury. The vaster the sales of the Model T, the more Ford could take comfort in a symbolic sharing of guilt, and, at the same time, the farther the car took the farmer from the farm, the more necessary to Ford were the tractor and the village industries and his plans to make men half-farmers, half-industrial workers.

Also increasingly necessary were his ill-conceived adventures into public life.

When the Model T was finally abandoned in 1927, the tractor went with it and so did the *Dearborn Independent,* the newspaper he had used as a vehicle for anti-Semitism. In the same year he made an abject apology to the country's Jews.

But in 1909 the car was just one year old, and even as Ford considered the Briscoe-Durant offers in 1910 the Model T design had been frozen. On the face of it this was slight testimony to the extraordinary symbolism with which the car was invested and which slowly became clear as the years passed. It was in fact the most adaptive position, given the reality of the time. The design of the T was in advance of its competitors; standardization on as wide a scale as possible meant constantly falling costs of production and an ever-increasing market as the economies of scale permitted the price to be cut year after year.

In a 1913 interview Ford emphasized these advantages:

As we see it, Model T is the acme of motor car perfection. Although slight improvements are made from year to year as our corps of expert, experimental engineers discover them, they are not of sufficient importance to warrant the changing of the car's model. Therefore since 1909 contrary to the policy of other companies, the Ford Company has made no yearly change in the model of its car. Many advantages accrue to the makers of a standardized car. Chief among these are economy and efficiency of manufacture, stability of product and in fact, all of those benefits which accompany concentration of effort.[99]

But as the company's manufacturing facilities expanded and production continued to climb, from 10,000 cars in 1908 to 472,350 in 1915 to 933,720 in 1920,[100] the Model T began to assume an explicitly symbolic value. And as this emotional commitment grew more and more evident, so did Ford's blindness to the need for change.

The "corps of expert, experimental engineers" was hamstrung. In his reminiscences Galamb gave a vivid description of the difficulties which developed as the car's design became obsolete. Complaints poured in from Ford agents: the car's brakes were unreliable, the planetary gearshift hopelessly unsatisfactory as the years passed in the light of the advances made by the company's competitors. While the latter steadily improved their designs, the Model T continued as it had begun: "The last Model T," said Galamb, "had to be built the same way as the first." In the meantime factories all over the country did a thriving business supplying Ford owners with improvements which Henry Ford refused to build.[101]

But Ford competed on price, and for as long as the prices of his competitors remained so much higher than his there was no need to change. And on this basis every element in the structure of his fixation locked into place: first, the car which had come to represent much more than reality ascribed to it—such a car could not be changed; second, the need to build the car by the millions—the production system which made this possible depended absolutely on a frozen design; third, the price which brought the car to the millions was itself a function of the frozen design and the production system to which it had given rise. Here reality and obsession walked hand in hand.

In 1924 Ford's refusal to permit any change in the car, and the symbolism with which he invested it, came together in some of his remarks during an illuminating interview:

For years and years the heaviest sort of pressure was brought to bear on us to change lines, change working parts— changes—changes—changes . . . had we fallen in with every suggestion that was made we wouldn't have an automobile . . . [and] the development of the automobile is the greatest single instrument for world peace that I know of. The United States is made up of many nations. These people live in peace and understanding because there is an easy interchange of ideals and ideas. There are no "remote places" in this country. The automobile has corrected that.

. . . There could not be civil war. . . . the people under-stand each other too well for that.

When the automobile becomes as common in Europe and Asia as it is in the United States the nations will understand each other. Rulers won't be able to make war. They won't be able to because the people won't let them. No man is going to fight with a neighbor he knows, and likes because some temporary boss drops in and orders him to start a free-for-all.

This is the biggest thing the automobile will accomplish—the elimination of war. The automobile is the product of peace.[102]

And so the magical link was forged—there could be no change in the car because to Henry Ford the Model T was not simply a car. "Our principle of business," he wrote in 1923, "is [to make for the consumer] something that, as far as we can provide, will last forever . . . we never make an improvement that renders any previous model obsolete."[103]

The Model T rode to obsolescence under its own power. Higher incomes, changing tastes, better roads, the excellence of competitive cars were there for everyone to see but Henry Ford. Even the Model T jokes which had circulated around the nation for many years, sometimes with the assistance of Ford himself, assumed a far less tolerant form. "The Modern Twenty-Third Psalm" was typical:

The Ford is my auto,
I shall not want another.
It maketh me to lie down beneath it,
It soureth my soul.
It leadeth me in the path of ridicule,
For its name's sake.
Yea, though I ride through the valleys,
I am towed up the hills,
For I fear much evil.
Thy rods and thine engines discomfort me.
I anoint my tires with patches;
My radiator runneth over.
I repair blowouts in the presence of mine enemies.
Surely if this thing followeth me all the days of my life
I shall dwell in the bug-house forever.[104]

In *My Years with General Motors,* Alfred P. Sloan, Jr., identified four new and crucial elements that transformed the automobile market in the 1920s. The first of these was installment selling, and General Motors in 1919 with the organization of its Acceptance Corporation was the first company to offer facilities for consumer credit. "We believed," Sloan wrote, "that with rising incomes and the expectation of a continuance of that rise, it was reasonable to assume that consumers would lift their sights to higher levels of quality. Installment selling, we thought, would stimulate this trend."[105] Interviewed in 1926, Ford said that installment sales were the bane of American business; the public was no longer buying, it was letting itself be sold: "We have dotted lines for this, that, and that, and the other thing—all of them taking up income before it is earned."[106]

Sloan's second new element in the market of the 1920s was the used car trade-in, and this worked to Ford's double disadvantage. A good used car more than met the price of a new Model T and with an installment plan the buyer could even trade up to a better car using his Model T for a sizable down payment. Sloan's third and fourth elements were the closed car and the annual model. Ford met demand for the closed car by putting a cumbersome body on the Model T without essentially changing its open-car design, but the annual model change he utterly rejected. "The Ford car," he said in 1926,

is a tried and proved product that requires no tinkering. It has met all the conditions of transportation the world over. We are developing broader markets in South America, Australia and Europe. Within ten years Russia will be a big customer. . . . The Ford car will continue to be made in the same way. We have no intention of offering a new car. . . . we do not intend to make a "six," an "eight" or anything else. . . . we have experimented with such cars as we experiment with many things. They keep our engineers busy—prevent them tinkering with the Ford car.[107]

Only a year later the Model T was finally abandoned following a crisis at the executive level of the company. Nonetheless, it was out of Ford's fixation that the gigantic factories rose, first at Highland Park and then at the River Rouge. Ford built them to make more, and still more, cars to a design that he hoped never to change. "Our big changes," he said, "have been in methods of manufacturing. They never stand still. I believe that there is hardly a single operation in the making of our car that is the same as when we made our first [Model T]."[108]

If the cars are to be built for the millions, runs the implicit theme, the means must be there. And the means *had* to be there because it was in production by the millions that Ford found surcease. This alone seemed to confirm his achievement. That Ford's fixation moved for so long in such consonance with the ordinary needs of ordinary men is, perhaps, the story of industrial creativity; that it should have driven him to blind rigidity and the need for absolute power is testimony only to its depth.

"One of the contradictions," wrote the author of an impressionistic biography of Ford, "is that the Ford car came first and the method afterward."[1] This quotation is taken from a chapter entitled "The Mad Way," and in it the author attempts to establish Ford's "obsessionary and extravagant" concern with the processes of production which, organized and controlled in new ways and on an unprecedented scale, were to give him cars, not by the thousand, but by the million.[2]

The argument to be put forward in this chapter will begin from a different point of view: that there is no contradiction in the fact that the car came first and the method later, since it is the car which is the concrete symbol of Ford's obsession. The Ford method—the production process which was to become so intimately associated with Henry Ford that even in Russia it was called Fordizatsia and assumed the stature of an industrial philosophy[3]—represents initially a highly adaptive attempt at coping with the conflicts which lay at the base of his obsession. That this adaptation was essentially regressive in character will be held in suspense for the time being; at this point it need only be noted that, as Hartmann has written, "there are adaptations—successful ones and not mere unsuccessful attempts—which use pathways of regression. . . . There is, for example, the detour through fantasy. Though fantasy is always rooted in the past, it can, by connecting past and future, become the basis for realistic goals."[4]

In Ford's case, out of the fantasy which gave birth to the Model T, there grew a very real willingness to face, and capacity to solve the problems which stood between the car's creation and its distribution in the millions. The highly individual way in which this process was carried through is a dominant aspect of Ford's style as a leader, and it has been summed up in the title of this chapter as "the need for control."

Alfred Sloan was to prove in his leadership of General

Motors that there were other and much more lasting ways of achieving mastery of the industry. He wrote in 1964:

Good management rests on . . . "decentralization with co-ordinated control." . . . From decentralization we get initiative, responsibility, development of personnel, decisions close to the facts, flexibility—in short, all the qualities necessary for an organization to adapt to new conditions. From co-ordination we get efficiencies and economies. . . . The balance which is struck between corporate and divisional responsibilities varies according to what is being decided, the circumstances of the time, past experience, and the temperaments and skills of the executives involved.[5]

It is testimony to Ford's conflicts that his style of leadership could foster none of these qualities and capacities. The need for control which brought with it the enormous success of the early years brooked no opposition. Ford's fellow shareholders were the first to face the trend; later, company executives, the government, and the unions were to share the same experience, but in intensified form for by then Ford had been confirmed by the very success which he had earlier achieved.

Linking all the stages of Ford's need for control—from the administration of the company to the manufacture of the car, to Ford's belief in his own infallibility and the wider horizons this opened to him—there is a single dominant theme. This is the need to act in the face of an external threat, the need for absolute control in order to ward off and where possible destroy the threat which existed somewhere "out there."

The first battle began in 1903, the year in which the Ford Motor Company was founded. By then the acquisition of the Selden Patent by the Electric Vehicle Company, which was noted in Chapter 1, had led to infringement suits which had been either decided in favor of the patent holder or settled out of court with the company sued acknowledging the validity of the patent.[6] The patent had been issued in 1895 and it had seventeen years to run; it had been held to cover in the broadest terms "the application of the compression gas engine to road or horseless carriage use," and this meant that it was within the power of the patent holder to establish a legal monopoly in the automobile industry.[7]

The Electric Vehicle Company, hard hit by the decline in demand for electric cars which followed the steady improvement in the gasoline engine, set out to use its acquisition to hold the growing industry to ransom. Using a far shrewder approach than a simple demand for royalties which would have left the market effectively open to every builder who cared enough to build, George H. Day, president of the Electric Vehicle Company, had transformed the Selden Patent into a means for suppressing competition, controlling the market, and directing the profits from automobile manufacture into the hands of a select few: the instrument used was the Association of Licensed Automobile Manufacturers.

Formed in March 1903, the Association began its existence with ten members; they included the Olds Company, Haynes-Apperson, Pierce, and Packard. In return for membership and a manufacturing license, these companies were required to pay to the Association a royalty of 1¼ percent of the selling price of every car they built, and the Association was invested with the legal right to grant or deny licenses.[8]

In February 1903, some four months before the organization of the Ford Motor Company, Ford discussed an application for membership with an Association representative. The discussions were continued into late 1903 with no decision reached, and then in 1904 the Ford Motor Company was officially invited to become a member. The invitation was rejected by the Ford directors.[9] The company decided to go it alone, and with this decision a very real threat to its corporate existence was openly and willingly courted.

In his analysis of the Selden Patent litigation, William Greenleaf has attributed Ford's decision to his pride in the car. Ford himself said later that he "knew [the car] was the product of his own brain and no man on earth was entitled to any 'rake-off' from that particular car." Other reasons for the decision were said to lie in the traditional distrust of monopoly which inhered in the Midwestern rural culture, as well as in Ford's opposition to the patent system; he later advocated its abolition on the grounds that the laws "exploit the consumer and place a heavy burden on productive industry."[10]

While all of these reasons are valid here, the behavior which they seek to determine was to become a pattern in the future. None would then serve as a satisfactory explanation; the pattern would grow in complexity and its coherence would lie not in reasons adduced to explain isolated incidents but in the overall theme of control—to make the car safe for the millions, despite, and in defiance of, external threat.

With the Ford Motor Company's refusal of their invitation, the Association of Licensed Automobile Manufacturers moved quickly to take the *Ford* case before the courts, but it was not until 1911 that the patent was finally held to be invalid. In the meantime, Ford battled against an Association which was controlled by the supporters of the high-priced car: in no year between 1903 and 1911 did the Association grant a license to more than four makers of cars priced at less than $1000.[11] This lent strength to Ford's argument, which was soon to be expressed in a widespread advertising campaign denouncing the Association, guaranteeing Ford buyers from loss if the Association took action against them, and proclaiming that he was fighting the privileged few so that he might give the millions a car they could afford.

The situation within the Ford Motor Company was later

described by Horace Rackham, one of the original share-holders:

The Selden Patent was always a matter of most serious concern to all of us. We realized that until it was disposed of it placed the entire fortune of the Ford Motor Company and the rest of us in hazard. I recall that we were advised by our counsel not to expand too much until this matter was disposed of. As a matter of fact, until the Selden case was out of the way, Mr. Ford and the company could not carry out their expansion program which we always had in our minds. Mr. Ford always had in mind quantity production of a low-priced car for the masses to meet the universal demand of the whole world, and when he went to Model T as the exclusive model, it was the beginning . . . but we were handicapped and could not proceed with . . . expansion . . . in the early years of Model T [because of] the Selden Patent case.

You cannot imagine how freed we all felt after the final decision against the validity of the Selden Patent. It was then that we could extend the expansion policy that was Mr. Ford's dream, and the sky was the limit . . .[12]

In fact this description betrays more of Rackham's timidity, which was shared by others on the board, than it gives an accurate account of the company's progress. In open defiance of the Association, Ford pressed on with expansion and even as he fought the war against monopoly, a war concerned with freedom from other men's control, the path which expansion should follow opened a new front within the company: with Alexander Malcomson's support of the trend to expensive cars, Ford was faced with an adversary whose strength and closeness to home demanded immediate and ruthless action.

The means which Ford chose to rid the company of Malcomson have already been described; what is of special interest is the relentless way in which the pressure was applied. Ford was not simply buying out a former partner with whom he disagreed on policy, he was defeating an enemy.

In 1919 Malcomson was in financial difficulties and appealed to Ford for help. None was given, but E. G. Liebold, Ford's confidential secretary, interviewed Malcomson and submitted a report of the discussion, which included an account of the methods Ford used to win control of the company. In the negotiations which led up to the sale of his stock, Malcomson stated that he had originally given an option to Ford on the 255 shares that he owned, in return for Ford's note for $75,000. In the meantime, Malcomson bought the shares held by two other stockholders, Bennett and Fry—a total of one hundred.[13]

Ford's option on Malcomson's shares was in itself sufficient to give him majority control with 510 of the 1000 shares issued, but this apparently was still not enough. According to Malcomson, the $75,000 note was about to fall due when Ford informed him that he had no intention of paying it, or of taking up the option, unless Malcomson was also prepared to sell the shares he had bought from Bennett and Fry. Malcomson had already discounted the note with his bankers and had used the money; faced with the need to make this good and without the funds available, he had no alternative but to surrender every share he held.[14]

Although the minutes of the Board of Directors record that Ford and Couzens acquired Bennett's shares in September 1907, Bennett himself stated that he sold his shares to Malcomson, and in circumstances which bear out Malcomson's version of events.[15] Since Ford borrowed the money with which to pay Malcomson, what seems likely is that the shares of both Bennett and Fry were held as security, and that Ford and Couzens acquired full title to them a year later when Ford took 65 and Couzens 35 shares.

The minutes of the Board of Directors and of the stockholders' annual meetings show little of the tensions within the company, but on at least one occasion before Ford finally achieved majority control the small stockholders did make an attempt to assert themselves. Significantly, it came in October 1905, the year in which Henry Ford's new certainty expressed itself in the development of the Model N. On October 16, 1905, at the annual stockholders meeting, Anderson moved and Rackham seconded that the company's bylaws be changed so as to require that directors' meetings be held once a week rather than once a month. The motion was rejected, with Ford, the Dodge brothers, Couzens, and John S. Gray voting against it.[16]

On Gray's death less than a year later, his son David became a director. He testified in 1926 that

He was a mere figurehead as a Ford director and his actions as such were purely perfunctory. . . . Plans were submitted and were voted upon in such manner as Henry Ford requested. Everything was cut and dried beforehand and the directors really had no say and no discretion. . . . When the expenditures for the Rouge and Dearborn plants were discussed, the amount involved being $14 or $15 million, [he] declined to vote for this as he was doubtful of the policy involved, and Henry Ford promptly broke with him. . . .[17]

With this as a background and abetted by a Board of Directors over whom he now exercised a supremacy which flowed no longer simply from his preeminence in design or from his grasp of the production process, but overwhelmingly from his control of a majority of the company's shares, Henry Ford turned his attention to the manufacture of his car and the expansion of the company's market.

His first step was "To make it all Ford"—and so read the title of an article in *Motor Age* in August 1906, some five weeks after the Malcomson sale:

the present Ford Motor Company and the Ford Manufacturing Company . . . will be brought together into one concern. Henry Ford has been working with this idea in mind for some time and now it is reported he is about ready to spring the scheme on his stockholders with every chance of putting it through. . . . At the present time the company is about five months back in orders and has something like 6,000 orders for 1906 on the books. . . . Ford's ambition is to put out 50,000 of [his] runabouts. . . . He thinks he has a car that hits the right chord and for that reason he announces positively he will not change the selling price of the little machine. He has been urged to do this by his branch managers but he believes the best policy is to stick to the figures he quoted when he first sprang the proposition on the public as early as last fall. . . . His aim is to reduce the manufacturing of automobiles to the same basis as sewing machines and typewriters, turning them out in quantities.[18]

The consolidation of the Ford Manufacturing Company, which had been formed to hasten Malcomson's departure, and the Ford Motor Company was finally effected on April 29, 1907, and a progressive layout system which had been initiated at the Manufacturing Company for the production of motors and transmissions was now introduced at the Motor Company itself. Max Wollering, superintendent of the Manufacturing Company, became superintendent of the Motor Company under the direction of Walter Flanders, a production expert who had joined the Motor Company in the summer of 1906. "Mr. Ford," Wollering said later, "was planning for mass production at that time. His great theory was interchangeability of parts. He knew that to get mass production interchangeability . . . was *the* factor."[19]

The machine tools which were to give uniformity and interchangeability to the production of parts were designed by Ford men, at night after the plant had closed. Ford and Wills, Wollering said, were at the plant nearly every evening to check on the progress of the designs,[20] and by February 1909, Ford was in a position to discuss the "Secret of Ford Output" with a Detroit reporter. "Quantity production," he said, "calls for the installation of the latest machinery and frequently the designing of special machinery. Fifty percent of the machines in use in our shop were designed by our engineers. Certain of our machines will with one man do the work of from three to ten men working with machines of even last year's best design. Such machinery would not pay unless kept working to capacity and capacity means in many instances parts for 150 to 200 cars a day."[21]

By this time Ford had of course made the decision to freeze the design of the Model T, and he froze it at a point ahead of the designs produced by his competitors. In the interview just cited he indicated the simplified design which rendered feasible the growing use of machine tools for mass production. Where a manufacturer with a more complicated design might need several machines to produce the components for a subassembly, Ford's design reduced the subassembly itself to one integral part. "In a well-known foreign built car," he said, "nine separate pieces are required for a certain operation which in the Ford is replaced with a single part."[22] The policy of standardization was carried directly into the realm of the buyer when in June 1909 the company announced that the Model T would adopt one standard color after the current stock of red and grey bodies had been shipped. The color would be Brewster Green "with black trimmings and red stripings."[23] Three years later, in a move to cut costs further, the trimmings and stripings would be dropped and the "any color so long as it's black" policy would be adopted.

As the movement to standardization and the mechanization of the production process went forward, prices fell and demand rose, and the company inevitably outgrew its existing plant. In January 1907, the directors discussed the purchase of land for the erection of a new integrated factory, and in April of the same year the company acquired 57 acres at Highland Park on the outskirts of Detroit.[24] Work on the new plant was begun in August 1908, and in December 1909 the company transferred its operations to the new site. Only one-fourth of the plant had been completed, but despite this, January production averaged 60 cars a day.[25]

The scope of the plant was testimony to Ford's defiance of the Selden Patent holders, and by October 1910 the company's claim that it now owned the largest automobile plant in the world was taken seriously enough by the *Detroit Journal* to warrant a front-page story.

After a description of the foundry in which 200 men produced cylinders, pistons, and brake shoes, the reporter painted a graphic picture of the emerging Ford system:

The machine shop is a veritable mass of machinery. . . . All parts of the motor car are made here in sequence of operation. . . . In the cylinder department special machinery has been installed which enables the machinists to turn out 15 cylinders at a time. Most factories turn out one at a time. . . . Each piece is machined in a jig, so that every one is absolutely interchangeable and will fit any car turned out of the factory.

In the assembly department as a result, the article reported, there was "no filing, grinding, sawing or hammering of parts to make them fit. . . . Everywhere there is simplicity of method."[26]

Then in June 1911 the company bought the John R. Keim Mills of Buffalo, New York. Previously an important supplier of parts for the Ford car, the mill now became an integral part of the Ford Motor Company: its equipment and managerial personnel were brought to Highland Park and in this way Ford acquired the services of W. S. Knudsen and John R. Lee among others.[27]

The company's management, like its plant, was now the strongest in the industry. Among those ranged below Ford, equidistant in terms of titles, which none carried, but distinguished by their ability and personal influence on Ford, was C. H. Wills, who shared his interest in design engineering and his commitment to expansion.[28] In charge of production, following the departure of Flanders and Wollering in 1908, were P. E. Martin and Charles E. Sorensen; of machine tool engineering and operational layout, Oscar Bornholdt, Carl Emde, and later Charles Morgana, an alumnus of the Keim Mills. Under Couzens, whose writ ran in every area of the company outside of design and manufacture, were Norval Hawkins in charge of sales; Fred Diehl responsible for purchasing; Frank Klingensmith, whose main job as accountant made him effectively Couzens's assistant; and John R. Lee, who was responsible for personnel.[29] Knudsen, whose work at the Keim Mills would have indicated a job in production, instead undertook the establishment of Ford assembly plants throughout the country, and in this capacity he worked under Couzens in association with Hawkins. Later he said that he "avoided becoming tied up with the factory side of the organization because he did not want to be placed under Mr. Martin or Mr. Sorensen . . . he was afraid that as a stranger he would not get fair treatment."[30]

Knudsen's statement is the mildest harbinger of the structural instability which would later develop, but for the time being Ford's preoccupation with expansion gave the company a momentum in which each executive could share. There was still so much to be done that the issue of overlapping jurisdictions was less a problem than a source of company strength. Hawkins, for example, introduced the first comprehensive accounting system and Lee carried it further.[31] Wills's contributions ranged from work on the design of the cars, to metallurgy, to the design of machine tools. He was concerned with purchasing, with make-or-buy decisions, and with pricing policy.[32]

Speaking early in 1913 to a convention of Ford branch managers Hawkins, summed up the company's past achievements. "The story of Ala-ed-Din and the Wonderful Lamp," he said, "is not more wonderful than the Story of Ford and His Wonderful Car. . . . By the end of February—the close of our first five months for [the] 1913 [financial year]—we will have shipped more than 56,000 cars as against 17,555 for the same period a year ago."

This was made possible, he went on, by a factory which

covered nearly 85 acres and was as complete as modern architecture and labor-saving machinery could make it; and by the work of more than 7000 dealers and 46 branch houses equipped with parts to take care of the needs of Ford owners. Ending on a note which owed more to Henry Ford than to the traditional philosophy of a sales manager, he said: "We build no annual models or multiplicity of models—and do not cater in any manner to the fancies or foibles of the fickle public, but we do continually increase our output and decrease the price of our standard car. We have only one price—with no special discount either to dealers or retail buyers. Our selling contracts are the stiffest in the industry and we force all the terms."[33]

In the 1913 financial year the company was in fact to produce 168,304 cars as against 78,440 for the previous year, and the employment figures would rise to 14,366 from 6,867.[34] In the following year production swept upwards again to 248,307 cars while employment was reduced to 12,880 men.

The development which made this tremendous increase in production possible was the coming into full-scale operation of the Highland Park plant. Writing in 1915, Arnold and Faurote reported that the cash cost of land and buildings had reached $3,575,000 by February 1914, and an additional $2,800,000 had been spent on machine tools. Still, it was Ford's plans for still greater expansion which engaged their awed interest:

The first building was erected in 1908 and additions have been in progress ever since. . . . Very large six-storey buildings are now (April 1915) in progress of erection on each side of the railway tracks, each track served by a travelling crane which will load and unload cars by crane-transfer direct to seventeen different landings on each floor of these new buildings. . . . Handling of materials and work in progress . . . is now the principal problem of motor-car cost-reduction, as the machine tools and the assembly processes and methods are now highly specialized; but the factory as now arranged employs somewhere from

800 to 1000 truck-men, pullers, and shovers, most of whom will be needless when the new buildings are completed and travelling-crane service is given fullest employment. The present machine shop will be transferred to the new buildings. . . . The foundry will occupy the top floor of one building and rough stores and the machine tools demanding most light will occupy the other top floors; work in progress will descend in the material course of operations until it reaches the train loading platforms ready for instant shipment.[35]

And all of this Ford had financed out of income in addition to paying dividends which by June 1913 totaled $24,713,000.[36] The Ford Motor Company had in fact reached a stage within the automobile industry analogous to Rostow's third stage of economic growth: "the interval when the old blocks and resistances . . . are finally overcome [and] compound interest becomes built, as it were . . . into habits and institutional structure."[37]

The principle underlying the Ford method was the process line, in which the car moved from the raw state to the finished product through a sequence of men and machinery. By 1913 the sequence of men and machines was already supplied by gravity slides; within months, moving conveyors would be introduced and the process line itself mechanized. The production system in other plants in the industry was still tied to the grouping of machinery by type; drill presses or milling machines, for instance, were herded together, and the flow of work in progress was made to conform to the location of departmental operations. A single part might move back and forth between departments before it was finally completed, contributing to higher costs in time and in-process inventory.[38]

Where other automobile companies had adopted the annual model change, the Highland Park plant in contrast had been built expressly to manufacture the Model T. Model changes involving as they did the scrapping of machine tools and inventory, lower worker productivity in the initial stages, and more strenuous advertising and sales efforts led to a capital burden which few companies could sustain without borrowing, and the cost of capital contributed in its own turn to the costs of production.

With the standardization of the Model T, volume permitted the rapid amortization of machine tools, even the prohibitively expensive single-purpose machines. And under the direction of Wills and W. H. Smith, another Keim alumnus, the Ford experimental shop developed new high-speed steels which gave still longer life and greater precision to the machines.

The company's engineers were free to concentrate on production methods, breaking down operations into the simplest steps and effectively eliminating the learning curve. In turn, these efforts at simplification had an enormously productive influence on the design of new and better machine tools: with the number of operations reduced to a minimum it was easier to design a machine to do the job, and for unskilled labor to replace the skilled workman.

In February 1913, F. H. Colvin, the editor of the *American Machinist,* visited Highland Park and later published a series of articles dealing with the company's manufacturing methods. Prior to this he had visited, among others, the Franklin, Pierce Arrow, Buick, Maxwell, Packard, Willys-Overland, and Reo plants: there was nothing in any, he testified, which compared with Ford's manufacturing efficiencies. None of these companies had, or could afford, the Ford machines which drew crankcases from flat sheets of steel; which produced the 95 tubes and nearly as many sheet metal pins in the radiator at a single stroke of a press; which soldered the 500 points of contact in the radiator in one operation.[39]

Ford was so far ahead that no other manufacturer could catch up with him. Even if they were to freeze their designs, none had the volume to allow for specialized machine tools, and, given the policy of model changes, the limited time in which specialized tools would be in use pushed their costs even higher than those of hand operation.[40]

The massive stream of cars which flowed from Highland Park moved to the company's branch houses as well as directly to its dealers. The branch houses were retail offices which carried stocks of parts and finished cars for sale to individual buyers as well as for delivery to dealers. The advantage of the branch system over the wholesale distribution method used by Ford's competitors lay in the close supervision of the company's dealers which it permitted: the company retained absolute control over the prices of cars, parts, and accessories, and could enforce the standards of service which were required by the dealers' franchise. Roadmen working out of the branch houses checked the dealers' repair methods and equipment, the condition of their showrooms, taught them how to handle advertising, keep accounts, and manage stocks of parts. And despite the inclusiveness of the company's control, the enormous demand for the Model T gave it the pick of automobile dealers in the country. By early 1913 there were more Ford branch representatives, roadmen, dealers, and dealers' salesmen coming into contact with the public than any other five manufacturers in combination could claim, and the company's distribution facilities were still in expansion.

In October 1911, the stockholders authorized the expenditure of 15 percent of annual net earnings, beginning from October 1, 1911, toward the development of a network of assembly plants across the country. Under Knudsen's direction, 28 assembly plants were established in the largest cities of 22 states. The plants were factories in miniature: they assembled cars from parts and motors shipped from Detroit and built, painted, and trimmed their own bodies. They extended the drive-away radius of finished cars and supplied dealers with stocks of parts over a wider range than the branch houses had previously handled. Most important of all, the system dramatically reduced the cost of freight.

Before the assembly plants came into operation, the company had at best managed to load a railroad car with only seven Model Ts, and even this was an advance over other manufacturers, the chassis of whose cars limited the load to four. With the shipment of straight car loads of parts—motors, gas tanks, tires, wheels, radiators—the Ford Motor Company now began shipping the equivalent of 26 Model Ts to each railroad car and in addition it could take advantage of freight rates which were lower for parts than for the assembled cars. Shipments could be diverted en route from one assembly plant to another; outside suppliers could ship direct to the plants without first going through Highland Park. The home plant itself benefited from the freeing of storage space which had previously been occupied by assembled cars and from the opportunity to produce stocks of parts for the assembly plants in the periods between production peaks. Of most advantage to the company was the fact that the new economies represented a clear profit: the cost of the car to the buyer remained fob Detroit in line with prevailing practice in the industry.

Adding to all of this were still other economies of scale. Purchases of raw materials and parts from outside suppliers had risen from $18.7 million in 1911 to $63.5 million in 1913. The manufacturing schedule for 1913 included requisitions for 90,000 tons of steel, 12 million hickory billets for wheel spokes, 800,000 tires, 2 million square feet of glass, 15,000 tons of molding sand, and 2 million cubic feet of gas a day. Faced with orders of this magnitude, suppliers were willing to quote lower prices, and where the supplier gave his entire output to Ford the prices were pared to a minimum.

Alfred Sloan said later that his first understanding of the intimate relationship of price to volume was taught him by Henry Ford.[41] At that time the Hyatt Roller Bearing Company was supplying Ford with more than half of its output. Wills demanded lower prices and got them after persuading Sloan that it was unfair to charge the Ford Motor Company with advertising overhead incurred in the search for other business.

To help other suppliers cut costs, Ford sent engineers into their plants to improve manufacturing methods, paid in advance for their products to give them capital for high volume machine tools, and used the company's enormous buying power to reduce the cost of suppliers' raw materials by taking over their purchasing. By taking advantage of cash discounts on all its purchases, the company earned nearly $2 million in 1913; in Rostow's phrase, compound interest had become built into the structure.

As far as demand was concerned, the future seemed limitless. In the farm market alone it was estimated that there were more than six million potential buyers of the Model T and the 1910 census indicated that there were 62,000 towns with populations of 1000 or under in which no Ford dealer had been appointed. The Good Roads movement was making steady progress and by 1913, 42 states had passed laws providing state aid for road improvement. Ford's continuing price reductions—the cost of the car had fallen from $950 in 1909 to $500 in 1914—were uncovering ever broader layers of demand.

It was with the clearest justification that the presidents of Packard, Paige Motors, Hupp Motors, and the chairman of the Dodge Company later agreed that competition with Ford in 1913 was impossible. The enormous cost apart, it would have taken one and a half to two years to put a competitive car on the market, and by that time the price of the Model T would in all probability have fallen below the level at which the new car was originally intended to compete. "A man would have been a fool," said the President of the Hupp Company, "to go into the business with the idea of competing with Ford in mind."[42]

Against this background of extraordinary achievement, a chorus of adulation inevitably began to make itself heard.

"Henry Ford," said a member of a British trade delegation that visited Detroit in 1913, "has shown us how to make motor cars better than any other man in the world. We dream of him at night. Had it not been for Henry Ford we would never have begun the making of motor cars in England."[43] The Highland Park factory became the cynosure of the industry. "The Ford Plant," said the manager of Germany's Benz Company, "is the most remarkable in the world; it is the very best in equipment and method."[44]

And the company itself contributed to the growing legend. "Henry Ford," ran a 1910 advertisement, "has been the greatest factor in the development of the automobile industry, greater than any other man in the world. . . . He is as well known in Europe as in America. [He] stands out, independent and alone, clear and strong, as the most dominant factor in the automobile industry of today."[45]

The sober fact was that it was all true: Ford's obsession stood vindicated by the market, by the industry, and by society at large. "The very fact," wrote Gitelson in a 1954 paper, "that in the narcissistic neurosis the ego maintains its capacity to perceive and deal 'adaptively' with external reality makes it possible for the intrapsychic conflict to be laid out on the framework presented by the environment, and to follow there a course which has the aspects of 'normality.' "[46] Ford's ouster of Malcomson, given the clear-cut objective of the mass car, was on the face of it a realistic clearing of the path, the neurotic component was exposed only in the means adopted. By 1911 when the Selden Patent was declared invalid, the opinion of the court condemned the threat to the industry against which Ford had fought—and here the element of conflict emerges only as part of a pattern made consistent by future actions. The drive to expansion, to build more and more cars of which Highland Park was so overwhelming a symbol, was again on the face of it a brilliant and daring synthesis of social needs with hitherto unobserved economic laws.

But the policy of price cutting did not grow out of a sophisticated appraisal of sociological and economic factors. It grew out of a need to extend the limits of obsession, to share with other men what he had done.

The cut-and-try method that Ford as an engineer so vigorously expounded found a place in management policy: as the money was made on the cars so it was poured back into making still more. Only then did the influence of volume on costs begin to emerge. "I hold," Ford said in 1916,

that it is better to sell a large number of cars at a reasonably small margin than to sell fewer cars at a large margin of profit. *I hold this because it enables a larger number of people to buy and enjoy the use of a car and because it gives a larger number of men employment at good wages. Those are two aims I have in life. . . .* This policy I hold is good business policy because it works—because with each succeeding year we have been able to put our car within the reach of greater and greater numbers, give employment to more and more men, and at the same time through the volume of business increase our own profits beyond anything we had hoped for or even dreamed of when we started.

Bear in mind every time you reduce the price of the car without reducing the quality, you increase the possible number of purchasers. There are many men who will pay $360 for a car who would not pay $440. We had in round numbers 500,000 buyers of cars on the $440 basis, and I figure that on the $360 basis we can increase the sales to possibly 800,000 cars for the year—less profit on each car, but more cars, more employment of labor, and in the end we get all the profit we ought to make. And let me say right here, that I do not believe that we should make such an awful profit on our cars. A reasonable profit is right, but not too much. So it has been my policy to force down the price of the car as fast as production would permit, and give the benefits to users and laborers, with resulting surprisingly enormous benefits to ourselves. The men associated with me haven't always agreed with this policy.[47]

Earlier, in 1912–1913, the price cuts had already assumed such importance for Ford that formal advertising appeared unnecessary. Moving out of his own sphere of action, he rejected detailed sales and advertising plans which Couzens had approved.⁴⁸ Again he was vindicated by the mounting sales of the Model T, and increasingly, by the actions of his competitors.

By 1915–1916, price cuts and the moving assembly line had become standard in the industry. In May 1915, Chevrolet announced a $235 reduction in the prices of its touring cars and roadsters. In the same years Oldsmobile and Hudson reduced their prices; Willys-Overland made price cuts of nearly 30 percent and Paige and Studebaker of 27 percent. Still, with the Model T runabout selling at $390, the best that Chevrolet could offer was a touring car at $490, and the cheapest Willys-Overland sold for $750. The Paige at $1095 and the Studebaker at $985 were out of the Model T's class.⁴⁹ All of these manufacturers cited "accelerated quantity production and improved production techniques and plant economies" as the means by which the price reductions had been achieved; they had in fact introduced the assembly line. An article in *Motor Age* reported in March 1916 that

Ford was perhaps the first to install the moving assembly scheme and to set an example for the rest of the motor world. It was marvelled at when it first became known that the Ford car did not stop in its process of manufacture until it was driven from the conveyor under its own power. Before long others saw the advantage of introducing the element of time relentlessly, and they set about to go the Ford plant one better. Today most of the big producers have installed the moving system with the modifications and improvements which the production departments of each deem best suited for the . . . class of cars being built.⁵⁰

The article cited Maxwell, Paige, Hudson, Packard, Studebaker, Dodge, Reo, and Saxon as having all adopted line production.

And so the man who would later say, "We have most unfortunately found it necessary to get rid of a man as soon as he thinks himself an expert," who would "refuse to recognize that there are impossibilities," approached a stage in which the confirmation in reality of his own infallibility—a confirmation which in fact attested to the "rightness" of his fixation—arose all around him.[51] There would be one further challenge to his authority within the company, and this would finally be dealt with by buying out his fellow shareholders, thus giving him total control.

The train of events began quietly enough in August 1913 when John F. Dodge resigned from the board and gave one year's notice of the termination of the contract between Dodge Brothers and the Ford Motor Company. From 1903 the Dodges, in addition to ownership of 10 percent of the company's stock, had been prime suppliers of parts. The terms of their final contract had required them to supply "at least 80 percent of Ford's annual requirements [for] transmissions, rear axle and drive shaft assemblies [and] drop forgings."[52]

The extent of their business with the Ford Company had provided the funds for the expansion of their original machine shop into a vast modern plant. Ford said in 1916 that the company had paid $27 million to the Dodges in the eleven years during which their contract ran, and this may have been an underestimate, for in 1912 alone the value of parts supplied by the Dodges was reported to be $10 million.[53] But as the Highland Park plant expanded, it became increasingly clear to the Dodges that their arrangement with the Ford Motor Company was fraught with risk. They were committing their entire output to a single customer whose private and public position was to exploit the economies of scale, economies made possible by the scope of his own operations, in order to reduce the price of the Model T. The Dodge plant was not subject to the close control the Ford Company wielded over its other suppliers, and Ford would undoubtedly soon refuse to pay the double profit the Dodges earned from Ford dividends and from the volume orders for parts.[54]

Rather than wait for Ford to terminate the contract, the Dodges took the initiative. They announced that they would go into automobile manufacture on their own account but that they had no intention of disposing of their Ford interests. "They are highly valuable interests," John Dodge told the press. "We received $1.1 million this year [1913] and over a million the year before."[55]

The dividends to which he referred consisted of a regular dividend of 60 percent annually on the official capitalization, which had been increased by a stock dividend of $1.9 million to $2 million in 1908, and special dividends declared several times a year by the board. The official dividend amounted to only $1.2 million annually and of that the Dodges received $120,000. The special dividends depended for their size and payment on the sanction of Henry Ford, but the Dodges evidently anticipated no reductions: the official capitalization represented only slightly more than 1 percent of the company's total investment.[56]

Then on October 12, 1915, Couzens resigned as vice-president and treasurer of the Ford Motor Company. The occasion arose out of Couzens's dissatisfaction with Ford's pacifist stand which had become increasingly outspoken in the months following the outbreak of World War I; the cause went much deeper.

The friendly relations that have existed between us for years have been changed of late, [Couzens said in a statement to the press]. Our disagreements daily become more violent. I finally decided I would not be carried along on that kind of a kite. I have never in my life worked for any man. Even when I was a car checker, a few years ago, I had no boss; but I was and am today willing to work with any man. I was willing to work with Henry Ford, but I refuse to work for him.

What Mr. Ford has to say is considered by many to be of wide importance, because the Ford Motor Company has been built up to such magnitude that the public eye is always on him. . . . [But] it was through my efforts that the Ford Motor Company was built up around . . . Henry Ford.[57]

And here was the crux of the problem—the issue of control.

In his own statement to the press Ford said that he knew of no reasons for Couzens's action other than disagreement over his pacifism. But E. G. Pipp, a close associate of Ford's who was then editor of the *Detroit News* and was later to be editor of Ford's weekly newspaper until Ford's anti-Semitism brought about Pipp's resignation, recalled later that Ford had already made up his mind to get rid of Couzens. "Jim sprung the thing about the [pacifist] article . . .," Ford reportedly told Pipp. "Fine, I thought, that's a dandy way out of it, so I stood pat."[58] In his reminiscences Ford's private secretary E. G. Liebold said he thought that "back in their own minds there was a bitter animosity between Mr. Ford and Mr. Couzens," and still other observers noticed the friction.[59] Some months later John Dodge discussed Couzens's resignation with Henry Ford; Couzens's departure, Dodge said, was to the company's disadvantage. Dodge testified later:

Mr. Ford then stated very emphatically that it was a very good thing for the company that [Couzens] had left, and that now they would be able to do things that before Mr. Couzens had prevented; that his restraining influence was gone and they were now going to expand. . . . he said they were going to double the size of the Highland Park plant and double the output of cars and sell them at half-price. . . . I told him that if he proposed to carry things to such an extreme . . . he should buy out the other stockholders, then he could run the business as he saw fit. He told me that he did not care to buy any more stock . . . he had control and that was all he needed. [He] spent most of the rest of the time telling about the shortcomings of Mr. Couzens with the aid of Mr. Wills.[60]

Ford's breach with Couzens thus assumes a shape quite different from that of a spur-of-the-moment break between the two men over an issue extraneous to the company's affairs. By 1915 Ford was already set on further expansion, and on a scale which would make Highland Park seem Lilliputian. The 1912 stockholders' resolution which had in effect limited expansion to 15 percent of annual net earnings was superseded in May 1915 by a new resolution which authorized the directors to decide on the sums to be spent.[61] But one needs to substitute Henry Ford for "the directors" if the stockholders' minutes are to reflect the facts. Interrogated in 1916 by counsel for the Dodges in the suit they were soon to bring in an effort to force the resumption of special dividends and set limits on expansion, Ford could remember no instance in which his directors had reversed his decisions.

Counsel: Your directors are very accommodating; whenever you ask them to ratify anything, they usually do it?
Ford: They usually do, yes.
Counsel: And if they don't do it, they wouldn't be there, would they? They haven't done anything for you to turn them out.
Ford: I don't turn anybody out.
Counsel: Because they have always done what you have asked them to do?
Ford: Not always.
Counsel: Tell us some instance where they haven't.
Ford: You look it up and you will find it.
Counsel: Just give us a single thing that the Board of Directors have refused to ratify, that you recommended.
Ford: I don't know of anything.
Counsel: You don't know of anything.
Ford: No . . .
Counsel: (pointing to Ford) This is the Board of Directors right here.[62]

The minutes of the directors' meetings, as in the Malcomson case, gave little indication of the tension between Ford and Couzens, but the assumption seems safe that it arose over Ford's invasion of areas of business which up to then had been Couzens's clear responsibility. In June 1915, four months before Couzens's resignation, Ford announced that he planned to build a blast furnace and tractor plant on a site of more than 1000 acres lying along the River Rouge.

"It is the intention of Henry Ford," reported the *Detroit Journal,* "to bring iron ore in boats to the blast furnace and turn the ore into motor cylinder heads and other auto and tractor parts without having either ore or iron pass through the hands of middlemen." Work on the project, Ford said, would begin that summer. Two days later Couzens contradicted him in print: "Nothing will be done for three or four years. . . ."[63]

Then on October 6, less than one week before Couzens resigned, Ford announced that construction of the tractor plant would begin immediately, and two weeks later ground was broken for the erection of a power plant.[64] In a statement to the press Ford made the first of a series of attacks on his stockholders:

In the new tractor plant there will be no stockholders, no directors, no absentee owners, no parasites, declared Henry Ford the other day, in a discussion of modern industrialism.
That is, there will be no incorporation, every man employed during the period of his employment, which the aim will be to make permanent, will share in the profits of the industry; but there will be no dividend to "stock" either at face or market value.[65]

In the following month a further announcement was made: the new venture would be a partnership under the style of Henry Ford and Son. Financed by Ford himself, it would not be hobbled by "absentee stockholders who do not labor but merely invest their money."[66] The profit sharers, the press reported, would be "those who supply the muscle and brain to build up the business."[67] So easily were the labors of Couzens and the Dodges dismissed.

Early in 1916, the Dodges subsequently testified, they approached Ford in an attempt to clarify the relationship of the tractor plant to the Ford Motor Company: they had been under the impression that it was a personal venture but had discovered that Ford was planning to use "the engine of the Model T and the facilities and resources of the Ford Motor Company to produce this tractor and still own the tractor plant himself." Ford reiterated his intention to keep the two companies separate, but of much greater concern to the Dodges, he said that "He did not propose to pay any dividends except the nominal [official] dividend; that the stockholders had already received a great deal more than they had put into the company, and he did not propose to pay any more; he was going to put the earnings of the [Ford Motor Company] back into the business so as to expand it."[68]

On February 2, 1916, the tractor issue was settled with a resolution passed by the Board of Directors. On the vote of Ford, Gray, and Klingensmith, who had succeeded Couzens as treasurer, the company released to Henry Ford by quitclaim all rights and interests in the tractor business as it had up to then been developed. Couzens alone voted against the resolution. On the following day in Couzens's absence, the stockholders unanimously approved it.[69]

Couzens perhaps more than any of the others had reason to remember the part played by the Ford Manufacturing Company in Malcomson's ouster. Then, as Henry Ford's closest adviser, he had helped establish what amounted to a rival organization, and it had been used against a director and important stockholder to force him into accepting Ford's terms. Although it is no more than conjecture, Couzens may have felt it unwise to concede so easily the issue of a separate company under Ford's control, and, in the event, he was to be proved right.

The Dodges, whose votes had contributed to the stockholders' unanimous approval of the quitclaim, were soon confronted with further problems. Early in August 1916, Ford announced drastic cuts in the price of the Model T. The touring car was now to be sold at $360, a cut of $80; the runabout at $345 and the chassis at $325 took price cuts of $45 and $35.[70] In the financial year to July 31, 1916, the company had sold 472,350 cars for a net profit of more than $57 million. Unfilled orders at the end of each month throughout the year had averaged 36,375 cars.[71] Gratuitously, and at one stroke, Ford had cut the following year's profit in half, and this would occur in spite of a phenomenal production increase to 730,041 cars.

But there was more to come. Ford had meant what he said to the Dodges when he discussed the tractor. On August 31, 1916, the *Detroit News* carried a report of an interview with Ford. "It was now the confirmed policy of the company," Ford said, "to discontinue payments of special dividends. The 1916 profits would be reinvested to pay for expansion. Work on the blast furnaces would soon begin."[72]

To the Dodges this must have been the final indication of Ford's contempt for his stockholders' opinions. The blast furnaces lay at the heart of Ford's vast dreams of expansion. The cost of the blast furnaces demanded for its justification an increase in production to one million cars a year. In turn, this meant enormously expanded storage facilities, plant, and equipment. And since the Highland Park site was now too small and crowded, expansion would have to begin with the acquisition of land.

Ford's personal holdings along the Rouge River were now extensive, so extensive in fact that it might appear only a small step, once the site was acquired by the company, to bring within the scope of the expansion program facilities for the manufacture of parts so far supplied by outside companies. Up to this point the Ford Motor Company was still buying springs, bodies, tires, coil units, wheels, and the bulk of its drop forgings from outside suppliers; and in spite of occasional delays and the setbacks which occurred when the plants of two suppliers were destroyed by fire, the contractors had grown with the company, contributing heavily to the consistent increases in production.[73] Ford's plans for expansion, it must have seemed to the Dodges, might well call for the unnecessary duplication of suppliers' facilities which had been built up over years of steady growth.

For all of these reasons work on the blast furnaces sounded

a call to action. They heralded a commitment of funds on an unprecedented scale, and directing the disbursement of these funds, and consolidating his control, would be Henry Ford. The Dodges were the only shareholders to resort to action in the face of deliberately slashed profits and the simultaneous proposals for enormous expenditure. That these policies seemed the negation of each other must have been uppermost in their minds. On September 25, 1916, they wrote to Ford:

We have for some time, as you know, been endeavoring to see you for the purpose—as you assumed and informed one of your associates—of discussing the affairs of the Ford Motor Company from the standpoint of our interest as stockholders, and with a view to securing action by the Board of Directors . . . [for] a very substantial distribution [of] dividends.

Not having been able to make an appointment to discuss the matter with you personally, as we very much desired to do, we write you this letter. . . .

The conditions shown by your recent financial statement—showing approximately $60 million of net profits for the past year and cash surplus in bank exceeding $50 million . . . would suggest, without the action being requested, the propriety of the Board taking prompt action to distribute a large part of the accumulated cash surplus as dividends to the stockholders to whom it belongs.

While we would be sorry to have any controversy over the matter, we feel that your attitude toward the stockholders of the company is entirely unwarranted. The statements that you have made—that the stockholders are and have been receiving as dividends all they are entitled to—shows a most extraordinary state of mind if it represents your real feelings.

While a dividend of five percent per month, 60 percent per annum on the capital stock of the company, $2 million, on its face would seem to be a large dividend, the fact is . . . that the assets of the company representing its surplus is as much the property of the stockholders as the assets representing the capital stock, and the stockholders are as much entitled to a dividend that will give them returns on their surplus investment as their capital stock.

. . . In view of the existing circumstances we ask that you promptly call a meeting of the Board of Directors to consider the situation and lay before them our views as stockholders as outlined in this letter, and we desire to say . . . that we conceived it to be the duty of the Board of Directors to distribute as a minimum a special dividend of not less than fifty percent of the accumulated cash surplus of the company.

Another matter that we desire brought to the attention of the Board is our contention as stockholders that the company has no right to use the company's earnings in the continued expansion of . . . plants and property . . . indeed from our point of view, they have already exceeded their authority in this direction.

We would be pleased to have your acknowledgement of the receipt of this letter and advice that you have called a meeting of the Board of Directors for the purpose of considering and acting upon the matters referred to in it.[74]

Ford did not reply to this letter until October 10 when he asserted that "it would not be wise to increase the dividends at the present time." He promised, however, to set the Dodges' views before the Board. Faced with the prospect of an indefinite delay, the Dodges on October 11 again wrote to Ford requesting an early meeting of the directors. They had seen reports, they said, of the company's "ambitious plans" for expansion, and they wished to be advised of the steps taken, since "it would be idle to have the Board of Directors consider the question of disbursing the cash assets of the company in dividends if, before the Board has considered our request, the same have been appropriated in the directions referred to."[75]

This paragraph may have helped determine Ford's strategy. His reply was delayed for more than three weeks, and then he advised the Dodges of the plans so far adopted by enclosing copies of the Directors' Minutes for October 13 and November 2. Acting unanimously, the directors had approved expenditure of more than $5 million for expansion at Highland Park. They had approved for $700,000 the purchase from Ford of the River Rouge site and had also approved the construction of blast furnaces, a foundry, and other buildings to be built at an estimated cost of more than $11 million. They had agreed to share the cost with Ford personally of dredging a canal and installing a turning basin since these facilities would lie between the company's site and the land retained by Henry Ford for his tractor plant.[76]

By then the Dodges had taken the issue to the courts. On November 2, they filed a minority stockholders' suit against the Ford Motor Company and its officers requesting inter alia an injunction to restrain the program of expansion, and the distribution of 75 percent of the current cash surplus, approximately $39 million. They also requested a decree to enforce the distribution of all future earnings "except such as may be reasonably required for emergency purposes." The bill of complaint attacked Ford's personal and absolute control of the company and termed his plans for expansion "reckless in the extreme."[77] Two days later Ford took his case to the newspapers:

The Dodge Brothers in their bill of complaint [say] that last year the Ford Company produced 500,000 cars at a profit of $60 million and had a satisfied public to deal with; that without taking any chances we should repeat the output, get the same prices we got last year, and produce the same margin of $60 million. . . .

Holding to that policy might be in the interests of the manufacturers of some other line of automobiles, but at this time we are interested in the manufacture of Ford cars and the people who look to us for cars and the men and women who look to us for employment.

. . . There is a complaint as to the amount of surplus cash we carry. That amount has been as high as $52 million at the close of the fiscal year. We did a business of $206 million last year and I don't think our surplus is any too large. . . . I have always wanted to have enough cash to swing our purchases without borrowing. I have always been opposed to going to Wall Street because I don't want them to get our hide. We are not afraid of them because we have the cash assets. . . .[78]

And then in a series of contradictions Ford took issue with the Dodges' contention that expansion should be deferred until the company could better assess postwar conditions. The uncertainty of conditions after the war's end, Ford said, was "just why we are using some of the surplus we have, to make our cost of production . . . secure on the present basis." Although he foresaw a decline in the price of steel, "we don't propose taking any chances even on that. We intend making our own iron. We have already contracted for blast furnaces. . . ."[79]

That the Dodges had referred to the uncertainty of public demand for the Model T escaped Ford entirely; it was the threat to his own sources of supply—premised on the near-messianic conviction of an ever-increasing public demand for the cars so long as he could build them—which obsessed him, and it was beyond his understanding that the Dodges did not share his conviction: "They say my course is likely to injure them. They own ten per cent of the stock and I own 58 per cent. I can't injure them $10 without injuring myself $58."[80] That the Dodges had no reason, conscious or unconscious, to lead them into risking their 10 percent was not an issue.

W. J. Cameron later said that Ford inherited from his "rural Populist background a terrible fear of monopolistic power holding everything down . . . [his] fear of this is evidenced by his building his own steel mills and buying his own raw material sources. He liked to have that safety."[81] The easy attribution to Populism of many of Ford's rigid prejudices has been taken further by, among others, Nevins and Hill.[82] But it needs to be borne in mind that Ford's "rural Populist background" in fact included a father who was a prosperous farmer, who supported the Republican party, and who never aligned himself with the Grange or with the Populists; who was an Episcopalian who nonetheless raised a family of religious freethinkers, quite at odds with the dogmatic Protestantism which was one of the mainsprings of the Populist movement. The Populist revolt of the 1890s in fact bypassed Henry Ford; he was then working for the Edison Company in Detroit, and Michigan itself was never the hotbed of Populism which developed in the cotton-growing South, the wheat-growing northwestern states, Kansas, Nebraska, and the Dakotas, and in the Mountain states where the price of silver had declined as disastrously as that of cotton and wheat. With greater insight, Keith Sward emphasized the transparency of Ford's Populist coloration.[83]

But an even clearer indication of the nature of Ford's fears comes from a contemporary journalist. In October 1916, an article in *Metropolitan Magazine* described Ford's recent rejection of a Wall Street offer for the Ford Motor Company, and, the writer continued, as a result of his refusal "Ford has heard various ugly rumors that the big interests are going to 'get' him in a simpler way—cut off his steel."[84] The "big interests" can only be Wall Street, and in fact in the spring of 1916 Hornblower and Weeks made an unsuccessful offer of $500 million for the company.[85] But of much more recent date were the negotiations initiated by Ford himself with the Morgan Company. Thomas W. Lamont had already visited Detroit at Ford's invitation, and in the correspondence which followed Ford's request for suggestions as to how he might divest himself of his holdings, it was *Lamont* who maintained that whatever financial arrangements might be reached it was imperative that Ford retain a position of importance in the company.[86]

The interests out to "get" him were beginning to assume in Ford's mind proportions which were out of touch with reality. They drew sustenance less from a background of Populism than from fantasy, and the fantasy was to be dominant in the drive to expansion at the Rouge. For his own peace of mind Ford needed control; nothing could be permitted to block production of the car. "I think the Rouge was pretty much like Topsy," said R. T. Walker later, "I think that it pretty much just grew. Mr. Ford . . . wanted to control to a greater extent everything going into the Ford car. That to him was important, not to be so dependent. . . ."[87]

The struggle for control which the Dodge brothers had brought to a head continued for more than two years in the courts. A circuit court decision favoring the Dodges was appealed to the Michigan Supreme Court whose judgment reversed the earlier decision limiting the company's expansion. The Supreme Court, however, upheld the lower court's direction that a special dividend equal to 50 percent of the fiscal 1916 cash surplus be distributed, less dividends paid in fiscal 1917. The total came to more than $19 million, and, in addition, the presiding judge held that "a business corporation is organized and carried on primarily for the profit of the stockholders. The powers of the directors are employed for that end."[88]

To Ford this must have been the most unacceptable feature of the decision. In spite of the dividend, the company was still in a position to afford its plans for expansion—the distribution left some $25 million of the 1916 cash surplus unaffected—but in revolt against the court's direction, Ford now set expansion momentarily aside and the issue became the existence within the company of men who would no longer be prepared simply to ratify his decisions. On December 30, 1918, in the first of a series of moves designed to rid the company of its stockholders, he resigned the presidency. "As you know," he wrote the Board of Directors, "I have intended to take this step for some time past, for a number of reasons, the most important of which is that my time must necessarily be given to other work less thoroughly organized than this, and I also wish to be relieved of all responsibility and obligations arising from holding a salaried position in the company. It is my desire to devote my time to building up other organizations with which I am concerned." On December 31, his resignation was accepted, and Edsel Ford was elected to succeed him.[89] Then on March 5, 1919, after a public silence of more than two months, Ford returned to the newpaper headlines. The *Los Angeles Examiner* published an exclusive interview with him at his vacation home in Altadena under the banner "Henry Ford Organizing Huge New Company to Build Better Cheaper Car."

I have decided on the new undertaking [Ford was reported as saying], and as matters stand intend to go ahead with it. . . . The $19 million decision . . . caused me to make this move. . . . Of that $19 million I have to distribute to myself about $12 million but I cannot in justice to myself put that back in the business because I have no way to oblige those who own the other portion to so employ it.

As I do not believe in subsidiary companies, I cannot resort to that method which many financiers employ. My only recourse is to get out, design a new car which can be sold cheaply and which will be in all details up to date. The only other venture I have gone into is our tractor company and this will be the method of handling the new car; that is, [through] Henry Ford and Son Incorporated. In this company all the stock will be held by my family.

For our new project we are already looking about for water power sites; the car itself is well advanced for I have been working on it while "resting" here in California. We shall have a plant on this coast, [and] all over the country, in fact we propose to dot the whole world with our factories because I believe that every family should have a car and it can be done.

Our company already has established its tractor business and is paying at the rate of $500,000 to $600,000 a month; it is capitalized at $5 million and has accumulated $12 million [in] assets. The old company? Why, I don't know exactly what will become of that; the portion of it that does not belong to me cannot be sold to me, that I do know.

I must do business on the basis I think right; I cannot do it any other. I do not like stock companies. I do not think the principle is the best that can be devised. . . .[90]

Similar articles appeared in other newspapers, and several stated that factory sites had already been bought.[91]

Ford was on the move once again. Still the champion of the car for the ordinary man everywhere, it was nonetheless bound inextricably to his need for total control of the company. The means which still lay open to him to increase the Ford Company's production went unheeded as the battle for control was joined. In the events that were to follow, Henry Ford would outmaneuver his stockholders at every turn, and control as a means of expansion would increasingly appear an end in itself.

Within weeks of the Los Angeles interview, the stockholders, one by one, opened negotiations for the sale of their shares. On March 14, 1919, the Gray shares were offered to investment bankers under a 15-day option at $9,000 each. On April 3, the Dodge brothers gave an option to a Rothschild associate at $12,500 a share, and the prices asked reflect the erosion of outside confidence in the company's future: in February 1917, S. K. Rothschild had offered the Dodges $18,000 a share.[92]

In the meantime the newspaper interviews continued. Liebold, questioned on the matter, said: "As the majority stockholder in a company of his own development, Mr. Ford finds himself in the position of an industrial master who is not master of his own industry. In [his] new venture he is not taking any chances with future troubles with stockholders. . . ."[93] Inquiries poured into the company's offices, many of them from people who could not afford even the cheapest stripped-down Model T. The Ford dealers, disquieted and anxious, were dealt with personally by Edsel Ford in a letter which gives a truer picture of the situation than the grandiose plans announced in the press.

In the first place [he wrote on March 21], a large majority of the reports afloat are greatly distorted and exaggerated. A new car may be manufactured, but as to when . . . we are not in a position to say, except that we do know a new car could not possibly be designed, tested out, manufactured, and marketed in quantities under two or three years' time.
There is nothing, however, indefinite about the present Ford car. . . . We intend to continue the production of the reliable Model T as aggressively as in the past, and feel that

we have the cooperation of our entire sales organization.
. . . Our factory and assembly plant production is being
pushed to the limit. . . .[94]

In the meantime, moving in calculated fashion through the
confusion he had created, Henry Ford made arrangements
in secret to buy out the minority stockholders. The negotiations began toward the end of March and were carried to
their conclusion by a vice-president of the Old Colony Trust
Company in Boston. Ford had in fact been in touch with
the bankers since January.

The price finally paid in July 1919 for $41\frac{1}{2}$ percent of the
company's stock was just under $106 million. To finance the
purchase Ford obtained a $75 million loan arranged by the
Chase Securities Corporation of New York, and the Old
Colony Trust Company and Bond and Goodwin of Boston.
In spite of his hatred of Wall Street, Ford went to the bankers to buy his company.[95]

Within a year the sharp postwar recession was to make the
threat of Wall Street control assume real proportions for the
first time, but in the intervening months Ford's increasing
dominance within the company was reflected in the resigna-
tions of C. H. Wills, John R. Lee, Charles Morgana, and
Norval Hawkins—four of the company's ablest executives.[96]

The friction between Ford and Wills was attested to by
Max Wollering as early as 1908. "Wills' job," said Wollering, "was watching Henry and Henry was watching him.
They used to watch each other, those two, believe me.
Henry was on the third floor; Wills would be on the second
floor. I don't know if it was jealousy but . . . they wanted
to know what [each] said to the various workmen."[97]

Wills had worked with Henry Ford before the formation
of the Ford Motor Company. He had contributed greatly
to the design of the Model T and to the use of alloy steels in
its construction. He had a written agreement with Ford
dating back to 1902 which entitled him to a share of Ford's
dividends. In his autobiography Sorensen later wrote that

"without Harold Wills' perfectionist mind, the early Ford cars would not have had sufficient mechanical excellence for evolution into the Model T."[98]

But Sorensen's *My Forty Years with Ford* is a strange book: it veers wildly from adulation of Henry Ford and a stress on Sorensen's ability to do everything Ford told him to do to extremes of egocentricity in which it is Sorensen who is responsible for every progressive development in the Ford Motor Company. So it is, that in spite of his praise of Wills's contribution, Sorensen could also write, "I found that one problem in getting things the way Ford wanted was Wills, who at times was extremely critical of his boss and his ideas. . . . [Wills] did not credit Ford with the ability he fancied he himself possessed and instead of giving him what he asked for, frequently tried to mold the Ford ideas to his."[99]

The truth more nearly lay in Wills's inability to accept the implications of one-man rule. His departure was prefaced by an incident recorded by Sorensen. For some time Wills had been passing on to Sorensen and Martin a small part of the dividend payments he received from Henry Ford. He was a collector of precious stones and had given Sorensen a diamond ring. "One morning in the late nineteen-teens," Sorensen wrote,

Mr. Ford asked me to come to his office. Wills was waiting there, apparently summoned. In plain language Ford told him he would have to change his living habits or he would be dropped if he did not do so. He also said that Wills should stop giving Ed Martin and me a share of his dividend payments and that he should quit giving presents to the staff.

"Charlie here has a ring you gave him. You get that back from him and stop that sort of thing. And one thing more; get to work every morning at eight o'clock like the rest of us."

Ford walked out of the office leaving Wills alone with me. I took off the ring and gave it to Wills and there wasn't much more to say. Ford was determined to put Wills to work the way he wanted, all of which was a shock to Wills, who always before had had a free hand. Instead of complying with the Ford ultimatum, Wills remained away more than ever. In 1919 he left the company.[100]

Here the issue of control is raised in a form that would soon dominate relationships within the company. With the external threats defeated and with the mechanisms of internal control more firmly in his hands than ever, with expansion assured, Ford was turning to the complex issue of control over the attitudes and relationships of his subordinates.

Step by step, the progression had inexorably led to this. From the fixation on the cheap car for the millions to the obsession with expansion in order to build it, Ford had been driven by a need to control, a need to have the power to act. It is as if fixation having become strategy, and the attempt at adaptation, policy, there was now once again nowhere else to go. And it should come as no surprise that it is at this point that the sycophant becomes an integral part of the company's management structure. Detached from concrete objectives, Ford's need for control would now become a need to have that control recognized, assented to, conformed to, and feared. It was as if he sought by these means to reconfirm the purposes to which his need for control of the company had earlier been put.

With the onset of the 1920 depression, the Ford Motor Company, like the rest of the industry, was faced with a rapidly declining consumer demand. Ford's financial position was weakened by the purchase of the minority shareholdings, by the expenditure of more than $60 million on the Rouge which had proceeded throughout the Dodge suit, and by the purchase of mines and timber tracts for sums in the vicinity of $20 million.[101] Nonetheless, he first attempted to stem the fall in sales by the largest price cuts in the history of the industry. For a time sales recovered, but by December 1920 the company was forced to close its plants. Between January 1 and April 18, 1921, it had to meet obligations totaling $58 million—the last installment of the loan for the minority shareholdings, federal income taxes, and an employee bonus. "At [that] time," Ford said in July 1921, "we had only $20 million in cash. That . . . is where the Wall Street bankers went wrong—they didn't see where we could get $40 million more to meet our obligations."[102]

The money was found by switching the plants from production to assembly of parts in stock, by shipping the finished cars whether ordered or not to Ford dealers throughout the country, who were compelled to pay cash or forfeit their franchise.[103] Instead of going to Wall Street, Ford sent his dealers to Main Street, and the company's funds were swelled by the proceeds of hundreds of loans contracted by dealers to pay for their consignments of cars. By April 1, $24.7 million worth of stock had been turned into cash.[104]

In addition, plans for inventory control were introduced, largely on the initiative of Ernest Kanzler, the brother-in-law of Mrs. Edsel Ford; and with the utilization of a recently acquired railroad, the Detroit, Toledo, and Ironton, the time spent by goods in transit was cut by one third, releasing $28 million from this source alone.[105] Employment in the offices and the plant was drastically reduced: the office staff was cut from 1074 to 528 and in the plant the number of men employed each day for each car produced fell from 15 to 9. Labor and overhead costs which had averaged $146 a car, were reduced to $93. By April 1, Ford's cash position, including foreign collections and the income from the sale of Liberty bonds and by-products, was reflected in a balance of $87.3 million, and his obligations were met in full.[106]

But within the company the crisis had produced further crisis. F. L. Klingensmith, the company's vice-president and treasurer, had favored borrowing to meet the demands placed on the company and had opposed price reductions on the Model T. On both counts he was guilty of supporting courses of action calculated to arouse an emotional response, and on January 3 he resigned.

Sorensen "automatically" supported Henry Ford, and it is from this point that his rise to power begins.[107] With Liebold, he executed the increasingly arbitrary decisions of his employer, and in the process the executive ranks of the company were decimated: out went W. S. Knudsen; C. E. Brownell, the head of advertising; W. C. Anderson, the company's European representative; Dean Marquis, who directed the Sociological Department; L. H. Turner, the chief auditor; H. E. Hartmann, Assistant Secretary and General Attorney. On a single day in 1921 thirty key managers were dropped from the factory staff.[108] "In [Ford's] presence," Marquis wrote later, "no one is ever entirely at his ease; at least that is true of his employees. . . . No living being knows what he is likely to say or do next."[109]

It was precisely this freedom to act without restraint which now lay open to Henry Ford and the executives who remained close to him were those upon whom he could depend for unquestioning obedience. The Ford Motor Company, Ford had often said, offered no titles to any man. "The Ford factories and enterprises have no organization, no specific duties attaching to any position, no line of succession or of authority, very few titles, and no conferences."[110] Set down in writing in 1923, this to a large extent reflects the aftermath of the executive exodus of 1919–1921. Gone by then were the men, who while they might not have held a title, were nonetheless clearly identified with a particular function or area of the company's business. These were the men whose identification with their own work inhibited blind acceptance of orders. And these therefore were the men who had to go, leaving a small group ranged around Ford and wearing as their sole badge of influence their closeness to him.

This came to be Ford's style of leadership in the ensuing years. It is a style which secured for him the power of a despot which had fear as its base. The executives capable of wielding any part of it would be those capable of making an identification with the aggressor. Ironically, Ford himself deprecated the effects of power in this form, but only as it concerned other men. "Foremen are only human," he wrote. "It is natural that they should be flattered by being made to believe that they hold the weal or woe of workmen in their hands. It is natural also that being open to flattery, their self-seeking subordinates should flatter them still more to obtain and profit by their favor. That is why I want as little as possible of the personal element."[111] Despite this, the structure Ford established after 1921 was based on a system of personal power which permeated the organization from the top. As a structure capable of dealing effectively with a changing environment, it was a failure; as a system of power it was extremely effective in the achievement of ends which bore little relationship to reality.

The company's progress after 1921 viewed from the standpoint of interpersonal relationships and their effects on organizational structure and effectiveness will be dealt with in a later chapter. What has been attempted in this one is to establish the reciprocity between fixation and the need for control—between the car and the process of production which was itself the very essence of Ford's adaptation to reality.

In the chapter that follows, a third reciprocal theme will be explored: it is the theme of "deliverance." In itself this word implies the existence of a threat or of an enemy, and it is used to bring coherence to a series of actions which on the face of it may appear unrelated. The relevance of this pattern of behavior to what has preceded it rests on its clear connection in time to the completion of the Model T and the development of the production system that could give Henry Ford the vast numbers of cars for which he strove.

The first of the many hundreds of accessions at the Ford Archives is a miscellany of documents, clippings, mementos, letters, notebooks—placed together because of their intimate connection with Henry Ford: the notebooks, for example, were Ford's, and they hold the scribblings, reminders, half-formed thoughts, and fully formed convictions of several decades. Among them there is one in which there are two entries within a few short sentences of each other: *learned a lot on the Peace Ship,* and *the motor car is finished.*[1]

Here, outlined by Ford himself, is the issue which this chapter will attempt to explore: it is the issue of Ford's choice of action once the car was built and the vast production system developed. It is an issue which represents the final step in the progression from fixation, through adaptation, because there is implicit in the need for new forms of action a recognition that the earlier work was done.

Yet this is to express it at its simplest: one might say equally that Ford had achieved what he set out to do, and now with more time at his disposal and the means at his command his range of interests widened and he could effectively act in their behalf.

In its barest outlines this was not a situation unique to him. Andrew Carnegie and John D. Rockefeller, for example, turned to philanthropy on an immense scale in pursuit of interests quite apart from the companies that they built. By 1919 Carnegie had given away more than $350 million, much of it to the Carnegie Corporation of New York, founded "to promote the advancement and diffusion of knowledge and understanding among the people of the United States"; to the Carnegie Foundation for the Advancement of Teaching; to the Carnegie Institute, which included the Institute of Technology; and to the Carnegie Endowment for International Peace. Rockefeller by 1937 had given nearly $600 million to the Rockefeller Foundation.[2]

The essential difference between the interests to which

4
THE "DELIVERANCE" OF MEN

these men gave expression and those to which Ford turned lies in the all-important element of time. Carnegie was nearly 66 when he began his philanthropic career and he had divested himself entirely of his holdings in Carnegie steel. For him it was in truth the beginning of a new life.

For Ford it was an instance of *plus ça change, plus c'est la même chose*. In 1912, Ford was 49, his business career was to continue for another 33 years. Only in his own mind had he achieved what he set out to do: the real world of changing public tastes and an advancing technology would soon demand changes in the Model T.

That Ford could not accept this is at the very base of the public career that he was so incoherently to adopt. From the bare outlines of similarity with the actions of men whose work was done in reality, *his* actions emerge in the early stages as a need to escape the consequences of what he had built—to sell the company, to give up responsibility—and then increasingly become suffused by the need to fight, first the threats to his own control within the Ford Company, and then the threats outside which seemed to face so many other men. "At certain points in history," Hartmann pointed out in a general discussion of the individual's relationship to the external world, "the ego can no longer cope with its environment, particularly not with that which it itself has created: the means and goals of life lose their orderly relation, and the ego then attempts to fulfill its organizing function by increasing its insight into the inner world."[3] Yet any individual's ability successfully to carry this through must depend on the flexibility of the mechanisms of defense. And since these mechanisms *"simultaneously* serve both the control of instinctual drive and adaptation to the external world,"[4] it must follow that save for a few exceptional individuals capable of questioning the unconscious process which has served them well in the past, an increased insight into one's inner world can rarely be arrived at successfully.

Instead, even as adaptation begins to falter, it is sought through an increasingly rigid reliance on the defense mechanisms which so far have worked. In itself this process means that adaptation to the real world is sacrificed to control of instinctual drives that now assume the characteristics of defusion. Aggression, previously bound and called into the service of a creative exchange with the external world, becomes increasingly autonomous; and on a level ranging from mild depression to melancholia it can be turned upon the self, or, within the extremes of self-justification and paranoia it can be turned upon the environment.

Ford eventually chose the environment. By 1912, he had moved beyond an adaptive relation to the men around him, to the car he had built, and as the future would prove, to the market he visualized. The creativity that had given birth to the Model T died under the weight of his fixation, but on a new and more restricted level he successfully fought to win control of the company and to build the largest and most intensively integrated plant in the world, in order to build still more Model Ts. Side by side with these developments came Ford's excursions into the public realm, and they began interestingly enough with the declaration of the $5 day in January 1914.

The announcement of the $5 day was, simultaneously, an announcement of a reduction in working hours from nine hours a day to eight. In addition, the company stated that it would arrange its annual production schedule in such a way that layoffs would be made in harvest time "to induce our men to respond to the calls of farmers for harvest hands."[5]

Ford's preoccupation with the farmer, an issue raised even in so extraneous a proceeding as the revision of the company's wage structure, has been consistently overlooked by his biographers in their accounts of the $5 day.[6] Yet its psychological significance is extraordinary. It is as if with the completion of the car for the farmer, other ways had to be found to help him, to free him from the burden he labored under. Anna Freud has written:

The mechanism of projection disturbs our human relations when we project our own jealousy and attribute to other people our own aggressive acts. But it may work in another way as well, enabling us to form valuable positive attachments and so to consolidate our relations with one another. This normal and less conspicuous form of projection might be described as altruistic surrender of our own instinctual impulses in favor of other people . . . the altruistic surrender of instinctual impulses seems, under certain conditions, to be a specific means of overcoming narcissistic mortification.[7]

The $5 day itself reflected no deeply held conviction on Ford's part, for the humanitarianism which seemed implicit in the gesture was soon to be negated. In 1923, Dr. Marquis described the transitory nature of Ford's interest as he moved from enthusiasm to indifference. A few days after the $5 day had become effective, Marquis wrote, Ford gave him the reasons for the decision:

There are thousands of men out there in the shop who are not living as they should. Their homes are crowded and insanitary. Wives are going out to work because their husbands are unable to earn enough to support the family. They fill up their homes with roomers and boarders in order to help swell the income. It's all wrong—all wrong. It's especially bad for the children. They are neglected from necessity. Now these people are not living in this manner as a matter of choice. Give them a decent income and they will live decently—will be glad to do so. What they need is the opportunity to do better, and some one to take a little personal interest in them—some one who will show that he had faith in them. . . . Blindfold me and lead me down there into the street and let me lay my hands by chance on the most shiftless and worthless fellow in the crowd and I'll bring him in here, give him a job with a wage that offers him some hope for the future, some prospect of living a decent, comfortable and self-respecting life, and I'll guarantee that I'll make a man out of him. All that man needs is an opportunity that has some hope in it, some purpose for the years to come.[8]

When Marquis resigned seven years later, the "era of co-operation and goodwill" had gone. The men closest to Ford were those who held that

the humane treatment of employees . . . would lead to the weakening of the authority of the "boss" and to the breaking down of discipline in the shop. To them the sole end of industry was production and profits, and the one sure way of getting these things out of labor was to curse it, threaten it, drive it, insult it, humiliate it, and discharge it on the slightest provocation; in short—to use a phrase much on the lips of such men—"put the fear of God in labor." And they were always thinking of themselves as the little gods who were to be feared.

Although, Marquis wrote, there were few men of this kind in the company when he joined it, those few "seemed to be in closer and more confidential relation to Mr. Ford than those who stood for the better things, *and this in spite of the fact that for the time being he seemed heartily in favor of the humane policies then in force.* Why he made familiars of men of this class was a profound mystery to those of us who saw only the other side—the nobler and better side —of him."[9]

By 1923, Ford himself had gone on record: "If a man is in constant fear of the industrial situation," he wrote, "he ought to change his life so as not to be dependent upon it. *There is always the land, and fewer people are on the land now than ever before.* If a man lives in fear of an employer's favor changing toward him, he ought to extricate himself from dependence on any employer."[10] And he went further. The 1922 edition of his autobiographical work with Crowther included the following passage which was altered in subsequent editions by the omission of the sentence in italics:

I pity the poor fellow who is so soft and flabby that he must always have "an atmosphere of good feeling" around him before he can do his work. There are such men. *They produce with a sort of hothouse fervor while they are being coddled, but the moment the atmosphere chills and becomes critical they become helpless.* And in the end, unless they obtain enough mental and moral hardiness to lift them out of their soft reliance on "feeling" they are failures. Not only are they business failures; they are character failures also; it is as if their bones never attained a sufficient degree of hardness to enable them to stand on their own feet. There is altogether too much reliance on good feeling in our business organizations. People have too great a fondness for working with the people they like. . . .[11]

The change in attitude attained tangible proportions in the executive upheaval of 1920–1921. "There was a great deal of apprehension," one employee said later, "because virtually every day or every few days, purges were going on. Departments were being eliminated overnight. These purges were not conducted on a scientific basis. Departments were completely wiped out."[12]

On the factory floor the fear and anxiety were much greater. In a 1921 article, E. G. Pipp described the methods used by "Ford Service," a department to which Harry Bennett would later give a structure and authority which competed with, and often defeated, the power of the functional organization centralized under Sorensen. Pipp accused Henry Ford of permitting his agents to use bribery, liquor, and easy women in their efforts to "get" individuals who stood in their way.[13] On the witness stand five years later these methods were attested to when Sorensen admitted "that he had used the Ford Company's secret police and women in an effort to trap" John M. Blair, a former Ford contractor: "Sorensen said that he caused the Ford police to arrange a party for . . . Blair with women in it, but denied that he threatened Blair with exposure before his wife."[14]

Among the workers, the Service Department maintained in addition a "spotter" system which came to be relied on as a means of reducing the work force; a former company publicist later described its operations. An employee whose job it was to drive the cars off a final assembly line at Highland Park frequently commenced work five or ten minutes early (for which he was not paid) so that the line would be clear and all in readiness when the department swung into action.

One day just about thirty seconds before lunch period, he delivered a car to the inspector, and knowing he did not have time to deliver another before the bell rang, he stepped over to a lunch wagon and bought a bottle of coffee. As he was paying for it the bell rang.

That evening when he went to punch his clock-card it had been removed from the rack. The time-clerk referred him to the superintendent, who at once ordered the clerk to make out a quit slip for this employee because he had bought a bottle of coffee before the lunch bell rang. Once more a "spotter" had done his deadly work as an aid to natural attrition.

No one was big enough or little enough to feel sure he was exempt from these spotters. So the haunting fear that their every movement was being watched was present in the minds of all.[15]

When the company reopened its plant after the 1920–1921 crisis, a relentless speedup was enforced along the production lines and the spotter system assisted in the decimation of the rank and file which accompanied it. *The Flivver King,* a tract in the muckraker tradition by Upton Sinclair, brings to vivid life the cuts in overhead and men employed per car:

They had been employing fifteen men per car per day. Now they had cut it to nine. In his public statements, Henry said: "This did not mean that six out of fifteen men lost their jobs. They only ceased being unproductive." If that statement had been true, the plant would have increased the production of cars by 66 per cent; but as a matter of fact they turned out just what they had been doing before the "reorganization," four thousand cars a day. They cut the overhead from $146 per car to $93, a saving of 60 millions a year. As a result, thousands of men took their places on the breadlines of Detroit and neighboring towns. . . .[16]

Nevins and Hill, writing of the polar changes in Ford's attitude to labor, noted that "conviction which is the result of enthusiasm is one thing and conviction growing out of character and steady purpose another, and in Henry Ford, except for a few beliefs like that in the cheap car, there was a singular lack of consistency and dependability."[17]

While there can be no doubt that this describes the issue, the immediate task is to explain it, and here theory sheds light on the facts. That altruism affords a means of overcoming narcissistic injury is a theoretical construct, used because it works. And to say this is in no way to depreciate the enormous social significance of the $5 day. It is simply to attempt the explanation of its psychological underpinnings in the mind of the man whose decision it was.

For Henry Ford the car was finished. It had not achieved the objective he had unconsciously set for it. More had to be done. He could try to lose himself in making more and still more cars. He could try, too, to find release through action in other fields, and it was to this that he did turn, only to abandon each attempt as its promise proved equally ephemeral. These were the convictions dismissed as "the convictions of enthusiasm." They sprang from an unconscious need which no achievement in reality could satisfy and reality in fact denied Ford even the semblance of achievement. Summoned into service as a result was an intricate conspiratorial fantasy that allowed expression of the hostility within him on a scale attainable only by a man of his wealth and power. And this in itself fed the fantasy, for action against the "enemies," helped "prove" that in fact they were there.

For the time being Ford continued to experiment with altruism and for the short period in which he did so he was cruelly ridiculed. The good that he wanted for other men was not so viewed by them, and perhaps inevitably, his vision of the external world began to assume the proportions of a projected nightmare.

The turning point came with two incidents, both the result of Ford's militant pacifism. The first, the voyage of the Ford Peace Ship, occurred in 1915; the second, a suit for libel brought by Ford against the *Chicago Tribune,* which had referred to him as an "anarchistic enemy of the nation which protects him in his wealth," took place in 1919.[18]

The *Oscar II,* the Ford Peace Ship, sailed from New York on December 4, 1915. Aboard it was a Henry Ford as passionately convinced of the rightness of pacifism as he had earlier been of the need to pay men more than a living wage. In taking the pacifist stand, Ford was fighting not only war but the makers of war as he saw them: "bankers, munitions makers, alcoholic drink, Kings and their henchmen, and school books."[19]

In April 1915 he said publicly that in the event the United States entered the war, rather than accept a single order for cars which might be used for military purposes, he would see his factory burned to the ground. In August he pledged his "life and fortune" to the quest for peace and attacked the campaign for military preparedness that was beginning to sweep the country. In September he gave $1 million to fight preparedness, and a few days later announced that he would increase the gift to $10 million. On November 12 he said that preparedness was part of a plan to keep the munitions factories at work.[20] So it was, that on November 19, when he interviewed two workers for peace at his home in Dearborn, he had already assumed a public position as a militant pacifist who was willing to spend enormous sums of money for the cause.

The two who came to see him were Rosika Schwimmer, a Hungarian feminist writer, and Louis Lochner, an American associated with the Fifth International Peace Congress.[21] They proposed a campaign aimed at arousing a public demand for peace which might encourage President Wilson to summon a conference of the neutral nations. Such a conference would then be called upon to establish a commission for "continuous mediation" between the warring sides in order finally to arrive at a formula for peace.[22]

Ford agreed to help, and on the following day left for New

York with Lochner. There, at luncheon with a group of prominent pacifists which included Jane Addams of Hull House, Oswald Garrison Villard, and Dean Kirchwey of Columbia University, he initially agreed to see President Wilson in an attempt to win Wilson's cooperation and official sanction for the project. Unfortunately for the credibility of the enterprise, the discussion did not end there: Lochner made a half-serious suggestion that a ship should be chartered to take the peace delegates to Europe, and the effect on Ford was immediate.

The *Oscar II* was chartered that afternoon in the face of protests from the other participants, and two days later when Ford met with Wilson it was already Ford's peace conference. It was his intention, Ford said, to finance a neutral commission, Wilson had only to appoint it.[23]

In a book written several years later, Lochner described Ford's ease of manner during the interview. He told Wilson a Ford joke which he had himself invented, and the theme of deliverance under the aegis of Henry Ford is so obvious that it seems a conscious, deliberate self-parody, except that Ford's mind did not work in this way. He was given to often brutal practical joking but not to irony which took himself as its object.[24]

The joke involved Ford personally: once when passing a graveyard, he told the President, he saw a huge hole being dug and asked the gravedigger whether he intended to bury an entire family. No, said the digger, the grave was just for one person. Then why was it so big? The digger explained that the dead man had been a very queer fellow; he had specified in his will that he should be buried in his Ford because the Ford had pulled him out of every hole so far and he was certain it would pull him out of this one.[25]

That it was from this vantage point that Ford approached the issue can hardly be doubted. He could save the peace. For him the objective was not to be reached in the give-and-take of negotiation. It was simply to stop the fighting, "to get the boys out of the trenches by Christmas . . ." to act and in his acting simultaneously to win his own private war. When the President said that he approved the idea of continuous mediation but that he could not be tied to one project only in the quest for peace, Ford's judgment of Wilson was that he was a "small man."[26]

The hurried arrangements for the voyage began, and by its end Henry Ford was to be given grounds for feeling even smaller than Wilson had appeared. At a press conference in New York on November 24, he announced that the Peace Ship would sail in ten days and that among others, Jane Addams and Thomas Edison would be on board. On the following day the ridicule began:

GREAT WAR ENDS CHRISTMAS DAY
FORD TO STOP IT

ran the headlines in the *New York Tribune*. The *Baltimore Sun* proposed that William Jennings Bryan should take command of the ship since, "If a brutal German submarine should sink her nothing would be lost." And to capture the centrality of Henry Ford rather than of peace in the project, as well as the mindless lack of planning which was its consequence, the editorial in the *New York World* resorted to verse:

I saw a little fordship
Go chugging out to sea
And for a flag
It bore a tag
Marked 70 h.p.
And all the folk aboardship
Cried, "Hail to Hennery!"

And so, without a quiver
The dreadful task they dare
Of teaching peace
To France and Greece
And Teuton, Celt, and Bear.
Ho for the good ship Flivver
Propelled by heated air.[27]

Invitations to join the expedition flowed out as on an ebb tide from Ford's New York headquarters, and as inevitably as the flood the refusals came streaming in: among those unable to go were Louis Brandeis, Thomas Edison, Cardinal Gibbons, Colonel E. M. House, William Dean Howells, William Howard Taft, the governors of forty-seven states, and finally, Miss Addams, whose presence might have lent some slight credibility to the seriousness of the enterprise.[28]

In the second volume of their history Nevins and Hill question why Ford so deliberately "stacked the cards against himself" by leaving so little time, first, for effective organization; and second, for the important men and women invited to make arrangements to travel; why indeed he had announced his plans before he had secured any support. "Why," they wrote, "did Ford set himself this all but impossible challenge? The answer lay in his own character. He had never followed conventional paths, and delighted in the seemingly impossible. Doubtless he felt that he and his associates could rise to the emergency and that the sensation would be the greater. Again, he craved action. For half a year he had been writing and talking against preparedness and war, and had built up a reservoir of explosive energy."[29]

This is reminiscent of the boy who asked "why" and was told "because." Ford clearly believed, as implicitly as he ever believed in the demand for the cheap car, that others in some way shared the need which led to the Peace Ship as a means of expression. For him, action was joined to affect in a relationship which precluded a realistic evaluation of means and objectives, and the compulsion to act in fact superseded any wish for success. For others, too, his assumption ran, action rather than reflection was the compelling force.

Played out on a national stage his actions assumed an exhibitionist character expressive of a need to have others support the illusion that he was acting effectively. When Jane Addams objected to the flamboyance which surrounded the

Peace Ship, it was this very aspect in fact which had attracted Henry Ford: "Men could see it. It would lift talk into action and arouse a sharper interest."[30] In putting his trust in action for its own sake it was as if he contemplated no end to it, for the end would bring still more disappointment.

In his own copy of Emerson's *Essays,* Ford listed the page numbers of passages he found of special interest. He wrote "good" next to page 97, and the passage marked on that page reads: "Only in our easy, simple, spontaneous action are we strong." A few pages earlier he marked: "We love characters in proportion as they are impulsive and spontaneous."[31] And this theme recurs in the jottings in his notebooks: "The only way to get happiness is to pursue it . . . happiness is in the pursueing [sic]"; and in rough paraphrase of Emerson, "Our spontaneous acteoin [sic] is always the best . . . you have got to keep doing and going."[32]

On the move without a thought, he defeated his own ostensible purpose, but there were gains notwithstanding this: they lay in the release which action afforded and in the pathways opened up for the deflection of responsibility and the projection of his own conflicts on a much larger scale.

The ridicule that surrounded the departure of the Peace Ship continued undiminished during the voyage. Reporters on board described the delegates as "a bunch of nuts," and when shortly after the ship sailed, Wilson's message to Congress advocated preparedness and an increase in the armed forces, the expedition split down the middle with one faction condemning preparedness and the other condemning the condemnation. "The dove of peace has taken flight," the *Chicago Tribune* reported, "chased off by the screaming eagle."[33]

Confined to his cabin with a cold for much of the voyage, Ford played little part in the wrangling, but he justified the venture to reporters: "I consider that the peace ship will have been worth while if it does nothing more than it has done already in driving preparedness off the front page of the newspapers and putting peace on the front page."[34]

On December 18, the *Oscar II* docked at Oslo. Ford made no public appearances at any of the meetings arranged for the delegates but he called in reporters on December 22. To their amazement he discussed, not the prospects for peace, but his farm tractor. Machines and not men, he said, would now be the drudges; he had not patented his invention, and he would attempt to prove to the arms manufacturers that they could make a larger profit by building tractors rather than guns. To one bemused newsman, it appeared that "[it] must be a very great man who permits himself to utter such foolishness."[35]

On the following day, Ford left Norway for the United States. With the Reverend Marquis who had accompanied him on the voyage, preceded by a bodyguard, and escorted by a flying wedge of local Ford employees, he braved the protests of those delegates who realized what was happening and simply left the others in their ignorance. Under the financial direction of Gaston Plantiff, Ford's New York manager, the delegates toured the neutral countries of Scandinavia and Holland, and the majority returned to the United States in mid-January 1916.

Tentative plans had by then been made for establishing a Conference for Continuous Mediation made up of like-minded men and women in the neutral countries. The selection of delegates to the Conference was to be highly informal: in Norway, Ford employees advised on the choice of members; the Peace Ship elected the United States delegates from among their own number, and in the other countries assorted peace societies appointed national representatives.[36]

In a letter to Henry Ford written from The Hague on January 11, Plantiff outlined the difficulties he had been compelled to face. The tour through the neutral countries had been far from smooth. "Mrs. Boissevain* whom I think you sized up properly by calling her a vampire, not having been selected a member of the administration committee, and not getting the limelight position which is so dear to her, presented a most insulting letter of resignation, attacking the delegates and the administration in a most unbecoming manner." The senior stenographer had already been dismissed and had threatened to bring suit against Mrs. Schwimmer and Lochner for slander. As to the administrative ability of the latter pair, Plantiff wrote with feeling:

the expense of this proposition, as you must realize, has been extremely large and I have hesitated at times in wonder at the enormity of it. . . . While I do not wish to take it upon myself to criticize the other members and peace delegates upon our voyage, yet I must in justice to myself say that Lochner, Madam Schwimmer and Publicity Agent Miss Leckie, have not the remotest idea of the value of dollars and cents and have incurred expenses which [but] for the sake of keeping harmony within the organization, I would never have permitted or authorized.

And about the difficulty of inducing to return to the United States those delegates who had not been selected to remain for the Conference, Plantiff wrote, "Many have wanted to stay as joy-riders but as they retard the progress of the mission and embarrass the accomplishment of what we have started to do, I have been strict in insisting on their return."[37]

While Ford continued to finance the Conference from Dearborn, the extent of his support was steadily reduced. By May 1916 the national delegations were reduced from five members to two and even so the costs evidently outran the gains: in the words of Dr. C. F. Aked, a United States delegate, although the members were "earnest men and women," the difficulty lay in that "they are not big men and women. There is not one great man or woman among

* Inez Millholland Boissevain, who is described by Nevins and Hill as a "Junoesque beauty and feminist."

us. I should hesitate to say that we have more than a fair average ability."[38]

Lochner was finally recalled to Dearborn on January 3, 1917, and by February 7, under Liebold's direction, financial assistance to the Conference was brusquely terminated. In the meantime, "the transformation of Henry Ford from Peace Angel to Vulcan" was effected in less than a week.[39]

The circumstances were extraordinary. Throughout 1916 Ford had waged an advertising and publicity campaign against preparedness. Buying space in the newspapers he had charged that "imperialists and profiteers were arming both sides for the purpose of exploiting the common people who would have to pay the bills."[40] In an interview with a reporter from *Metropolitan* magazine, he had said:

I don't believe in boundaries. I think nations are silly and flags are silly too. If the country is rotten, then the flag is rotten and nobody ought to respect it. Flags are rallying points, that's all. The munitions makers and the militarists and the crooked politicians use flags to get people excited when they want to fool them. I am going to keep the American flag flying on my plant until the war is over, and then I am going to pull it down for good and I am going to hoist in its place the Flag of All Nations which is being designed in my office right now . . .

War is a foolish thing, anyway. It's not only that the people are killed and wounded—I don't lose any sleep about that—but it's the extravagance and waste of it, and the oppression of people that follows it and the raising of prices everywhere, and the stopping of machinery that might be making things that people want.

The munitions makers build up wars so that they can make a profit and the business men build up war so they can get concessions. But these are not the people who are really responsible for it. The real people behind this war business are the big money lenders, the International Money Trust.

I don't believe in preparedness; it's like a man carrying a gun. Men and nations who carry guns always get into trouble. I am going to spend my life and my money putting a stop to war, by telling the people about it. I won't fight under any circumstances. . . . I'll stand up and be shot for that too. . . . In this country most soldiers are lazy, crazy, or out of a job. Well, we'll see that they have jobs—and there [are] not enough lazy and crazy men left to worry us. Pretty soon people all over the world are going to insist upon universal disarmament and peace. The European war is almost over. Before very long we are going to see the folly of the whole thing spring right up and ripen up, you watch![41]

In 1916, too, an incident occurred which in 1919 would embroil Henry Ford in yet another blaze of ridicule. His pacifist stand was construed by the *Chicago Tribune* to mean that he opposed the calling up of the National Guard, which had taken place in June in the face of unrest on the Mexican border. A Ford spokesman had in fact stated that any Ford employee who answered the call would forfeit his job. No such measure was later taken by the company—but the *Tribune,* dealing with what was "news," published an editorial which called Ford an anarchist and an ignorant idealist. Ford answered with a libel suit claiming damages of $1 million.[42]

The irony was that it would take three years for the suit to come to trial and the erratic convictions upon which the Peace Ship was launched would then be exposed to the full glare of publicity *after* their holder had become master of a vast war machine.

On February 3, 1917, Wilson severed diplomatic relations with Germany, and two days later Ford announced that "in the event of a declaration of war [I] will place our factory at the disposal of the United States Government and will operate without one cent of profit."[43]

Having earlier attested to the strength of Ford's pacifist convictions ("His was no wild, perverse crusade: he was marching along the same road that Hay, Root, Taft, Bryan and others had travelled, and millions in spirit marched with him"[44]), Nevins and Hill now advanced an explanation for the sudden change from peace to war which is notable for its sheer inconsistency. First, Ford's new "bel-

ligerence" is seen as a higher form of pacifism: "I am a pacifist first but perhaps militarism can be crushed only with
militarism. In that case, I am in on it to the finish."[45] Second, Ford's pacifism is held not to have been so deeply
rooted after all: "Ford never preached pacifism to the point
of non-resistance."[46]

But that he had is incontestable. It was Ford and not a
spokesman for him who declared that he would burn his
plant to the ground rather than produce for war. It was
Ford who suggested on December 1, 1915, that the soldiers
in the trenches should call a general strike.[47]

These are the contradictions inherent in a confusion of issues. The Ford historians have chosen to take Ford's actions
at their face value, and at this level his inconsistencies breed
inconsistent attempts at explanation. The simpler truth
was that for all his protestations, Ford was not a pacifist in
any real sense: his were not the beliefs of a Quaker. Pacifism
for him was a means of expressing emotion unencumbered
by conviction, and his subsequent actions clearly bear this
out. At a deeper level his behavior is of a piece with the
earlier reversal from the $5 day. The components had now
unmistakably shaken loose, and the aggression which clouded
his vision was consistently acted on. The belligerence, earlier
turned against war and the makers of war, was now expressed in waging it.

In the first months of the war, Ford himself suggested a
one-man submarine: "Carrying a man apiece, they will run
out below the biggest battleship afloat, touch off a bomb beneath it, and blow the ship out of existence."[48] The company became an arsenal, producing cars, trucks, ambulances,
ships, tanks, and Liberty engines. Ford personally proposed
the tactical innovation of overwhelming Germany with
bombers: his company, he said, would build 150,000 planes
at a cost of 25 cents a pound.[49]

Throughout this period he maintained that he would return every cent of profit on war work to the government, yet

he never did so. In June 1922, a laudatory biography by Sarah T. Bushnell, written from material supplied by Mrs. Henry Ford, stated that Ford had already returned $29 million in war profits to the government.[50] The Secretary of the Treasury, Andrew Mellon, personally refuted this, and Ford denied any awareness of the contents of the book.

The sum involved varies with the biographer, from a low of $926,780, arrived at by Nevins and Hill, to a high of 60 percent (the proportion of the company's floor space given over to war work) of $45 million (Ford's personal share of the company's net profit after taxes in the years 1917–1918), or a total of $27 million, which has been estimated by Keith Sward.[51] Were one to accept the low figure, and Nevins and Hill had access to the facts and were extraordinarily careful researchers, the point would be proved even more effectively: Mr. Ford simply didn't care. The return of less than $1 million to the government would have caused him no hardship and it would have lent conviction to his stand. That Ford's involvement was a passing thing is best expressed in his own behavior: by the war's end, he was already embroiled in still other "causes."

The *Tribune* suit, which was finally heard at Mt. Clemens, Michigan, in the summer of 1919, was decided in his favor, but the jury of farmers made it a hollow victory. The million-dollar claim for damages was settled by an award of six cents.

During the course of the trial, the extent of Ford's ignorance once the automobile was set aside was painfully delineated by counsel for the newspaper: Ford's stand against preparedness and an increase in the armed forces, based on a belief that the army was then adequate for defense, was made to look ridiculous when he admitted that he had no idea of the size or distribution of military forces at the time.[52] He could not define an anarchist or give the meaning of "ballyhoo."[53] Aggression meant "to burglarize"; he did not know when the United States was founded; he thought Benedict Arnold was a writer.[54] Counsel for the *Tribune,* attempting to make the case for Presidential intervention on the Mexican border in 1916, was brought up short against the tractor even as the Norwegian reporters had been several years before:

Counsel:
There have been several governments overthrown in Mexico during that period, haven't there?
Ford:
I think there have, but still you can go down and travel.
Counsel:
Were you able to travel in 1915 and 1916?
Ford:
You are able to travel now.
Counsel:
I said in 1915 and 1916.
Ford:
Got 300 tractors there in the last six months.
Counsel:
Did you hear my question? I move to strike that out as not responsive.[55]

The light which his own testimony shone on Ford was reflected in newspapers throughout the country. "Now the mystery is finally dispelled," ran a typical editorial at the trial's end. "Henry Ford is a Yankee mechanic true and simple; quite uneducated, with a mind unable to 'bite' into any proposition outside of his automobile and tractor business, but with naturally good instincts and some sagacity."[56] The enterprise to which he was soon to turn would leave even those qualities in doubt, but for the time being he was caught up in the results of the 1918 senatorial election in Michigan.

At Wilson's suggestion, Ford ran as the Democratic candidate. His unwillingness to enter politics had initially been such that Wilson won him over only by a strong personal plea, and in the face of this, Ford's earlier estimate of the President evidently underwent a sea change.

Mr. Ford [Wilson told him] we are living in very difficult

times—in times when men must sacrifice themselves for their country. I would give anything on earth if I could lay down this job that I am trying to do, but I must carry on. . . . I know it would be a very great sacrifice for you to make, but you are the only man in Michigan who can be elected and help to bring about the peace you so much desire. I ask you therefore to overcome your personal feelings and interests and make the race.[57]

On the following day, June 14, 1918, Ford's candidacy was announced. The campaign was to be notable chiefly for the candidate's lack of participation. In September Ford said:

The President has asked me to become a candidate for United States Senator from Michigan. I know nothing about parties or party machinery, and I am not at all concerned about which ticket I am nominated on. . . . I shall not spend a cent nor make a single move to get into the Senate. I shall not have a campaign organization, nor pay any campaign bills. . . . I do not care anything about parties or politics or politicians. I would not walk across the street to be elected President of the United States, I certainly would not make a public speech to get the nomination or to be elected.[58]

Ford had in fact never made a public speech in his life nor did he attempt to do so during the course of the campaign.

The intimacy politics called for, the endless involvement in planning, the day-to-day assessments of tactics, the need to appeal to other men's self-interest in the give-and-take of negotiation, all held little attraction for him. In the 1920s, when there was a serious movement afoot to nominate him for the Presidency, F. L. Black, a staff member on Ford's newspaper, asked him whether he really wanted to be President. Black said later, "He startled me with—'I'd like to be down there for about six weeks to throw some monkey wrenches into the machinery.' "[59]

The detour through words, which is the chief constraint on the results of political action, was anathema to a man now accustomed to the luxury of acting on impulse. On a different level, the election was yet another test of Ford's professed pacifism, a test to which he was indifferent despite a ringing press statement: "[Wilson] was put into his present office to put an end to war, and under his leadership we are going to administer to militarism and its champions such a thorough and crushing defeat that no nation will dare to start a war so long as people remember this one."[60] The President, shortly to be embroiled in the battle for the Peace Treaty, would need every Senate vote he could command, yet Ford's lack of interest almost certainly lost the election. Of a total of more than 432,000 votes cast, he was defeated by a margin of less than 8000.

Undeterred by the responsibility he bore for his own defeat, Ford now turned on the victor with an energy never exhibited before the election. Truman H. Newberry, the successful Republican candidate, and a member of a prominent Detroit family, was haled through the courts on charges of corrupt practice and bribery brought at the instigation of a corps of private investigators hired by Henry Ford. Sentenced in 1920 to two years' imprisonment and a $10,000 fine, Newberry was not exonerated until 1921, when the Supreme Court held that the federal law under which he had been convicted was unconstitutional.[61]

Ford maintained throughout that "Wall Street interests" had bought Newberry his seat, but the small army of investigators in the field could find nothing to prove it, and the contradictions in Ford's position, as far as the spending of money was concerned, were made resoundingly clear in a letter from Theodore Roosevelt to Newberry shortly before the election:

The expenditure on behalf of pacifism by Mr. Ford in connection with the Peace Ship and in connection with his great advertising campaign in favor of the McLemore resolution and of the pacifist and pro-German attitude against our participation in the war, was thoroughly demoralizing to the conscience of the American people as anything that has ever taken place. The failure of Mr. Ford's son to go into the army at this time and the approval by the father of the son's refusal, represent exactly what ought to be expected from the moral disintegration inevitably produced by such pacifist propaganda. Mr. Ford's son is the son of a man of enormous wealth. If he went to war he would leave his wife and child immeasurably distant from all chance of even the slightest financial strain or trouble, and his absence would not in the smallest degree affect the efficiency of the business with which he is connected. But the son stays at home, protesting and appealing when he is drafted, and now escaping service. Your two sons have eagerly gone to the front. They stand ready to pay with their lives for the honor and the interest of the American people, and while they thus serve America with fine indifference to all personal cost, the son of wealthy Mr. Ford sits at home in ignoble safety, and his father defends and advises such conduct.[62]

The pacifist was now producing for war, ostensibly to bring peace to the world. But the opportunity to take part in the deliberations that might have led to peace was cast aside. The war to end war had to be fought without the participation of Edsel Ford. Even the sums expended on pacifism were to an extent recouped by war profits, and yet in the postelection battle against Newberry it was Newberry's expenditures in behalf of his own convictions which were the main issue.[63]

Newberry finally took his seat in the Senate in January 1922. Townsend, the senior senator from Michigan, had supported him, and for this Townsend went down to defeat in the same year: the *New York Times* reported that Ford employees disbursed "a steady golden stream" to prevent Townsend's reelection.[64] In November 1922, Newberry resigned from the Senate barely ahead of a movement to expel him which was organized by the Democrats following their majority victory in the year's congressional elections. In his letter of resignation, Newberry referred to the "political persecution" with which he had had to live from the day of his election, and to the "hundreds of agents [who] had hounded and terrified men in all parts of [Michigan]."[65]

The man appointed to succeed Newberry was James Couzens, and a year later, when the Ford presidential boom was
gathering momentum, Couzens used both his old relationship with Ford and his new political position bitterly to de-
nounce Ford's candidacy. Couzens told the Republican Club
of Detroit:

Ford wants to be president. His failure to withdraw from
the Nebraska primary proves that. Why does he refrain
from announcing his candidacy? Because he is afraid. He
realizes that it would prove just as great a fiasco as his peace
ship. . . . He has never gotten over his defeat as a candidate for United States senator. . . . This man who has
made more unfulfilled promises than any man in America
is now trying to guide or to criticize others. . . . Why Ford
for President? It is ridiculous. How can a man over 60 years
old, who has done nothing except make motors, who has no
training, no experience aspire to such an office?[66]

The ridicule which had begun with the Peace Ship had
followed relentlessly on the heels of Ford's every public action since. Although he was widely admired among farmers
and factory workers, other than his own, although he was
looked up to by pacifist and prohibitionist alike, these were
not the people who controlled the newspapers or wrote the
wounding editorials. In self-defense Ford now adopted two
seemingly separate strategies: he made himself far less ac-
cessible to the press, he literally withdrew behind a wall of
secretaries and publicists; and he bought his own newspaper, a weekly that would continue under its original name
as *The Dearborn Independent*.

In reality these decisions complemented each other. Ford's
isolation, intended to keep the world away from him, cut
him off from ready contact with any but the flunkys and
hacks who surrounded him. They filtered, and where necessary blocked, the unpleasant responses which his actions
evoked. *The Dearborn Independent*, which was shortly to
launch a vicious and sustained anti-Semitic campaign, allowed Ford to take positions for which he need bear no re-

sponsibility; the costs, in which at its most basic the assumption of responsibility is rooted, no longer needed to be paid if only because no bill could be presented. Within his heavily guarded borders Ford could do what he pleased and avoid the consequences.

For the first one and a half years of its life the newspaper confined itself editorially mainly to support of Wilson and the League of Nations.[67] But from the beginning, Ford had seen it as an instrument of enlightenment. "I am going to print the truth," he told Upton Sinclair in 1919. "I am going to tell the people what they need to know. I am going to tell them who makes war, and how the game of rotten politics is worked. I am going to tell them how to get the idle land into use. Above everything else, I am going to tell the young men to find useful things to do, because that is the way to be happy in this world."[68]

The first priority was thus allotted to "who makes war." The Peace Ship debacle rankled. It had been Ford's first grandiose failure. Incapable of accepting his own overwhelming contribution to the futility of the enterprise, he fastened the guilt onto other men and acted all the more vigorously and self-righteously to strike them down. Once again he found release in action from the doubts he carried with him.

Unleashed on an international scale, Ford's prejudices contributed to a state of mind which eventually condoned the murder of millions of innocent people. "It is not only the Old World that [the Jew] holds thus enmeshed," Hitler wrote in 1924, "the same fate menaces the New. It is Jews who govern stock exchange forces of the American Union. Every year makes them more and more the controlling masters of the producers in a nation of one hundred and twenty millions; only a single great man, Ford, to their fury still maintains full independence."[69] Externalizing his own conflicts and acting in the world of fantasy he so created, Ford justified his attacks on the freedom of other men with the simple statement that he was bringing them real freedom for the first time: he was delivering the "good" Jews from the "bad" who persecuted both "good" Jews and Gentiles alike. Several months earlier an article in the magazine *Forum* noted the connection between the sense of personal persecution and the $5 day: "Ford has the idea that he is persecuted. He believes the press began to hound him after the $5 day," the article reported. Ford himself was quoted as saying that "There is a good part, not all, of the American press that is not free. It is owned body and soul by bankers. When they tell it to bark, it barks. The capitalistic newspapers began a campaign against me. They misquoted me, distorted what I said, made up lies. . . . The invisible government got at its work."[70]

During a camping trip with Ford, Edison, and Firestone in August 1919, the same month in which the *Forum* article appeared, John Burroughs the naturalist noted that "Mr. Ford attributes all evil to the Jews or the Jewish capitalists —the Jews caused the War, the Jews caused the outbreak of thieving and robbery all over the country, the Jews caused the inefficiency of the Navy of which Edison talked last night . . ."[71]

Anti-Semitism brought into clear, more manageable focus all the hitherto differentiated targets of aggression. The warmongers, the munitions-makers, the bankers; the vendors of depravity who made films and composed jazz; the distillers of alcohol, and the manufacturers of cigarettes could all now be subsumed under the word "Jew." Even the gold standard could be attacked as the invention of "Jewish Wall Street."[72]

The first *Independent* article that was exclusively dedicated to anti-Semitism appeared on May 22, 1920. Under the banner, "The International Jew: The World's Problem," the paper announced:

There is a super-capitalism which is supported wholly by the fiction that gold is wealth. There is a super-government which is allied to no government, which is free from them all and yet which has its hand in them all. There is a race, a part of humanity which has never yet been received as a welcome part and which has succeeded in raising itself to a power that the proudest Gentile race has never claimed— not even Rome in the days of her proudest power. It is becoming more and more the conviction of men all over the world that the labor question, the wage question, the land question cannot be settled until first of all this matter of an international super-capitalistic government is settled. . . . If all this power . . . has been gained and held by a few men of a long-dispersed race, then either they are supermen whom it is powerless to resist, or they are ordinary men whom the rest of the world has permitted to obtain an undue and unsafe degree of power. Unless the Jews are supermen the Gentiles will have themselves to blame for what has transpired and they can look for rectification in a new scrutiny of the situation and a candid examination of the experience of other countries.[73]

For twenty consecutive weeks the series continued. The threat of the "international Jew" was said to lie in the covert leadership they gave to Jews all over the world; their master plan was so to demoralize the lives of Gentiles by war, revolution, and disorder that the control of world politics, finance, and commerce would fall into their hands.

Given this all-encompassing conspiracy, everything and anything found its own gocd place: morals had declined since the war because the Jewish money interests were working "to render them loose in the first place and keep them loose." Rents were skyrocketing because "the Jewish landlord" was at work. The short skirts of the flapper era "came out of Jewish clothing concerns." Gambling, pornography, even nightclubs—"every such activity has been under the mastery of the Jews."[74]

At the start of the series, Ford received a letter of protest from Detroit's leading rabbi, Dr. L. M. Franklin. Dr. Franklin had been a friend of Ford's. As the years passed, Ford had presented him with several Ford cars, but on June 14, 1920, Franklin wrote:

With deep regret and after mature deliberation I feel it is my duty to return herewith for such disposition as you may choose to make of it, the special sedan which you so thoughtfully presented to me some months ago.

This gift—like previous ones received at your hands—I have enjoyed and valued less for its intrinsic worth than for the fine thoughtfulness it betokened on the part of a man whose friendship I have never failed to appreciate.

Now, however, it appears from the last issue of the *Dearborn Independent* that with the desire of establishing the truth of an unfortunate idea that has taken possession of you, you are determined to continue the series of articles that must inevitably tend to poison the minds of the masses against the Jews. Under such circumstances, I cannot in self-respect continue to be the beneficiary of your well-meant courtesy.

You claim that you do not intend to attack all Jews but whatever the thought in your own mind may be, it stands to reason that those who read these articles—inspired and sanctioned by you—will naturally infer that it is your purpose to include in your condemnation every person of the Jewish faith.

[I hope] that you may come to realize the enormity of the injury which you are doing to a people whose sufferings and sacrifices for the sake of humanity have through the ages been beyond measure.[75]

The appeal might never have been made. It was not Ford who replied, but Liebold—and in terms which bespoke a new arrogance:

It is of course to be regretted that you have seen fit to . . . sever the relations of friendship which have heretofore existed between you and Mr. Ford. I sincerely hope, however, that conditions will so adjust themselves as to eventually convince yourself that Mr. Ford's position is correct, as resulting therefrom the world and all its people may benefit thereby. No man can have and follow a principle unless he is ready and willing to make whatever sacrifices are necessary.[76]

The point was that Henry Ford made no sacrifice. He did not even pay the personal price, however small it might have been, of acknowledging that he had one friend the less.

The anti-Semitic articles were to continue through ninety issues of the newspaper. Reprinted in book form under the general title of *The International Jew,* they were published in four volumes: *The World's Foremost Problem, Jewish Activities in the United States, Jewish Influences in American Life, and Aspects of Jewish Power in the United States.* All of these books were widely circulated.[77] From Philadelphia a reader who claimed to be a Russian by birth, American by naturalization, but who bore a pristine German name, wrote urging the publication of the books in Germany: "I should like to see your books translated into German. It would help the cause *very greatly,* for the sales in Germany would be enormous; fully as large as here, if indeed not *much larger than here,* because the Germans—usually—lock their stable before the horse is stolen. They overlooked this precaution once—before the recent war—and the cost of it will prevent another oversight I trust."[78]

To this effusion it was again Liebold who replied: "we wish to advise that Volume I of The International Jew, has been published in Germany and may be obtained from Hammer-Verlag (Th. Fritsch) Leipzig. As we have given our entire attention to the problem in the United States, we are not contemplating the publication of this book in foreign languages preferring to leave this to the people of the respective countries where such would be of benefit to them."[79] By March 1923, the Munich Correspondent of the *Chicago Tribune* reported that the books were "being distributed by the millions throughout Germany to aid Hitler's campaign against the Jewish people in Germany."[80]

The backbone of the articles was the czarist forgery of "The Protocols of Zion" which Liebold acquired in June 1920 from Boris Brasol, a Russian émigré.[81] In December 1920, the *New York Times* condemned the forgeries as "about the strangest jumble of crazy ideas that ever found its way into print."[82] But by then Ford's abdication of responsibility had become total. In January 1921, Gaston

Plantiff, who had earlier been the Peace Ship's financial overseer, wrote Liebold that he had recently talked to Herman Bernstein, an editorial writer on the *New York Times*. Bernstein had himself been a member of the peace expedition and, Plantiff wrote, "he is very anxious to see Mr. Ford personally, as he says that he can convince him he is on the wrong track and that it is nothing but fraud that he has."[83] Liebold's reply is notable for the ease with which the problem of forgery is turned aside and for the extent to which his own personal authority had clearly superseded Henry Ford's:

The slightest acquaintance which Mr. Ford has had with individual Jews has been used to the limit for purposes of getting interviews and attempting to accomplish Bernstein's same purpose. *The matter has gone too far for us to stop and consider now just where it is wrong.* This has been carefully weighed and considered long before we started. If anything we have published is untruthful, the Jews have thus far failed to show it.

Bernstein's reference to fraud is evidently in connection with the Protocols. If you will carefully read our articles, you will find we have at no time guaranteed their authenticity. We have merely stated what they contain and have paralleled this with what actually took place and are leaving it to the mind of the public to judge. I have no objections whatever to talking with Bernstein except I have found that the moment we open ourselves and extend interviews to the Jews, it is only used for the purpose of misquoting and publicity which has no bearing whatever on the issue and attempts to [deride] the individual members of our organization.

So far as Mr. Ford is concerned, he has nothing to say to anybody. The matter is being handled entirely by the organization of the publishing company and so long as Mr. Ford personally keeps out of it, I am confident that it can be brought to a successful end and will personally leave him free to take whatever action he chooses at the right time.[84]

Although it was with his own conflicts that anti-Semitism so securely meshed, on the evidence Ford could have had no clear idea of the extent to which he had been committed by the men around him. It would be going too far to say that he held anti-Semitism as lightly in principle as he had held the issue of peace: the Jews offered far too inclusive a target. Yet, as abruptly as it had begun, the campaign was later to be abandoned. Like the Peace Ship, anti-Semitism offered a pathway to action but only a temporary release from the same unconscious conflicts which only in externalization were rendered tolerable.

Liebold, in the meantime, went on to build up a network of secret agents. In Germany, a certain Lars Jacobsen attempted to win the support of the ex-Kaiser to the Ford cause:

I will ask you to use a great deal of care in communicating with me, [he wrote Liebold] and to use all possible care that the letters are not intercepted, because while I dislike to think of myself as a coward, on the other hand I have no delusions about what the Jewish revolutionary party in Germany will do to me if they find out that I am communicating with the Hohenzollerns on behalf of Mr. Ford, in order to secure information that will show the Jews up. If that happens, I am certain that you will not hear from me any more. . . .[85]

One can only speculate as to the extent of Liebold's consternation when early in 1922 Ford ordered the series discontinued. "I want you to cut out the Jewish articles," he told Cameron. "Put all your thought and time to studying and writing about this money question. The Jews are responsible for the present money standard and we want them on our side to get rid of it."[86] It was evidently of little consequence that his books were at that very time trumpeting a call to action: the day was at hand, Volume I of *The International Jew* declared, when the country's "flabby tolerance" toward the Jews would be abandoned and there would be a Jewish exodus from America.[87] What Americans needed was simply "the gristle to attack."[88] And, reassuringly for those whose urge to action found expression difficult, it was "not without reason" that the Ku Klux Klan was undergoing a revival in Georgia.[89]

For the next two years, although the books continued in circulation, the newspaper's anti-Semitism was sporadic, concerned less with the overarching "menace" than with the individual actions of munitions makers, Wall Street bankers, and Hollywood producers.

Then in 1924–1925, the articles began again. In the intervening years Ford had been defeated in his bid to take over Muscle Shoals, a complex of partially completed dams, power installations, and plants for the manufacture of nitrates, on the Tennessee River. Under government control it was eventually to be developed into the Tennessee Valley Authority.

The Ford bid for Muscle Shoals was an offer to lease the dam for 100 years at an annual rental of 4 percent of the construction costs, estimated at $68 million, which the government would incur in completing the project on a scale to furnish 850,000 horsepower. The power so produced would be at Ford's disposal, but he offered to pay in addition to the rental offer an annual sum for maintenance, and a semiannual contribution to a sinking fund that was calculated to realize over the 100-year term of the lease, $49 million if invested at 4 percent, or $70 million if invested at 5 percent. Government engineers estimated that taken together the amount offered for maintenance *and* the sinking fund contributions fell short by $150,000 of the annual cost of repairs to the dams.

Of equal importance in the Ford bid was an offer to buy outright for $5 million the nitrate plants, the quarry, and other installations at the site. Their cost to the government had been $85 million, and their estimated scrap value was $8 million. But if the offer were accepted, Ford undertook to manufacture annually approximately 110,000 tons of ammonium nitrate for fertilizers that would be sold directly to the nation's farmers at a net profit of not more than 8 percent.[90]

The offers bound Ford to produce neither cheap power

nor cheap fertilizer, and it violated the spirit of the Federal Power Act of 1920 which had set a 50-year limitation on power leases.[91] Yet its appeal to the imagination of small farmers everywhere was phenomenal. In Congress Ford was called the friend of "the great agricultural and labor interests of the country, the people who toil from morning till night."[92] In an impartial analysis of the Ford bid, the *New York Times* concluded that

Ford is the modern miracle worker, in the farmer's eyes as well as in those of many other citizens. His success as a maker of cars has overclouded his failure as a peacemaker and his poor taste in journalism. The mere rumour that he was to take over Muscle Shoals persuaded many a farmer, especially in the South, that a new day was to dawn. This impression was cleverly strengthened by statements made by propagandists that Mr. Ford had undertaken to "cut the price of fertilizer in two."[93]

Ford had in fact undertaken to cut the price in four. "We'll make [fertilizer] for a great deal less because we'll cut out four profits now going to manufacturers and middlemen by making a complete fertilizer and selling it direct to the farmer."[94] In reality, as the *Times* article was at pains to point out, the process under which Ford hoped to produce cheap fertilizer was so inadequately developed at the time that "neither Mr. Ford nor any one else really knows how much it will cost. . . ."[95]

Testifying before a congressional committee, Ford's Chief Engineer, W. B. Mayo, shed further light on the bid:

Questions by several committeemen developed that it was Mr. Ford's intention to use all the power developed by the water projects and other plants for his own purposes at Muscle Shoals. It was not the intention, Mr. Mayo stated, to establish a power selling company to compete with commercial companies engaged in that enterprise. A part of the power created, it was explained, would be consumed in the manufacture of automobile parts from raw materials. This statement by the witness revealed for the first time that it was the intention to operate the plants in connection with Mr. Ford's automobile business and was construed as implying the production of light metals, possibly of aluminum, which would enter into the construction of automobiles at the Detroit Factory.[96]

The congressional battle that ensued over the Ford bid finally resulted in Ford's withdrawal on October 15, 1924. In the face of strong opposition from Senator Norris of Nebraska, it was clear that a favorable decision could not be reached, and Ford abandoned the fight.[97] Before he did so, however, he excoriated his opponents even as he attempted to make his motives clear. Mayo's testimony notwithstanding, he declared:

My purpose in taking over Muscle Shoals is not to benefit us or our business in Detroit or any other part of the country— my one purpose is to do a certain thing that will benefit the whole world. . . . If the Government accepts my offer for Muscle Shoals as we have made it and will consider completing the dam according to [the] financing plan which I have in mind, we can here do an epochal thing—literally, I mean it—an epochal thing. We shall eliminate war from the world. . . . The cause of all wars is gold. . . . There's profit in war. I don't mean moral profit or increased religious interest or spiritual uplift through trial by fire, nor any of that kind of bunk—it's money profits I mean, profits in gold—that's the one and only reason for wars. . . . There's a group of international bankers who today control the bulk of the world's gold supply. They have their members or their agents in every country. No matter to what country they as individuals claim allegiance, they all play the same game, to keep the gold they have in their own hands—and to get just as much more as possible. . . . With the international bankers the fostering, starting, and fighting of a war is nothing more nor less than creating an active market for money. . . .[98]

In this interview Ford went on to suggest that the way to defeat the international bankers and so eliminate the causes of war lay in moving the nation's currency away from the gold standard, printing the money to pay for Muscle Shoals and retiring the entire "non-interest bearing" currency issue out of the earnings of the plant. No details were given but the essential point is the entirely consistent attribution to others of the wish to make war. By so doing, Ford was free to make war on the makers of war: "In Muscle Shoals lies the freedom of American industry. During the war the country turned its every resource to help free the world from militarism—a militarism fostered by an international money power. Now in the same way we are going to fight to the last ditch to free American industry and American agriculture from that same money power."[99]

The Muscle Shoals bid was withdrawn in October 1924, but by March of the same year the *Dearborn Independent* had resumed its anti-Semitic articles: the hoped-for rapprochement with the bankers in order to eliminate the gold standard had failed.

In this second series of articles, the issues closest to Henry Ford combined to make the newspaper's attacks the most libelous which had so far ensued. Anti-Semitism, the Jewish money power, and the exploited American farmer were explicitly thrown together for the first time. Aaron Sapiro, a Chicago lawyer who had been active in the organization of farmers' cooperative marketing organizations, was accused of being a tool of a Jewish group bent on the exploitation of the American farmer and eventually of the farmers of the world. Linked to Sapiro were the inevitable "Jewish combinations," "international banking rings," and "Jewish international bankers."[100] Sapiro himself, the articles proclaimed, had personally cheated the farmers for whom he worked.

Sapiro's response was a $1 million suit for defamation of character, which came to trial in 1927. After six weeks of hearings the court was compelled to declare a mistrial because a woman juror in an interview with a Detroit newspaper was reported as saying, "it seems to me that someone is trying to keep this case away from the jury."[101]

According to a *New York Times* report, the Ford lawyers had "let loose a swarm of detectives recruited from the Ford organization to spy upon the coming and going and conversing of all the members of the jury."[102] Harassed to an unbelievable extent by Ford investigators who produced affidavits ranging from alleged perjury on her part to the allegation that her husband ran a speakeasy, the woman had attempted to defend herself to a newspaper reporter whose interest may have exceeded the purely reportorial: in his decision the presiding judge attributed the mistrial to the fact that "justice [had] been crucified upon the cross of unethical and depraved journalism."[103]

Ford had, prior to this incident, strenuously sought to avoid being served with a subpoena to appear as a witness for the plaintiff, and when the Sapiro forces finally succeeded in serving him, an accident occurred on the night before he was due to appear in court. Two weeks later he was still unwell. It was at this point, just as Sapiro's lawyers were about to require an examination by an impartial physician, that the mistrial was declared and further hearings postponed for six months.[104]

In the testimony given in the first weeks of the trial, W. J. Cameron assumed total responsibility for the newspaper's anti-Semitism. Ford, he said, had never read the *Independent* in his presence; no advance copy had ever required Ford's approval; he had never discussed "any article" or "any Jew" with Ford; he had never discussed the position taken by the paper on any public question with Ford.[105]

On July 6, 1927, three months after the trial's end, whatever integrity Cameron might have managed to retain was dealt a grievous blow when Ford released a sweeping retraction of, and apology for, the *Independent*'s anti-Semitism. Interviewed by the Associated Press, Cameron said he could not "believe Mr. Ford would make public such a statement" without advising him. "It is all news to me," he said. "I cannot believe it is true."[106]

But that it *was* true was incontestable.

In the multitude of my activities [Ford's statement ran], it has been impossible for me to devote personal attention to their management or to keep informed as to their contents.

It has therefore inevitably followed that the conduct and policies of these publications had to be delegated to men whom I placed in charge of them and upon whom I relied implicitly.

To my great regret I have learned that Jews generally, and particularly those of this country, not only resent these publications as promoting anti-Semitism, but regard me as their enemy. Trusted friends with whom I have conferred recently have assured me in all sincerity that in their opinion the character of the charges and insinuations made against the Jews, both individually and collectively, contained in many of the articles which have been circulated periodically in the *Dearborn Independent* and have been reprinted in the pamphlets mentioned, justifies the righteous indignation entertained by Jews everywhere toward me because of the mental anguish occasioned by the unprovoked reflections made upon them.

This has led me to direct my personal attention to this subject, in order to ascertain the exact nature of these articles. As a result of this survey I confess that I am deeply mortified that this journal, which is intended to be constructive and not destructive, has been made the medium for resurrecting exploded fictions, for giving currency to the so-called Protocols of the Wise Men of Zion, which have been demonstrated, as I learn, to be gross forgeries, and for contending that the Jews have been engaged in a conspiracy to control the capital and the industries of the world, besides laying at their door many offenses against decency, public order and good morals.

Had I appreciated even the general nature, to say nothing of the details, of these utterances, I would have forbidden their circulation without a moment's hesitation, because I am fully aware of the virtues of the Jewish people as a whole, of what they and their ancestors have done for civilization and for mankind toward the development of commerce and industry, of their sobriety and diligence, their benevolence and their unselfish interest in the public welfare.

Of course there are black sheep in every flock, as there are among men of all races, creeds and nationalities who are at times evildoers. It is wrong, however, to judge a people by a few individuals, and I therefore join in condemning unreservedly all wholesale denunciations and attacks.

Those who know me can bear witness that it is not in my nature to inflict insult upon and to occasion pain to anybody, and that it has been my effort to free myself from prejudice. Because of that I frankly confess that I have been greatly shocked as a result of my study and examination of the files of the *Dearborn Independent* and of the pamphlets entitled "The International Jew."

I deem it to be my duty as an honorable man to make amends for the wrong done to the Jews as fellow-men and brothers, by asking their forgiveness for the harm I have unintentionally committed, by retracting as far as lies within my power the offensive charges laid at their door by these publications, and by giving them the unqualified assurance that henceforth they may look to me for friendship and goodwill.

Finally, let me add that this statement is made on my own initiative and wholly in the interest of right and justice and in accordance with what I regard as my solemn duty as a man and as a citizen.[107]

Publication of the *Independent* was abruptly discontinued at the end of 1927. It was the same year in which the Model T was finally abandoned and the manufacture of the tractor transferred to Ireland. At one stroke Ford appeared to cut himself loose from the interests which up to then had dominated his life; and in fact, from this point forward his actions increasingly reflect a preoccupation with violence—a preoccupation now shorn of the rationalizations which had earlier given at least a shadow of social meaning to his behavior.

The struggle as Ford appeared to see it, first with the government over the New Deal and the National Recovery Act, and then with the UAW over recognition, was one in which the issue of sheer power was uppermost. The government and the unions, Ford believed, were out to "get" him. In the attempt to fight back he came increasingly under the influence of Harry Bennett, an ex-boxer who was head of the Ford Service Department. Bennett's ties to the Detroit underworld were notorious, his involvement in Dearborn politics corrupt; and he was the leading figure in the "Terror" that enveloped the Ford plants in the thirties. A responsible labor leader writing in 1938 described the miasma of dread and intimidation for which Bennett was responsible:

There are about eight hundred underworld characters in the Ford Service organization. They are the Storm Troops. They make no pretense of working, but are merely "keeping order" in the plant community through terror. Around this nucleus of 800 yeggs, there are, however, between 8000 and 9000 authentic workers in the organization, a great many of them spies and stool-pigeons and a great many others who have been browbeaten into joining this industrial mafia. There are almost 90,000 workers in River Rouge and because of this highly organized terror and spy system, the fear in the plant is something indescribable. During the lunch hour men shout at the top of their voices about the baseball scores lest they be suspected of talking unionism. Workers seen talking together are taken off the assembly line and fired. Every man suspected of union sympathies is immediately discharged, usually under the framed-up charge of "starting a fight," in which he often gets terribly beaten up.
Harry Bennett's power extends beyond Dearborn to Detroit. In certain localities in Michigan, judges and other state officials cannot run for office without a petition with a specified number of signatures. Bennett simply puts such petitions on the conveyor belt, and in one afternoon the prospective candidate has all the signatures he needs.[108]

Bennett indulged Ford's aggression, and worse, used it for his own purposes. Later, in an extraordinarily brutal book he wrote of Ford's "profound morbid interest in crime and criminals," but it was an interest which at the time he did his best to foster by playing upon the nightmares of a sick and aging man.[109]

It is upon this destructive note that the theme of "deliverance" comes to an end. The progression from conflict to adaptive defense to a return of the repressed to projection and near paranoia had carried Ford from the great creative years of the Model T, to the expansion and technological advances at Highland Park, and then hopelessly to a series of adventures which were invested with a restitutive fantasy that nothing in reality could sustain. Ford's anti-Semitism embodied the fantasy's central elements, for it was the bridge that linked altruism to unrestrained aggression toward others—and the parallel fear of aggression directed at himself.

In an examination of the psychological roots of fanatical anti-Semitism, Norman Cohn has pointed out that at the deepest symbolic level the Jew represents to the anti-Semite both the "bad" son, ridden by murderous wishes toward the father, and the "bad" father, the potential killer of the son. First, as Christ killers, the Jews assumed the guise of unrepentant parricides; second, as the older religion with a God who did not combine the father-son attributes of the Christian Trinity—a God who was father only and the merciless father of the Old Testament in addition—Judaism and the Jews were "ideally situated to receive the Oedipal projections associated with the 'bad' father."[110]

The relevance of this unconscious pattern to an analysis of Ford's behavior lies in the coherence it gives to the theme of "deliverance." It is not too much to say that at a symbolic level Ford first tried to help the "sons," and, when this failed, turned to the destruction of the "fathers." The early altruism by the 1920s had been transformed into aggression, yet there was still an element of restraint. Ford was freeing the "good" Jews from the "bad." But from 1927 onward, it was the destruction of anyone more powerful than he which drove him on to the excesses carried out by Bennett in his name.

Ford's great burst of creative inspiration followed his father's death in 1905. At a conscious level he had repudiated his father's help, denying that it had ever been given him. He continued to do so throughout his life, and it is as if he had to prove to himself that his father had abandoned him. But the reality was that he had left the farm; he "forgot" that his father had found him work when he first went to

Detroit; he denied his father's gift of the land which permitted him to marry; he rejected his father's offer of financial help in the early years. And it was only with his father's death that he found himself.

A pattern of guilt emerges in which the element of restitution predominates. Ford's fixation on the car, a fixation beyond the reach of the pressures of reality, can mean only that it had come to symbolize for him a way back, a means of expiation. The Model T was the farmer's car—and the farmer for whom it was built was, even as Ford's father had been, the farmer of the nineteenth century who struggled over half-cleared tracks and through snow and wind to get to town; who needed a car capable of sawing wood and pumping water, a car which was durable, bereft of frills—and cheap.

The fantasy with which the Model T was invested was ultimately incapable of realization, but for a time it worked. The design was frozen at a point where its usefulness was beyond question in conditions which had changed little from the 1880s. And then the drive to produce the cars in ever vaster numbers assumed dominance. To achieve this, Ford battled for control of his company and created the conditions for the great advances in the production process which were the concomitants of expansion. In ever-increasing numbers the farmers of the country—and others, but they were less important—bought the Model T.

The early altruism was as much the result of his own success at expiation as it was a herald of failure; he had been a "good" son but he had still not done enough. Other men too might be helped even as he had helped himself. Now that the Model T was finished, there were still other ways in which the unconscious sense of guilt could be appeased. And so, symbolically, he turned to help the "bad" sons, among whom now he stood and now he did not.

But here, too, reality denied him any lasting surcease, and the more cruel the denial the more intense became the need to externalize. The pre-Oedipal pattern of projection became Ford's dominant mechanism of defense and the greater the unconscious sense of guilt the more fearsome was the imaginary enemy: he turned to the destruction of the "fathers," the men who threatened the power he held.

The dynamics of individual conflict and equally of a style of adaptation lie in the earliest experiences of the external world, in the relationships which are established with others, in the opportunities which exist for self-expression. The following chapter will attempt to trace the dynamics of both conflict and adaptation in the personality of Henry Ford, and the critical themes of fixation, control, and "deliverance" which have so far been explored will be shown to have their genesis in early unconscious attitudes that later tended to determine conscious choice. It is from Ford's choices—his predisposition to certain kinds of action, his selection of types of situations and relationships—that the definition of his style will hopefully emerge.

The preceding chapters have attempted to establish the validity of three dominant behavioral themes. In the course of this attempt the assumption was made increasingly explicit that Ford's actions, although consciously decided upon at many different points in time and in relation to a diversity of objectives, achieved consistency because of the unconscious meaning with which they were invested. To say this is in no sense to argue for psychological determinism—there was nothing predetermined for example in Ford's choice of anti-Semitism as such. Had there been any other movements which were capable of presenting the issues of good, bad, weak, powerful, of redemption and destruction, it is conceivable that Henry Ford would have aligned himself with them. It is less the isolated choice of action than the issues idiosyncratically held to, which permits a definition of style.

The movement back in time which aims at establishing the earliest emergence of Ford's concern with the themes and issues unconsciously dealt with is equally not to be construed as a form of reductionism centered on rigidly viewed infantile antecedents. As Rochlin has pointed out in his analysis of the relationship between loss-restitution and creativity, "Being born in a stable does not make one a donkey. The problem of creativity seems to lie elsewhere . . . [it] is a special or particular mental activity. It remains to show what function it performs, what conflicts it serves to resolve. . . ."[1]

The issue thus is one of *process.* Accepting the structural concepts of psychoanalytic psychology one must, as far as the data will permit, look to the strength and quality of significant relationships in Ford's early life, as he and others remembered them, for an explanation of the unconscious themes that were later to become dominant.

Ford's memories of his childhood are striking for the closeness and immediacy with which his mother is re-

5
THE NARCISSISTIC STYLE

called, and for the hesitation, indifference, and even hostility which characterize his recollections of his father.

Allan Benson, the earliest Ford biographer who wrote in 1923 from material gathered in interviews with Henry Ford, devoted several pages to Ford's memories of his mother: "She was of that rarest type of mothers—one who so loved her children that she did not care whether they loved her. What I mean by this is that she would do whatever she considered necessary for our welfare even if she thereby temporarily lost our goodwill. . . . When mother made up her mind to anything, she never stopped until she had accomplished her purpose." In these pages Ford talked about his mother's sense of cleanliness and order and attributed his own to hers; he described an incident in which she remonstrated with him for trading the bread from his school lunch for cake; he said "that his wife and his son's wife are the same type of women as his mother." And then, in two brief paragraphs he dismissed his father. "My mother had a mind of her own," he said, "but she would have had no respect for a man who permitted his wife to rule him. I often consult with my wife with regard to business affairs because I know her judgment is good and many times take her advice. But I am always the one to decide what I shall do."

Benson, recording the information that Ford had given him, then went on to write:

William Ford, father of Henry, lived to be 79 years old. He had inherited the remaining 200 acres of his father-in-law's farm and was, therefore, throughout life in comfortable circumstances. He was a good, honest, upstanding farmer, with all the virtues of good citizenship, but with none of the daring that has led his eldest son so far. William Ford was content to be a warden in the village church, to till his farm and to live in peace. To him, a bird in hand always seemed to be worth a good many in the bush.

This might be easily disregarded were it not for the curious juxtaposition: "My mother had a mind of her own, but she would have had no respect for a man who permitted his wife to rule him. . . . William Ford had inherited his father-in-law's farm and was, therefore, throughout life in comfortable circumstances. . . . [He had] none of the daring that has led his eldest son so far."[2]

There is an implicit undercurrent which many years later Ford made explicit. In a discussion one day with Edward Litogot, the grandson of his mother's brother, he pointed to the old farmhouse in which he had been born and brought up and which he had restored as part of Greenfield Village—his own reconstruction of nineteenth-century rural America. "You see that home across the street there?" he said to Litogot. "That's my mother's home. My father just walked into that place. That belonged to my mother. That was my mother's home. It was her home and my father just walked into the place."[3]

In an interview published in July 1923 in the *American Magazine,* Ford talked about his mother more extensively to Edgar Guest. The interview took place in the old farmhouse.

As a tribute to his mother Henry Ford has restored the home she loved. It stands today exactly as it was in 1876; if not with the same furniture, with exact reproductions. There is no evidence that she is no longer here. . . . We were in her kitchen—the kitchen as it was when she was here doing for her children; spotless and orderly as she always kept it, now missing her presence, but radiant with something you could feel—a son's reverence for her.

The symbolism is perhaps overdone by the saccharine character of Guest's style, but it is there nonetheless: Henry Ford was keeping his mother's house exactly as she would have kept it. The question is: When she was alive for whom preeminently was it kept?

Ford's restoration of the house attests to the intensity of his early interest in the things his mother did, in the ordinary household furnishings among which she worked.

Can you remember [wrote Guest], the name and model

number of the stove which stood in your sitting-room when you were a boy? Henry Ford could and did and it took him eighteen months of constant and diligent search to find its duplicate. But perhaps the stove was easy to remember. Then can you remember the exact pattern and coloring of the Brussels carpet which covered the parlour floor of your home when you were a boy? If you wished to find one like it today could you describe it to another so exactly that no mistake could be made either in pattern or color? Henry Ford could and did. . . .

Ford, in fact, restored his mother's original set of dishes by dredging up broken bits of china from the land surrounding the house. He bought shawls similar to those his mother had worn to fill her bureau drawers, he placed slippers like hers under her bed. When she died, he told Guest, "I thought a great wrong had been done to me. . . . Now and then friends have suggested that it is too bad she could not have lived until now. They think I could have made her very happy. I have thought of that too; but I believe now it is better as it is. I believe that her work here was finished. She had done all that she could do for us and she was called away." This is not a surprising statement coming as it does from a man to whom it meant much that his uncle should tell him that he was "just like" his mother; "he smiled as he said [that]," Guest wrote, "as though he was recalling . . . the incident which had prompted his uncle's comment."

Then, in a contradiction that escaped Guest, Ford talked about family ties. Edsel Ford and his family, he said, often spent an evening with the older Fords at the farmhouse and ". . . we don't need visitors when we have each other. Maybe that's what it is—what the modern family needs to learn—the art of being happy with each other. It was Mother's idea. More than once I have heard her say in this room that if we couldn't be happy here in this house, we'd never be happy anywhere else. I was happy here too until she was taken." And after that? "Oh, after that it was different, and three years later I walked out of the front gate and headed for Detroit. . . ."

In this interview the relationships which Ford consciously established with the first and most significant figures in his life begin to take form. To his mother he owed everything. He was "like" her, he had always tried to do what she would have wanted: "I believe I have done as far as I could just what she hoped for me." Yet here again he added a curious qualification: "Perhaps my mother would be satisfied; but I am not. I have not done half enough either for her or for the world. I count my life in things accomplished, and there is still so much I ought to do."

This leaves the conscious avowals seeming a little less true. There is a note—contempt is perhaps too strong a word— but there is the attribution to another of satisfaction with an achievement which is below one's own high standards. Earlier there was the acceptance that his mother's death was for the best—and he left unsaid that she died giving birth to her eighth child and that he himself was only 13 years of age at the time: ". . . it is better as it is. I believe that her work here was finished. She had done all that she could do for us." There is the contradiction too between the acceptance of his mother's idea that "if we couldn't be happy here in this house, we'd never be happy anywhere else"—and—"I was happy here until she was taken . . . three years later I walked out of the front gate and headed for Detroit." Try as he might later to make her beliefs his own, they failed to work for him when he needed them most.

The conscious picture is perhaps a little carelessly drawn, for its edges have begun to blur: "to my mother I owe everything" seems less true than "to a certain image of my mother, which I try to keep carefully in place, I prefer to believe that I owe everything. To my father, by implication, I then owe nothing." The universal heritage of ambivalence toward parental figures was thus resolved by division: his mother became for Ford the symbol of all that was good, and the tie to the father to which ambivalence toward the mother would have led was defended against by attributing to him the hostility that had been lifted out of the mother-son relationship. But it was a resolution that he had endlessly to fight to maintain.

In the Guest interview which runs to some seven pages, Ford's father is mentioned only at the very end:

A tractor was working in a nearby field, a field his father had plowed over many times.

"I never had any particular love for the farm," he said; "it was the mother on the farm I loved."

He watched the tractor whizzing over the ground, and then turned to me with this:

"You know, farm work is drudgery of the hardest sort. From the time I left that front gate as a boy until now my only interest in a farm has been to lighten its labors. To take the load off the backs of men and put it onto metal has been my dream. If I can do that I shall have rendered a real service to humanity—the sort of service she tried to teach me to perform."[4]

It is perhaps appropriate that the interview should have ended on this note, for Ford's manifest devotion to his mother, and rejection of his father, was paralleled by the deepest need for restitutive action. However much he attributed the form to his mother—as when he said, for instance, that "People often ask us why we keep our shops immaculately clean. My mother was a great woman for orderliness and cleanliness. I want my shops to be as clean as my mother's kitchen."[5]—however much he repeated this, the function of what he did served his father.

The connection was as distanced and as remote as he could make it. The symbolism was "The Farmer," an abstract entity for which he could admit a compassion that was entirely lacking in his conscious relationship to the elder Ford. Time and again he told his biographers and the journalists who interviewed him of the battle he had fought with his father: first, over his mechanical bent; second, over his wish to leave the farm; third, over his belief in the future of the automobile. Benson's description is typical and his information came from Ford himself:

The next thing that William Ford knew his son Henry was repairing watches and clocks for a few nearby neighbors, charging nothing for his work. That was all right. . . . But there came a time when William Ford was not so well pleased that his eldest son had become clock and watch repairer for the whole neighborhood. The elder Ford's dissatisfaction arose from the fact that the boy still continued to charge nothing for his work, tho [*sic*] the excellence of his craftsmanship had caused his business to extend for many miles around. People said that when Henry Ford fixed a watch or a clock that the job was done right, and William Ford thought that if the boy was so good a mechanic, he was good enough to be paid for his work. William Ford was the kind of a man who always gave and demanded exact justice, hence his insistence that the laborer in this case was worthy of his hire. . . . Finally, Henry Ford's father could stand it no longer and forbade the boy to go out nights to do free work. Henry was working hard all day on the farm in summer, and the father felt that he needed his rest.

"I couldn't quit," said Mr. Ford, "so I used to go to my room at 9 o'clock at night and wait until I thought my father had gone to sleep. Then I used to creep out of the house, go to the barn, saddle a horse, and ride away—sometimes many miles—to a place where I knew there was a watch or a clock to repair. Many a time I did not get home until 3 o'clock in the morning. Yes, I always worked on the farm the next day just the same. The loss of sleep did not seem to hurt me any."[6]

This heroic picture of the persecuted small boy who stole out of the house at night in defiance of his father's commands has been flatly contradicted by Ford's eldest sister, Mrs. Margaret Ruddiman. "His father never forbade him to repair neighbors' watches," she said in her reminiscences. "I never knew of him going out at night to get watches and bringing them back to repair them. Those are largely imaginative stories." Mrs. Ruddiman doubted, too, that Ford's father would ever have insisted that his son should be paid for helping the neighbors. ". . . Father was a prosperous farmer. We had the things we needed, but we were taught not to be extravagant. Possibly some of the neighbors recompensed Henry for his work, but I know that Father never told Henry he should charge for the work he did on the neighbors' watches and clocks."[7] As to the relentless demands for labor on the farm and the callous disregard of the boy's lack of sleep: "My brother had some particular chores around the farm that were assigned to him by his father," Mrs. Ruddiman said, "but I don't know of any particular thing that he had to do. He was allowed to stay late in bed. There was no particular reason for it except that he was sleepy. The rest got up and went about their duties and he stayed in bed. That didn't happen every day, but it was a habit that he formed."[8] It was a habit that evidently proved hard to break. In Detroit in the 1890s Fred Strauss recalled that "[Henry] never came to work until after nine o'clock. . . . He never could get around in the morning."[9]

The measure of the concession that sleeping late represented must be taken in relation to life on a farm in the 1890s. Apart from the constant care of the farm animals and the intensive labor at planting and harvest time, there was still land to be cleared of standing timber—the hardest kind of work for men who had only teams of oxen to help them. "My father would get up about six o'clock and do the chores at the barn," Mrs. Ruddiman recalled. "[We] had sheep, eight or ten cows, pigs and horses. [We] raised chickens too and when we had extra eggs we sold them. . . . My father tilled the soil and raised wheat, oats and corn. . . . He sold part of what he raised and used part— hay for the horses, cornstalks for the cattle, and corn for the hogs. . . . He was most always clearing new land."[10]

On Saturdays the results of the week's labors were taken

to Detroit by wagon. "Hay, grain and wood were some of the things father had orders for and delivered regularly; apples, potatoes, and other small farm products were seasonal and were taken to market when there was a surplus. The hay and grain were sold to livery stables . . . wood was used by many families for both heating and cooking. During the year a cord at a time was taken to market."[11] Although the Ford farm was larger than the average, Henry Ford's boyhood was affected by fewer hardships than beset his contemporaries.

Ford's need to create a harsh punitive father where none existed is reflected equally vividly in a legend that he encouraged about a workbench built in his room. His father so detested his mechanical pursuits, it runs, that after his mother's death Ford took his tools upstairs, and locked in his room away from his father's displeasure, he worked late into the cold winter's nights with a lantern between his feet to keep him warm.[12] When he restored the farmhouse at Greenfield Village, the workbench was built into his old room. But in commenting on the restoration of the house, Mrs. Ruddiman said: "There are several changes, if I ever had the permission, that I would like to make [because] if it is to be open to the public it is not right. The workbench is one. That should be at the east window in the kitchen. There was nothing upstairs except his dresser and a little stand that he kept trinkets in, and his bed, of course."[13]

In a written memoir for a Michigan historical journal Mrs. Ruddiman described precisely the function that the kitchen window served: "From the east window Mother could watch the goings and comings of her family about the barns. . . . *She could watch for Father's return from town as there was a good view down the road. It was at this window that Henry later had his workbench and tinkered with his watches.* This was an important window in an important room in the house."[14] But Henry Ford was later unable ever to admit that he had sat at that window working on a neighbor's clock and watching the road for his father's return from Detroit.

Nor could he admit that far from thwarting him or threatening him, his father had helped him as best he could. The elder Ford maintained a workshop on the farm where repairs were made to farm tools and equipment, and as a boy Ford had had full access to the shop.

As Henry grew older [Mrs. Ruddiman recalled], Father gave him the opportunity of fixing things at home. Then as he gained experience, he helped the neighbors with their repairs. Since Father was handy with tools he was very proud that Henry had inherited his ability to fix things. . . . The farm gates were heavy to open and close, so Henry made hinges for these gates and a device for opening and closing them without getting off the wagon. Father was quick to recognize Henry's ability in making new things. He was very understanding of Henry's demands for new tools for the shop and ours was one of the best equipped in the neighborhood. . . . Thus many of the neighbors came to Father when an emergency repair job was needed. . . .[15]

Mrs. Ruddiman's concern with the misleading accounts which were circulated about Ford's relationship with his father led her to make her own attempt to set the record straight, and the passages quoted from her memoir indicate this. But in the course of expressing her dissatisfaction she included a statement that is more revealing of her brother's state of mind than any simple refutation of the myth:

For many years, I have been very concerned about the stories indicating a lack of understanding between Henry and Father. *Henry and I discussed this many times, but he put off doing anything about correcting the stories.* . . . There were family discussions and differences of opinion as there are in all normal families, and no doubt there were many times when Father questioned the wisdom of Henry's decision but at no time were there any serious quarrels or any kind of family trouble. This phase of Henry's life has been so dramatized that to many it is reality, and *since Henry did not correct these ideas,* many persons have assumed that it was true that all was not well between father and son.[16]

The point was that the ill feeling between father and son was of the son's own making and it was at his urging that it found its way into print. When at the age of sixteen Ford left the farm for Detroit it was not, Mrs. Ruddiman said, a dramatic instance of "the farm boy running away from home in order to pursue his life's work."[17] Yet this is precisely what Ford made it out to be. "Without saying a word to anyone," he told Benson, "I walked nine miles to Detroit, rented a room in which to sleep and sought employment in a machine shop."[18] To Arnold and Faurote who included a biographical sketch of him in their *Ford Methods and Ford Shops,* Ford told a similar tale:

Henry Ford's mind and fancy both drive him to things mechanical, while his father wished him to become a farmer, the result being that the boy decided for himself that his schooling was completed at the age of sixteen, and that he would not be a farmer and would be a mechanic. Following the bent of his irresistible inclination toward things mechanical, the boy Henry left the farm, against his father's commands, went to Detroit, eight miles eastward, and entered Flower Brothers' machine shop. . . .[19]

Once again Mrs. Ruddiman felt it necessary to correct the misapprehensions:

I wish to make clear the fact that we knew that at some time Henry would go to Detroit to learn more about steam engines and machinery. However, no time had been set and we did not know just when he would feel that he should begin his work and study. I am sure that Father and Henry had discussed his leaving and the time had been left up to him. Of course Father was disappointed that Henry did not wish to continue life on the farm, but if learning about machinery was what he wanted to do, Father would not hinder him.[20]

Although Ford was never to discuss it subsequently—and, on the evidence, at one point attempted to suppress it—it was his father who found him a steady job in Detroit at the

Flower Brothers Machine Shop. Fred Strauss subsequently recalled his first meeting with Ford at the Flower shop where he was already employed: "One morning I brought some valves into the office and while there I saw Henry Ford's father, and Henry was with him. I didn't know who they were but the next day Henry came to work. . . . They put Henry in with me and he and I got chummy right away. Henry was to do the same work I did. . . ."[21]

Many years later Strauss wrote a folksy letter of reminiscence to Frank Campsall, one of Ford's private secretaries:

When I wrote this letter to Mr. Campsall about Henry, Henry denied that he had ever worked at Flower Brothers at all. He told [Campsall] that I must be mistaken, that I must have taken someone else for him. He said he had never worked there. I got a letter from Mr. Campsall telling me this. . . . [then] some years after, when I met Henry, he told me, "Fred you were right. I remember very well when the both of us worked at Flower Brothers." He never wanted anybody to know that he had worked at Flower Brothers.[22]

The Flower brothers were in fact old friends of Ford's father and often visited at the Dearborn farm, yet what Henry Ford chose to remember was a fantasied struggle which he had won all by himself. His early biographers repeated Ford's version of how he made ends meet in the first days in Detroit. He was earning $2.50 a week and the cheapest boarding house he could find cost $3.50, so "after working ten hours a day in a machine shop, the boy worked from 7 to 11 each evening repairing clocks and watches, for which he received $2 a week."[23]

To turn once again to the deflating Mrs. Ruddiman: "Henry did not have to walk the streets trying to find a boarding house whose weekly rate would meet his wages, for he stayed with Aunt Rebecca Flaherty, Father's sister, who lived with her family in Detroit."[24]

In 1882 Henry Ford returned to his father's farm and he was to remain there for nine years. He was then nineteen, he had received his mechanic's papers and yet he turned his back on the machine shops of Detroit—which had earlier exerted so powerful an attraction. Benson's explanation, which undoubtedly came from Ford himself, is significant for the note of enticement which is attributed to the father and the heroic strength ascribed to the son. "Right here," Benson wrote, "came a point in Mr. Ford's life that, if he had been a youth of weaker purpose, might have wrecked him. His father gave him 40 acres of land. It was a bait to get the young man back to the country. William Ford did not want his son to be a factory worker in a city. It seemed so foolish to the father, when the son might as well enjoy the free, independent life of the farmer."[25]

The facts were that the gift was not made until late 1886 or early 1887, and the land extended over 80 acres, not 40.[26] After several years on the farm, Mrs. Ruddiman said: "Father gave Henry the use of the Moir eighty acre farm which he had acquired some years before. . . . It was a good farm with fertile soil and quite a large piece of timberland which could be cut and sold for a profit . . . about 1886 or 1887 . . . Henry set up a sawmill and portable engine on his own property."[27]

And again Mrs. Ruddiman set out to correct the misinterpretations. "It has been said," she wrote, "that the reason Henry returned to the farm was because Father was ill and had demanded that he give up his work in the city to manage the farm. . . . That was not the reason. . . . Father, the boys [her brothers John, aged 17, and William, aged 11] and a hired man had been getting along very well. . . . [Henry] wanted time to think and plan."[28]

Ford in fact, at a symbolic level, wanted time to resolve as fully as he could the old ambivalence toward his father. And the means finally came in the guise of an offer from his father of financial help: the father, attempting only to give the son what he said he wanted, offered him money to help build the first car. "It is true," Mrs. Ruddiman recalled, "that my father offered to put money in the first automobile but my brother wouldn't take money from my father or any member of the family. . . . I don't know why my brother told my father not to invest money in the first car, but he did just that."[29]

This incident is of vital psychological importance because it is the first step toward Ford's attempt at a final resolution of his conflicts. His hostility toward his father was now to be grounded in what he unconsciously felt to be his father's abandonment of him. His father wanted and needed him so little that he could offer him money to build the car that would take him away from the farm. The second and equally important step came with the elder Ford's death in 1905. In the intervening years Henry Ford experimented endlessly, but it was only in the months following his father's death that he finally accepted his own vision and designed the first mass car. The discrepancies which have so far been cited between Ford's memories and the facts, were, every one of them, subsequently recorded, and in a sense his father's offer made them inevitable. Ford had now accepted an unconscious fantasy of abandonment which gave focus to his aggression but at the same time involved the deepest sense of loss: at a conscious level he coped with this by becoming not the son abandoned but the son strong enough to leave home.

The fantasy of abandonment was the expression of a fundamental narcissistic loss, and, despite his attempts at reversal, Ford's awareness of it was sometimes conscious, in the sense that symbolism and imagery which meshed with the conflicted rage and longing within him would evoke a response. Up to the time when he first left Detroit at the age of sixteen, Ford told Benson, his favorite book had been *Herbert Mattison, A Bound Boy*. The hero of the book had been "bound out" by his father to work for a neighbor until he was twenty-one. This, Benson noted

in passing, was "a common thing in America 50 years ago,*
the boy who was bound out receiving only his board and
clothing and a small amount of money."[30] The bound boy
in fact was effectively rejected by his father. Cast out to
make a living as best he might, he was the very symbol of
a son abandoned.

This review of fantasy and reality has hopefully brought
into relief the narcissistic implications of reversal: while
Ford maintained that his father had always opposed him,
that he never wanted him to leave the farm—what he was
simultaneously maintaining was that he meant so much to
his father that the elder Ford could not release him, could
not let him go. Out of reversal there emerged the manifest
belief that it was not he who needed his father. And,
equally important, it was he who had had the strength to
do what he truly wanted to do in face of his father's need,
and against his opposition.

What one is looking at here are the dynamics of conflict
within an individual whose talents and abilities permitted
him, at least temporarily, to bind them by enormously creative action in the real world—and the attempt to trace the
sources of conflict is thus inversely an attempt to follow the
development of the creative process by establishing the
functions it performs [and the] conflicts it serves to
resolve.[31]

In his discussion of the complex of loss and abandonment,
Rochlin has given it a centrality which rivals that of the
Oedipal resolution. The Oedipal resolution in fact is seen
as a development in which loss is come to terms with on a
sweeping scale for the first time:

The child's oedipal wishes fail to be realized. Up to this
point fulfillment was expected in relation to the parent.
But with the recognition that it will not come about, the
child's greatest libidinal experience fails. It turns into a
colossal loss. Whatever the compensations may be, and to
whatever degree repression may either succeed or be evaded

* Benson's book was published in 1923.

through sublimation, the fact remains that the highest level of libidinal aspiration is thwarted and must be foregone. *The element of object loss is introduced into and becomes a part of . . . libidinal experience.* With that the loss complex is firmly rooted.[32]

The relationship to both parental figures is bound into the losses associated with the Oedipal resolution and in the individual case the nature and strength of the loss must come from the evidence.

For Henry Ford the evidence runs strongly in favor of the hypothesis that the loss he endlessly attempted to make good concerned his relationship to his father. Ford's earliest memory was one that he recorded himself, a circumstance notable in that it must be set against his intense dislike of dealing in the written word. This memory concerned his father.

The first thing that I remember in my life is my father taking my brother John and myself to see a bird's nest under a large oak log twenty rods East of our Home and my birthplace. . . . John was so young that he could not walk. Father carried him. I being two years older could run along with them. This must have been about the year of 1866 in June. I remember the nest with 4 eggs and also the bird and hearing it sing. I have always remembered the song and in later years found that it was a song sparrow. I remember the log layed in the field for a good many years. This field was pasture. There was a well close to the log where the cows used to drink. Now [1913] there is a slight depression where the well was and the field is a fine meadow. . . . The next thing I remember is having the ague the summer I was six, 1869. I would be all right in the forenoon and would have chills, fever and shake in the afternoon. I remember my father hauling wood and seeing the redhead woodpecker, swallows, bluebirds and robbins. My Grandfather told me the name of all these birds. My Grandfather was my mother's foster father. He was born in Cork city Ireland on the 17th of March 1804. He came to this Country about 1825. After my mother married he and my Grandmother lived with my parents. She died in 1870 and he in 1881. I do not remember her very well. But I spent many happy days with him. When I was in Ireland in 1912 I [went] to the church in Cork and found the record of his birth. His name was Patrick Ahern. Her name was Margaret McGinn. My mother's name was Mary Litegotte. My father's William Ford. From seven on I had a mechanical turn. I made water wheels and steam engines. The first was a water wheel in the ditch and then at School where we drove a coffee grinder and ground clay which was very slow. Then I got a ten gallon tin can. Made a furnace of clay and brick-bats. Made turbine steam engine with tin blades and Pop gun Elder for steam pipe and blocks of wood for elbows and couplings. The steam gauge was a lever arranged on the bottom of the can so that when the pressure raised the bottom sprang out, indicated the pressure on a half circle. We never got over ten lbs. of steam. The turbine ran very fast. Three thousand RPM. It did not develop much Power. About ten of my schoolmates would go to the RR and pick up Cole to burn. The boiler finally blew up and scalded three of us and I carry a scar on my cheek today. It set the fence on fire and raised ned in general.[33]

It would perhaps be trite to say that here together we have the father, the younger brother, and the road to sublimation. What does bear exploration is rather what Henry Ford made clear by omission: the reference to his mother, one short sentence indicates the importance he attributed to her—and this in his earliest memory. His father in contrast is the major figure in the recollection. It was only in the 1930s when Ford was in his seventies that he eventually admitted to Ann Hood, a schoolgirl with a journalistic bent, that his father was "kind and just but a man of few words," yet his mother loved his father "with the deep love of a woman who never had parents." He respected his father, he said, but it was "to his mother that he turned for love and understanding."[34]

Ford's attachment to his mother, it seems evident, was rooted in identification. It is as if as a result the small boy too came to want so much from his father in fantasy that reality could deal him only disappointment. In fantasy the equation of disappointment with abandonment was made—and dealt with by the displacement onto his father of the hostility inherent in the relationship between mother and son.

In turning to his mother, Ford attempted to abandon the father who had abandoned him. The sense of loss was dealt with by a heightened narcissism in which he saw himself as the chosen son of his mother and reality supported him. "[My mother] believed in Henry's childish tinkering with tools," Mrs. Ruddiman wrote. "She encouraged him, and her patience and understanding were appreciated by him. There was a closeness between mother and son which Henry missed after her passing. . . . Henry told of incidents in which Mother seemed to know what he was thinking about and planning to do. She had what we call intuition. Henry was very much like her in that respect."[35] And, it might be added, he wanted to be "like" her. In her memoir Mrs. Ruddiman recalled how carefully their mother's image and ideals were held up to the children by their father and this forms part of the unconscious pattern: it was the mother whom the father loved, not the child; in being loved by the mother the child's narcissism could find a new outlet and in being "like" the mother he might come to resemble more closely the object the father had chosen.

It is significant that Ford himself recalled that it was his mother who had disciplined him as a child. Guest asked him if his mother had ever whipped him. No, Ford said:

The answer came instantly and almost sharply as though I had offended both him and her to ask the question.

"I was never whipped, but I was punished when I deserved it."

"How?"

"I was made to pay the penalty of my misconduct. I was humiliated. Shame cuts more deeply than a whip. Once, when I told a lie, Mother made me suffer the experience of a liar. For a day I was treated with contempt and I knew that I had done a despicable thing. There was no smiling at or glossing over my shortcomings. I learned from her that wrongdoing carries with it its own punishment. There is no escape."[36]

But the hostility that must inevitably have been evoked by these necessary measures was thoroughly repressed. There is no hint on Ford's part that the punishments he received at his mother's hands were other than he deserved. She "presided over [the household] and ruled it," he said later.[37]

In contrast to her dominance was his father's mildness. Mrs. Ruddiman recalled in her memoir that disastrous experiment with the steam engine which Ford himself set down in writing: "It blew up near the Miller School. They burned down the fence around the school. I saw it at the time and [Henry] had all the other boys working for him. He didn't do much. He only told them what to do and they very willingly did it. They made a fire. . . . Then there was another party bringing chips and wood and things like that. All at once the fence was on fire. . . ." Yet for the prime instigator, the consequences were light indeed. "My father had to help repair the fence," Mrs. Ruddiman wrote. "He didn't object to that too strongly, only in his quiet way. I can't remember hearing what he said except explaining the matter, that it was dangerous."[38]

Despite the contrast, in later life Ford drew his mother's image with unusual tenderness and reserved his hostility for his father. In doing so he endlessly reworked the complex of loss and abandonment, the unconscious pattern of which had now been set. In its earliest stage the sense of loss was dealt with by the attempt at disengagement from his father and by a narcissistic investment in himself. His father had abandoned him but he became the chosen son of his mother. Later would come the more massive denial in which the protagonists in the conflict would be reversed: he would be the one who abandoned his father—and what was passively endured would in the classic cycle be actively reversed. At a conscious level this would be shorn of its underlying meaning; Ford's decisions would be rational, objective. The rage and longing associated with the fantasy of abandonment and loss would be repressed. But guilt over the destructive wish and prototypical fear of future loss would remain, and both guilt and fear demand relief.

"The experience of a loss," Rochlin noted, "or the sense of it, whether it occurs in fact or fantasy, is an engine of change."[39] For Henry Ford the arena of change would be the environment, reality would be altered, restitution made for the destructive wish, and the real world so controlled that the fear of loss might be held in abeyance. But for any man these ends are attainable only in the process. They can never attain finality because the impetus to their achievement lies in an ineradicable unconscious pattern which endlessly requires action—whether it be flight at one extreme or the resolution to stand and fight relentlessly at the other.

It is out of this background that an individual style of engaging reality emerges, and the attempt to define it, by focusing on the issues Ford held to, begins with his return to Detroit in 1891. He was then 28. Erikson has written:

To be adult means among other things to see one's own life in continuous perspective, both in retrospect and in prospect. By accepting some definition as to who he is, usually on the basis of a function in an economy, a place in the sequence of generations, and a status in the structure of society, *the adult is able to selectively reconstruct his past* in such a way that, step by step, it seems to have planned him, or better he seems to have planned it.[40]

At a conscious level Ford had reached the decision to build the car. Symbolically he had reached the point where he could at last abandon his father because finally and unequivocally his father had abandoned *him*. His father did not want him enough; his offer of financial help to build the car was the final and symbolic expression of his indifference as to whether his son stayed with him on the farm.

This should in no way be held to imply that there was an open breach between father and son; the evidence indicates that Henry Ford simply wanted to go it alone, to do it himself.[41] He was now at the point where he could, in Erikson's words, "selectively reconstruct the past in such a way that . . . he [would seem] to have planned it." And the past now became one in which, against his father's opposition, he fought to realize his own vision.

That this maneuver could be only partially successful has already been indicated. Behind the facade of action in the environment there lay the unremitting unconscious sense of loss, and the need to guard against it—to be independent of other men, to make them dependent on him so that, in crisis, he would be the one who abandoned them. This was an implicit theme to which Dean Marquis returned again and again in his 1923 biography.

The Ford executive has added to those two uncertainties in life—taxes and death—a third that is discharge. Of the man climbing up in the Ford organization it may be said that he hath but a short time to live and is full of misery. He cometh up and is cut down like a flower. He never continueth for long on the job.

A judge of national repute once said to me, "I have a great admiration for Henry Ford, but there is one thing about him that I regret and can't understand, and that is his inability to keep his executives and old time friends about him." The answer is that it is not a matter of inability, but disability. He can't help it. He is built that way.[42]

And again, in a discussion of the 1920–1921 decimation of the company's executive ranks:

a finer, more capable, and more loyal group of men never backed a chief. They are not with him now on the upper levels of success, but a number of them were with him when he was making the climb. Granted that he has shown that he no longer needs them, he must admit that much of the momentum that makes the going easier is the stored-up energy of the men who put every ounce of strength in them into the tug of the early days. He may not need them now but there was a time when he did. He has been a very apt pupil. He is quick to recognize the merits of another man's idea and to appreciate it. But such was the devotion to him of the men about him that they were glad to have him take the credit for all achievements.[43]

The bond that Ford established with other men was a narcissistic bond; he could take but he could not give. Sorensen wrote later that "he never had a close intimate friend." His annual camping trip with Edison, Firestone, and John Burroughs was an essay in publicity,

with squads of newswriters and platoons of cameramen to report and film the posed nature studies of the four eminent campers . . . aside from this annual . . . get-together and an occasional Edison visit . . . [Ford] seldom saw [him]. With Harvey Firestone the relationship was of business origin . . . [and] although Ford and John Burroughs had a common interest in birds, the naturalist was primarily Edison's friend. Henry Ford saw Burroughs only on the annual well-publicized camping trips.[44]

The absence of close ties to men outside of his company was paralleled by a similar absence within it and by a rejection even of his own brothers. Sorensen wrote:

He lived a life so secluded that few ever saw him in his own home. I know of only two members of the Ford staff who ever spent a night with the Fords. One was our English manager Lord Perry. I was the other. . . . Sometimes a boyhood friend or two would see him at his office, but I never knew him to look them up. . . . I knew his two brothers, William and John, but never saw them in his home. They hated him, either because they envied him or because they expected him to do more for them. . . .[45]

One can only speculate that Sorensen's source for this final statement was Ford himself, but it rings true: "Mr. Ford was quite a strong family man, another associate recalled subsequently. [But] the interesting part was that he didn't get on too well with his own immediate family. I'm quite sure that he didn't get along with his brothers, Bill and John, anywhere near as well as he did with his wife's family . . . he felt more friendly toward his sister than he did toward his two brothers."[46]

In a magazine article in which Ford discussed the four

women in his life—his mother, his wife, his mother-in-law, and his sister—Mrs. Ruddiman was credited with being "a real sister" to him after his mother's death, and Ford did help her on a modest financial scale during his lifetime. But for his brothers he did little in comparison with what was done for his wife's large family, and there was nothing whatever left to them in his will.[47]

The rejection of the masculine figures in his own family was counterpointed by a close tie not only to his mother and his wife, whom he termed "the believer" for her unquenchable faith in him, but to his mother-in-law as well. At her death Ford said that she had been one of the most important factors in his success; and in an interview on his fiftieth wedding anniversary his views on marriage put stress on the need to "pick a good mother-in-law . . . a father-in-law isn't so important."[48]

In this way the underlying pattern found expression, and Ford's style was characterized by aggression toward, rejection of, and the drive to dominate the men around him, but to women he showed a consistent tenderness. His need to guard against loss was based on the deepest and most elemental fear. Bound into it were the aggressive rage at the one who had abandoned him, and the libidinal longing which sought to deny the existence of loss and through restitutive action to bring back the time when loss had never existed. While guilt over the destructive wish found surcease in restitution, at the same time it might be dealt with by the attribution to others of the very aggression which brought it into being, and here a complex of rationalizations took form.

Action taken in the service of restitution was by far the more amenable to rationalization than was action taken in the service of retaliation, of actively reversing the fantasy of abandonment. Action of the first kind was addressed to "The Farmer," and to freeing men from the troubles that oppressed them, but the dividing line was thin. At any time the transformation into action of a retaliatory kind might occur, and with this, aggression unleashed. At this point the process of rationalization would grow strained, not even Henry Ford could seriously have believed that his *Independent* articles were aimed at saving the "good" Jews from the "bad."

If one takes an example closer to him and accepts as plausible that Ford did tell Sorensen that his brothers expected too much from him, then the help he gave freely to his wife's family must be discounted and his views on work, utility, and charity called in to rationalize his lack of generosity.

It is a complicated procedure. Ford's views were colored by the conviction that men must stand on their own feet, that salvation lay through useful work, and that charity which did not provide a man with a chance to work was useless. Yet he could make exceptions not for his own brothers but for his wife's.

The discussion so far has attempted to put forward the two recurrent issues to which Ford unconsciously held. At the risk of oversimplification they may be described as the need to retaliate against the "bad" father and the need to deny through restitutive action (although I left the farm I am still a "good" son) the sense of loss and abandonment. They overlap each other.

In *The Problem of Anxiety* Freud noted that

The ego which has experienced the trauma passively, now actively repeats an attenuated reproduction of it with the idea of taking into its own hands the directing of its course. We know that the child behaves in such a manner toward all impressions which he finds painful, by reproducing them in play; through this method of transition from passivity to activity the child attempts to cope psychically with its impressions and experiences. . . . But the crux of the matter is the initial displacement of the anxiety reaction from its origin in the situation of helplessness to the anticipation of the latter, the danger situation. There then ensue the further displacements from the danger itself to that which occasions the danger, namely, object loss and the modifications thereof . . .[49]

This is to state with precision the overlap between the unconscious issues that engaged Henry Ford. Retaliation, the transformation from passive endurance of loss to active reversal, with Ford himself now the actor, has been traced in the relationship between Ford and his father. Its displacement to his relationships with other men, notably those he maintained with his own executives, has been briefly examined, and its effects on the organizational structure of the company will be explored in the following chapter. The need to deny the sense of loss out of which reversal grew and which is actively expressed through the attempts at restitution, has been referred to only in passing.

But, as the second of the two main unconscious issues that define Ford's style of leadership, its relevance is extreme. The first issue, that of retaliation, and its concomitant need to control others, to maintain his own independence while demanding subordination from other men—this issue defines the style of Ford's interpersonal relationships. The second is concerned with his approach to the concrete world of things.

It was through the work of his own hands that Ford sought symbolically to say that although he had left the farm he was still a farmer's son. The depth of Ford's fixation on the Model T, the extent to which this car was built for the farmer, and Ford's adamant resistance to change in its design have already been outlined. The gap that grew between the demands of reality and Ford's own actions attested to the fantasy in which the car played a central part. In 1934, shorn of any disguise, the fantasy's shape was revealed to the public. The stage chosen for it was the Ford exhibit at the Chicago Exposition.

An unpainted weatherbeaten barn of wood sits in Mr. Ford's back yard at Chicago in striking contrast with his huge exposition building in its modernistic dress. The little wooden structure bears a homely board sign:

BARN FROM THE FARM OF

WILLIAM FORD

FATHER OF HENRY FORD

BUILT 1863

BROUGHT HERE TO DEMONSTRATE THE

POSSIBILITY OF A CLOSER RELATIONSHIP

BETWEEN AGRICULTURE AND INDUSTRY[50]

Inside the barn there was an assortment of machinery, which according to Ford, "most any farmer [could] rig up at home from odds and ends," and with which he could go on to produce goods for the industrial manufacturer.

Back at Dearborn [Ford said] we are in the farming business on a big scale. So in Chicago we are talking as one farmer to another. And the old Barn here is our Speaker—it tells the story. What we call the "farm problem" must be solved by each farmer acting for himself. Just as soon as the individual farmer can make money, the "farm problem" will vanish for good and we think most of our other economic problems will go with it. . . . By means of this old barn—and there are thousands of barns just like it all over the United States—and the simple machinery in it, we are trying to pass along what we've learned for the benefit of any farmer who cares to make use of it.[51]

In the fairy tale too the prince cast out by his father returns to save him, and he returns because the bond is still there. Ford returned again and again throughout his life.

First, he took the car. Mrs. Ruddiman's statement that their father offered his son financial help notwithstanding, Ford told a repetitive tale of rejection. "His first trip he took with his car was to his parents' home," one of the employees at Greenfield Village remembered Ford telling him. "He thought he really had something and his dad got mad about it. He didn't like it at all. He thought it was something that would scare all the horses off of the road. . . . He could never get his father interested in his idea, his father wanted him to be a farmer. The first trip when he went home to his Dad, his father . . . was very disappointed."[52]

As must now seem inevitable, Mrs. Ruddiman's version differs:

It was characteristic of Father that he would not ride in the car on his first day. He was as interested as all of us in the fact that here was the horseless carriage about which we had been hearing. He looked it all over and listened with interest to Henry's explanation of it, but he refused to ride in it. . . . Father was a conservative farmer of those times. He saw no reason why he should risk his life at that time for a brief thrill from being propelled over the road in a carriage without horses. . . . Despite his refusal to ride in the car on that first Sunday, Father was very proud of Henry's achievement. He talked about it to us at home and he told his neighbors about it . . . [and] on later trips of Henry's to the farm, Father rode in the car.[53]

This of course was Ford's first car, completed in 1896. The car that would in truth drive the horse from the farm and lay the farmer's burden on steel and motors was still to come. It would take ten years more before the first real attempt at the mass car would be put on the road and by then the real father would be dead. But in symbolic terms he lived throughout Ford's life, and Ford returned to him again and again. After the car came the tractor and accompanying them both was the interest in the land: "After he began to get some money, he acquired farm property, not that he had any idea of a goal for the company that might need property. Because he was a farmer and loved the land, he acquired all the property he could. It is that old adage about the farmer believing in the land. . . . That is why he bought ground. . . . It was his idea to ease the [farmer's] burden. . . . That's what got him into the tractor business. . . ."[54]

The Ford farms were used as a testing ground for the tractor and for crop experiments which would benefit the country's farmers. Ford's work in soybean processing was ahead of its time. From the beans an oil was extracted and a plastic developed which were both used in the manufacture of Ford cars.[55] The soybean project was an attempt to give the farmers a secure cash crop for the industrial market.

A. M. Wibel, who eventually became the head of the company's purchasing department, remembered Ford at the Dearborn luncheon table endlessly discussing with his senior executives the importance of helping the farmer: they were the basic stuff of the country; they could be helped by building them a more efficient power unit than the horse, the horse ate all winter and worked only in good weather; the tractor was the best way of helping the farmer.[56]

Tractor production was carried out at a loss and Sorensen, Liebold recalled, made strenuous efforts to have Ford consider the situation and do something to remedy it. Finally, Ford asked for the loss figures; they were estimated by Sorensen to be about $55 on each tractor. "Well," Ford said. "That's about the best information I've had. I'm glad of it. If we can give the farmer $55 with every tractor that's just what I want."[57]

By 1940 the Ford farms extended over nearly 11,000 acres. Ford had in addition built a series of "village-factories": neglected waterpower sites were restored; old mills were renovated and dams repaired or rebuilt in order to give farmers the chance to process their crops themselves and earn an income from industry as well as from the land.[58] "He was interested in any stream where he could put in a dam and make a little power plant," one of the earliest Ford employees recalled. "He wanted to build these plants so he could make a little community and hire the farmers around. They could work on the farm and work in the shop too. He wanted to make a better way of life for them."[59]

In 1940, announcing his support of the National Farm Youth Foundation, Ford finally repudiated what he himself had done: "Young men of the farm have not realized their opportunities on the home soil. As a result many of them have left the farm. . . . The family system of farming has suffered and we want to see it rebuilt."[60]

Earlier, during the worst of the Depression, a journalist from the *New York Times* had described the state of mind which led up to this:

He sees the world sadly out of plumb, and because he moves by instinct he is trying to work out not by formulation but on the ground, what he calls "a sample" of a better balanced scheme. Instinct leads him back to the soil. He began on the farm and he knows something real is to be found there. . . . Industry itself, used for its proper ends, cannot hurt the world, but something has, he says; there is a tendency in all great industry to devour life. When that happens it becomes necessary to restore the balance, to go back and see where we took the wrong turn.[61]

And so he did go back—with the village-factories, and the crop experiments, with the tractor and the car, all of them concrete manifestations of an unconscious need to say it was not so, that he had never left the farm, that the sense of loss did not exist.

Against this background the issues of restitution and retaliation emerge as central to a definition of Ford's style. That these issues themselves have common ground in the themes of guilt and expiation is no less true for the attempt that has been made to hold them separate. Separation has permitted a narrower look at the broad field of unconscious motivation and displacement and will permit as well the isolation of clusters of component issues. In some instances these component issues will again appear to overlap. The active/passive dichotomy, for example, and the susceptibility to impulse as against the ability to delay, are relevant to both the issue of retaliation which dominated Ford's interpersonal relationships and to the issue of restitution which governed his actions in the world of things. On the other hand, loyalty, power, and rivalry are specific to retaliation; and concrete thinking and the sanctification of work are bound into the issue of restitution.

But before these component issues are considered, it may perhaps be useful to restate the relationships that have so far been drawn. Retaliation is symbolic of loss and disappointment. It is the Law of the Talon, the expression of a narcissistic reinvestment in the self which is no less aggressive because it is a defensive maneuver. The attempt at restitution is a concrete manifestation of the loss and disappointment which narcissism is invoked to defend against. In itself it is an expression of narcissism because the fantasy involves the conviction that restitution can be made: in this way the sense of omnipotence enters in to color the individual's view of what can be achieved.

Ford's hyperactivity has been described in entirely physical terms again and again. Its more intellectual expression is represented in the inability to settle down with any issue for long which did not touch upon "The Farmer." "When I started with him," said an early Ford employee, "he was like a bunch of springs, quick in action, nothing slow about him. He was always on the go. You'd think his body was built of springs."[62]

In his description of Henry Ford, Dean Marquis noted both the hyperactivity and the irresistible inclination to impulsive action:

A still picture of Henry Ford would be impossible for the simple reason that there is something in him that is never still. He thinks quickly and he acts quickly, and he is always thinking and acting. His normal state seems to be that of mental agitation, and it is an agitation that is contagious. In his presence no one is ever entirely at his ease; at least that is true of his employees. You come to feel certain of but one thing, and this is that with any work which he has to do, the unexpected is bound to happen. There is about him the fascination of an unlimited uncertainty. No living being knows what he is likely to do or say next. . . . As in every other man, there is in Henry Ford the mingling of opposing elements. In him, however, the contrast between these elements is more pronounced than in the average man. Phenomenal strength of mind in one direction is offset by lamentable weakness in another. Astounding knowledge of and insight into business affairs along certain lines stand out against a boasted ignorance in other matters. Sensational achievements are mingled with equally sensational failures. Faith in his employees and, at times, unlimited generosity toward them are clouded on occasion by what seems to be an utter indifference to the fate and feelings of men in his employ. There seems to be no middle ground. . . . There is no line discernible that I have ever been able to detect, that marks the resultant of the opposing forces within him, and to which one may point and say, "this is the general trend of his life." . . . His moral qualities . . . have never been compounded and blended into a stable, unified character.[63]

The choice of words is suggestive of the analysis that has been undertaken so far. "The opposing forces" of retaliation and restitution made action—at some points in Ford's life almost any action—imperative. He was unable simply to sit still: "he was always fiddling with something, keeping his hands active in some way." And his face was an unerring index to his moods: "there were days when Ford executives feared to see him coming down the hall . . . people would definitely avoid him when his moods were bad." Men on whom he had showered attention yesterday were today given "the silent cure" and ignored utterly.[64] Action on impulse was carried through to the most serious of business decisions. Liebold said later:

Whenever I knew that a problem could be taken care of, I never as a rule discussed the details with Mr. Ford unless I knew he was interested. When he came into my office I never knew whether Mr. Ford was going to stay there two minutes or an hour. I always hesitated in talking about some things when there were other matters of more importance that I wanted to get across to him. . . . He never cared much about what the books would tell him about the conduct of the business. At the end of the year when he came to set the price of the car, he'd say, "Well, how much money did we make?" Suppose we made $60 million and we built two million cars, Mr. Ford would know right away he made a $30 profit. He'd say, "All right, we'll cut the price $30." . . . That's how Mr. Ford grabbed his market.[65]

And the master's impulse was law to the Ford employee. "If you didn't agree with Mr. Ford," said one, "you would no longer be useful to him. The fellows that yessed him were fellows in his favor."[66] But even they could feel small security. "He would tell you that he was going to do a certain thing and he'd turn right around and deliberately do the opposite . . . you could never count on anything. You didn't know what he would do from one day's end to the other."[67]

The arbitrary exercise of power was paralleled by a sense of his own infallibility: "Mr. Ford thought that he could do anything," Joseph Galamb said, "and this was extended into a dislike not only of experts but a belief in the futility of using testing equipment on the components for his cars."[68] His attitude to the men around him at times bordered on the sadistic:

Characteristic of any engineer that ever went to work for Henry Ford, he would start to treat them nice at first; then he would start to either completely ignore him or treat him mean, or build him up to a fall and then knock the props out from under him. It seemed he used to take fiendish delight in playing those tricks. He got his pleasure out of work, but yet at the same time he used to like to see people suffer by giving credit to someone else for what you had done. . . . He used to test you and see how you'd react against it. . . .[69]

The "testing" of men was often carried to an intensely provocative extreme. L. S. Sheldrick, the company's chief automotive engineer in the 1930s, recalled an incident that will be cited at length because of the light it sheds on Ford's underlying need to provoke aggression against himself—an aggression, it goes without saying, which he could then triumphantly counter with his own, in this way leaving the sadomasochistic outlines of the fantasy clearly visible.

About this time Mr. Ford was becoming interested in certain young students over at the Edison Institute, boys who appeared to have something on the ball, and he thought he could make something out of them. . . . He took them around with him, exposed them to a lot of conferences, explained everything that was going on in these conferences. He took them on trips with him, and, in some cases built these boys up into such a state that there was no being with them at all. They were just little supermen because they had the personal attention of Mr. Ford about five hours a day. . . . I knew [one of them] well and he was a mighty fine boy. My heart ached for what was going to happen to that boy. . . . I knew that some day the slats were going to be kicked out from under him.

[Mr. Ford] built these boys up to the point where they'd go around giving orders. [This boy] used to walk in and give Sorensen orders. Sorensen hated that kid's guts like nobody's business. Henry Ford would take these boys' counsel and advice in preference to the older men. He gave that impression, I mean. He just did it to get the older men's goats, I guess that's why he did it.

When Mrs. Ford would be away somewhere he would take [this kid] over to the residence to live with him. [The kid] used to sleep over there when Mrs. Ford was away. I know in one case he drove Mr. Ford down to New England, to the Wayside Inn and back. He was only a kid about fifteen or sixteen, just old enough to have a driver's license.

Well, all of a sudden one day [the kid] was in the dog house. The boss wouldn't even speak to him. Nobody knows what the reason was. I thought the kid would just go to pieces. It was a terrible blow.[70]

Adding to the configuration of hyperactivity, impulse, infallibility, and thinly disguised aggression aimed at "breaking" men, was a vanity that rarely came through to outsiders. "Henry Ford was not modest," Sorensen wrote. "He did a lot for people he liked, but he didn't want his staff to be in the public eye. No one else in the organization could stand out above him. He pretended to be humble when with people who did not know him. . . . This was an act. He could never be humble when around us."[71]

Sheldrick described an incident during World War II when, on a tour with a British official through the Pratt and Whitney engine plant, Sheldrick's photograph was taken by reporters. It appeared in the evening edition of the *Detroit*

Free Press, but in the next morning's edition it was gone. A member of the newspaper's staff told Sheldrick later that Henry Ford had called the paper that night and asked for the deletion.[72] "He sought publicity," Sorensen said. "There was nothing shy about him in that. Shyness is a tendency to shrink from observation. He wanted to be observed."[73] And in an ironic aside for a man who wielded the discharge ax for Henry Ford more often and more brutally than any other, Sorensen added: "After the name of Henry Ford became a household word, men in the Ford Motor Company who might temporarily get more publicity than he did aroused his jealousy. One by one they were purged."[74]

The style that emerges from this catalog of components was apparent as early as 1915 when Arnold and Faurote described the structure of executive authority within the company:

The general scheme of the Ford Motor Company's operations has been largely of Mr. Ford's origination, but the details of organization have been carried out by others. So far as a close observer can discover, Ford himself has no premeditations, but acts wholly upon inspiration. In reply to a direct question he disclaimed any systematic theory of organization or administration, or any dependence upon scientific management, and seemed to lay emphasis wholly upon the personal equation. As he put it, "I know what kind of help I want and I look around until I find the man I am sure will give it." He has thus built up about himself not so much an organization as a staff of aides—all ranking as equals, none in command of any one department, all [out] ranking any titular department head, each eager both to meet any suggestions Ford advances or to volunteer suggestions for his decision, each as likely as the other to be put in charge of any shop-betterment idea Ford may conceive, because he observes no discrimination in lines of service. This alone makes the Ford establishment unusual, to say the least, in its direction. It also makes the establishment his own absolutely throughout, though, as he said, leisurely looking out of his office window, "I have no job here—nothing to do."[75]

If one looks for the analytic prototype of this style it lies in Freud's description of the all-powerful primal leader:

His intellectual acts were strong and independent even in isolation, and his will needed no reinforcement from others. Consistency leads us to assume that his ego had few libidinal ties; he loved no one but himself, or other people only in so far as they served his needs. To objects his ego gave away no more than was barely necessary.

He, at the very beginning of the history of mankind, was the "superman" whom Nietzsche only expected from the future. Even today the members of a group stand in need of the illusion that they are equally and justly loved by their leader; but the leader himself need love no one else, he may be of a masterful nature, absolutely narcissistic, self-confident and independent.[76]

This, it must be emphasized, is a model, a first form. In 1931, ten years after this severe abstraction had been put forward, Freud made its shape more easily recognizable in his paper, "Libidinal Types":

The characteristics of the third type, justly called the *narcissistic*, are in the main negatively described. There is no tension between ego and superego—indeed, starting from this type one would hardly have arrived at the notion of a superego; there is no preponderance of erotic needs; the main interest is focused on self-preservation; the type is independent and not easily over-awed. The ego has a considerable amount of aggression available, one manifestation of this being a proneness to activity. . . . People of this type impress others as being "personalities"; it is on them that their fellow-men are specially likely to lean; they readily assume the role of leader, give a fresh stimulus to cultural development or break down existing conditions. . . . Aggressiveness and activity go with a predominance of narcissism. . . . People of the narcissistic type, who, being otherwise independent are exposed to frustration from the external world, are peculiarly disposed to psychosis; and their mental composition also contains some of the essential conditioning factors which make for criminality.[77]

This might have been written of Henry Ford. In his case one is dealing preeminently with the derivatives of narcissism superimposed upon object loss. In the aggression directed at other men there is the retaliation for the original loss and the forestallment of future loss by the inhibition of libidinal ties. Ford is "free" to act ruthlessly, and action nonetheless is rationalized by an ethic of "work" and "service" even as expiation is sought in the concrete product of that "work" and "service."

Ford's views on charity in themselves offer an introduction to his ethic of work: they are steeped in the conviction that men should stand on their own feet, that salvation lay through useful work and that charity which did not give men a chance to work was useless. "Henry Ford," Marquis wrote, "decries charity. He makes no attempt to conceal that fact. He believes that money should be made to work, and that men should work for money. He insists that anything that can't pay its own way has no right to exist."[78]

No man, in other words, had a claim on Henry Ford. He owed others nothing. If a man worked, he could claim his just reward. If he did not, such a man held no rights over the work of any other.

The obligation to others which is a derivative as much of a libidinal tie as it is of guilt was dispensed with by Ford's idea of "service." Ford conceived his own work as service to others, a service notwithstanding that it was he who set its terms.

Interestingly enough, this mechanism has been seen to be at work on a much vaster social scale, operating to justify the absolute power of an entire ruling class. The concept of production for use rather than for individual profit had its political counterpart in the absolutism of the feudal system.[79] The arbitrary use of power was justified by the good it was held to achieve.

So it was with Henry Ford. Service was work. Public service he told Upton Sinclair, was "the only true kind of happiness. No man can be really happy if he is just thinking about his own happiness; he must be doing things."[80] Work in its own turn was activity: "The solution of all this discontent," he said in 1921, ". . . is just keeping busy."[81] Two years later he told a delegation from the International Labor Office of the League of Nations that the one sure cure for world unrest was "a job for every man. Let the people of the world once get the idea that all they need is to do a good day's work six days every week, and that in this way they can make their own prosperity, and there will be no more talk about unstable conditions, for instability will have ceased to exist." And, in unconscious equation of work and the binding of aggression, he declared that "if everyone has a job that interests him he will be too busy to think about making war."[82]

Inseparable from the issues of activity, work, and service was the making of things, concrete things that people used. "Making things," he told Sinclair, "will lead the way to freeing men for higher things."[83] Things were the tangible proof that work was worthwhile and it was in his fixation on the concrete that both his greatest strength and weakness lay.

Knowledge of the world, Ford believed, came through the sense of touch.[84] He read blueprints with difficulty, but, according to Sorensen, "his mind worked like an electronic calculating machine and he had the answer to what he wanted. The trick was to fathom the device or machine part that was on his mind and make the object for him to look at."[85]

Like a researcher in pursuit of the dimly remembered facts, Ford might scour the country for an old engine with which he had once been familiar. The universal joint for the Model T came from an old steam engine he had seen in the 1880s.[86]

In 1915, when the steel mill was being built at the Rouge site, Ford countered Knudsen's suggestion that the mill should be situated downriver at Trenton where there were limestone deposits, with "I can't take in all that land. Why it's fifteen miles from where I'm buying to Trenton. I can't do that. I want all Ford manufacturing behind one fence where I can see it."[87]

Progress, he believed, depended on "the engineering type of mind. . . . Everything is an engine, finance is an engine, industry is an engine, medicine is an engine, education is an engine; when we get financial engineers and health engineers and educational engineers and industrial engineers then these departments serve humanity as they were intended to do; otherwise not."

The extreme cathexis of the inanimate found its most publicized expression in Ford's famous statement after the *Tribune* Trial that history was "bunk." The history made by kings and generals and statesmen, he said, was not true history. "I'm going to start up a museum and give people a true picture of the development of the country. That's the only history that is worth preserving. . . ."[88] His museum today is filled with the artifacts of a century of industrial progress, the nineteenth century. They were bought, said one employee, unevenly, over a period of years: "Sometimes it would be a car-load a day, and then again it might be only one a week. Again it might be three car-loads a day. I'm referring to *freight-car* loads."[89]

In his essay on "Ego Development and Adaptation," Hartmann noted that

thinking, and particularly causal thinking, implies not only synthesis and fitting together, but also differentiation. We are dealing here with the coexistence of differentiation and integration familiar in biology. The development of this function of differentiation finds psychological expression not only in the formation of the mental institutions but also in reality testing, in judgment, in the extension of the world of perception and action, in the separation of perception from imagery, cognition from affect, etc. The equilibrium of these two functions may be disrupted, for instance, by precocity of differentiation, relative retardation of synthesis. . . . Since we somehow connect the synthetic function of the ego with the libido . . . it is plausible to assume an analogous relationship between differentiation and destruction.[90]

For Henry Ford, differentiation and integration remained fixed at the level of the inanimate, and in its libidinal aspect this is fully in keeping with the analysis which has so far been advanced. The synthesis he achieved in his understanding of the world of machines was unsurpassed in the early years of the industry. It was when he moved beyond the machine that his attempts at synthesis collapsed disastrously. He could not see the connections. His overriding hatred of the money power, Wall Street, and the bankers drew sustenance from his belief that they threatened the world of productive work. Bankers were parasites who lived off other men's labors. The money system hampered and destroyed the production system. Grasping only the most concrete aspect of the process, the things produced, he could say in all seriousness that "all the money in the world could be dumped into the sea, and as long as men could put one stone on top of another and till their ground, they would have products to barter and exchange and world commerce would go on without interruption."[91]

Industry is concerned with the concrete, the production of goods, and Ford's creativity at this level brought a great productive enterprise into being. The issue of restitution, which informed with personal meaning the concepts of work, service, and to an extent, his sense of the concrete, provided the unconscious background for his industrial achievement. When the Model T was finished, the issue remained, and Ford carried over into other fields totally unsuited for its application a style bred of conflict and the need to master it. The degree of adaptation which he had achieved in the real world had brought with it enormous power: it made action on impulse feasible, it made aggression a luxury he could afford. But it is not enough to say with Lord Acton that power corrupts; power, rather, provides the setting for regression on a massive scale.

With the Model T an assured success, the instinctual fusion that had made it possible broke down, and driven by a reexperiencing of the unconscious loss there was little to which he could turn. In the regressive fantasies that ensued, it was aggression, the issue of retaliation, which became dominant. Had Ford been something other than a brilliantly insightful mechanic, had his vision of the world been less concrete, there might have been other pathways to adaptation, to some new form of synthesis. As it was, he worked with what he had, and the need to deny loss, the narcissistic investment in himself, the omnipotence associated with the fantasy of restitution and supported in the real world by his vast wealth made of him, as far as a man can approach a model, the exponent of the narcissistic style. The effects of this style on the company's organizational structure, which will be explored in the chapter to follow, were little short of catastrophic.

Between 1919 and 1925 construction at the Rouge and the vast plan for integrated manufacture had cost Henry Ford at least $360 million.[1] The company owned iron mines, timberland, and saw mills in Michigan's Upper Peninsula; coal mines in Kentucky and West Virginia; glass plants in Pennsylvania and Minnesota; rubber plantations in Brazil. Raw materials and finished products alike were carried in Ford ships or over a Ford railroad in Ford freight cars. The Rouge produced coke, iron, steel, castings, engines, and bodies for Highland Park and the outlying assembly plants, and it built the company's tractors. Starters and generators, batteries, tires, artificial leather, cloth, and wire were all Ford-made. Ford production in 1925 was 20 percent greater than the entire industry's in 1920.[2]

The underside of the strategy of expansion, the need to create a structure and to establish mechanisms of control, was not even implicit—as an issue it did not exist. As late as 1933 a *Fortune* reporter could find it worth noting that the Ford Motor Company had passed its formative period and needed an administrator at least as much as it needed a creator "taken as a whole, the company reflects most sharply the strengths and weaknesses of its founder. There are too many people who will do what Mr. Ford thinks and there are not enough people who can influence what Mr. Ford thinks."[3]

"What Mr. Ford thinks" had initially been the company's greatest strength: the decision that there should be no change in the Model T had led to enormous economies of scale; in turn, these had made price reductions a phenomenally successful marketing policy, and expanded demand had encouraged further integration in the interest of still further economies. In the end Henry Ford had come to control the processes of production from the raw ore to the finished car.

But "what Mr. Ford thinks" when applied to the interpersonal process was freighted with disaster. There was in the

6

EXECUTIVE RELATIONSHIPS

Ford Motor Company at the executive level no structure of authority derived from position: there was a structure of power whose gradations were defined by a man's closeness to Ford.

Decision-making lay secure in Ford's hands. The executive exodus of 1920–1921 had cleared the ranks of the larger share of independent men and of those who remained, the closest to Ford and thus the most powerful, were implementers of his decisions rather than contributors to their formulation. In the first half of the 1920s, for example, although production climbed steadily, the prime stimulus to demand was Ford's continued reliance on price reductions. Between 1920 and 1924 eight successive cuts were effected.[4] These decisions were taken by Henry Ford before any assessment of production costs was arrived at, and the task of fitting a profit into the new price was left to production—a speedup on the assembly lines; to purchasing—"hammering down the suppliers" by threatening to withhold orders; and to sales and distribution—a loss on one model it was hoped would be absorbed by a profit on another. In addition, the dealer organization might have its discounts reduced. In 1924, when production levels were setting new records, Sorensen supported Ford's belief that the dealers were making too much money: "They are all getting fat and lazy sitting on their fat ———. [A discount cut] will make them go out and go to work."[5]

For a company ostensibly in the business of building cars, the company's financial statement for the year ending February 1924 made strange reading: of a net profit of more than $82 million, the profit on cars sold amounted to $4.1 million while the profit on spare parts alone was $29 million.[6]

The price-cut decisions, once an overwhelming source of company profits, had by the mid-twenties become decisions that Ford made by rote and with which his executives concurred like automatons. The much more basic issue, that of change in the Model T, was left untouched. When it was finally raised in 1926 by Ernest Kanzler, one of the few talented men left in the company, Ford effectively fired him.

The issue which no one dared to raise was written into the company's declining share of the market. In 1921 Ford had sold 67 percent of all cars built in the United States, but by 1926 his share had fallen to 46 percent.[7] As early as 1922, Chevrolet, with 240,000 cars, had registered a production increase of 220 percent on the previous year; Ford production had advanced by 27 percent. Writing in 1923, two industry analysts declared that "if any inference were justifiable from the facts, Ford's share of the nation's output would slowly decline in the future with a corresponding advance by other makers."[8]

The erosion of the company's position as pace setter to the industry was only too clearly a function of Ford's leadership. As he said in his autobiography—and it bears repetition—"the Ford factories and enterprises have no organization, no specific duties attaching to any position, no line of succession or authority, very few titles and no conferences. We have only the clerical help that is absolutely required; we have no elaborate records of any kind and consequently no red tape . . . the work and work alone controls us."[9]

In the earlier years this system had worked primarily because Ford's objectives were concrete and definable. The drive to build the mass car was the binding force in the years immediately preceding 1908. It drew to Ford talented engineers who shared his own exhilaration at creating a car which was ahead of its time and who shared, too, in the prestige of the Model T's success and in the renown that the Ford Motor Company swiftly achieved. There was a sense of movement in the company which the Highland Park expansion served to accentuate. There was more than enough for any man to do. A man, it was felt, set his limits for himself. The more prosaic aspects of the company's life, the tiresome details of administration, control, finance, purchasing, sales, and distribution were dealt with by James

Couzens and dealt with so effectively that Ford was consistently to underrate their importance in the future.

The drive for control of the company which followed hard on the Model T's success helped to destroy the earlier ties that work on the car had cemented. It was true that control of the company gave Ford the vast sums eventually needed for the Rouge expansion but at the same time it set the seal upon autocracy. For a man like Wills who seemed initially to see only the need for expansion,[10] the outlines of one-man rule grew clear so quickly that he left the company before any of the plans to which he had contributed became a working reality.

The point was that Ford himself had set a style of identification with the job, or more precisely with its product, which could be sustained neither by him nor by anyone else once the immediate and tangible challenges of design and production, marketing and expansion, had been overcome. What the company clearly needed at this juncture was a new definition of purpose: in effect, an ideology that would have permitted a wider definition of a man's work.

Ford was incapable of developing this. From a concern with the concrete he moved, under the impetus of the company's growth, to a preoccupation with interpersonal processes, and he took with him to apply out of all useful context the omnipotence which had led to much of his early manufacturing success. The single-minded pursuit of lightness, cheapness, and durability in the car, for example, had provided even if by decree a framework for executive action to which the company's success gave meaning. But in the 1920s Ford's fixation on the Model T destroyed any rational relationship to the environment and the organization turned upon itself in an orgy of self-destruction. Over it all Ford presided, relentlessly demanding a degree of individual submission which could no longer be justified by reference to any external, objective necessity. It became increasingly clear to Ford executives that they worked not for a company with a definable purpose to the attainment of which they could contribute, but for a single eccentric individual—Henry Ford. By the mid-twenties, on the evidence, an executive given to reflection would have been compelled to wonder whether the Ford Motor Company had given up the automobile market for the spare parts trade.

This extreme personalization of the company's organizational structure was the inevitable outcome of Ford's history. Left with nothing to which he could turn as wholeheartedly as he had to the Model T, the issue of retaliation now defined his style and it was the drive to dominate, to keep men in a state of submission which provided the impulse to action within his company. This necessarily precluded the existence of a more rational, bureaucratic structure which, as Weber noted in his description of the extreme case, "develops the more perfectly the more the bureaucracy is 'dehumanized,' the more completely it succeeds in eliminating from official business love, hatred, and all purely personal, irrational and emotional elements which escape calculation."[11] Poised at the opposite extreme, Ford's style brought to the surface of executive action an emotional content that inhibited rational processes.

The single source of power within the company was Henry Ford. Below him authority was fragmented and conflicting and to this the egalitarian masquerade of "no titles" contributed heavily, since it served further to entrench Ford's dominance on the one hand and his executives' dependence upon him on the other. Authority was respected only where it was recognized that the executive who exercised it held Ford's personal favor and support, and it was equally recognized that Ford's shifting moods might without warning upset the balance of the moment. For a Ford executive each day might bring new groupings of power to be contended with. "There is only one dominating spirit in the whole organization," wrote E. G. Pipp in 1924, "and that is Henry Ford. All others are tools, some subtle tools, some tools with initiative perhaps, but all tools to serve that spirit's purpose."[12] In such an atmosphere sycophancy blossomed, competitive strivings which had earlier been tied to a definable task centered on a man's closeness to Ford. "I have lived in the atmosphere of one of the Ford front offices for more than a year," Pipp wrote soon after he resigned from the editorship of the *Independent*. "I have seen the intrigue, men literally pushing each other in the scramble to get close to the throne; and to get away from it at times I have gone for relief to the wholesome atmosphere of the foundry, the blast furnace, the heat treat, the machine rooms, the assembly room. . . ."[13]

The executive structure of the company was a de facto structure. The lines of command which emanated from Ford's position were the radii of so many concentric circles. They could be arbitrarily retracted or extended and the rationale for either decision as often as not was grounded in Ford's "philosophy of conflict."[14]

He constantly played man against man [F. L. Black said subsequently]. Mr. Ford's idea was that both men would work much harder because if one man lagged he would soon lose status. . . . He would give one of the men a job to do and at a later date he would give the other a job along the same lines and before long they both realized they were working on the same job. This is the way Mr. Ford pitted Martin against Sorensen. After Kanzler left as Vice-President, I was asked by Mr. Ford to prepare a story announcing the selection of Martin as Vice-President. Mr. Ford gave me the impression that this would put a burr under Charlie Sorensen.[15]

Conflict, Ford believed, was the most effective way not only of stimulating competitive effort but of sorting out weak executives who were of no use to the company. He worked, said Frank Hadas, a Lincoln plant executive, on the principle of " 'Let's you and him have a fight and see how we come out.' If you decided to drop it, well you were the weaker one."[16]

The rivalry and confusion which these methods generated

were compounded by the passing nature of Ford's interests. In design engineering in particular executives were at the mercy of Ford's whim. "He would often forget projects or drop them at any stage of development," one engineer recalled. "It was almost impossible to develop a car under Mr. Ford's supervision because he was constantly changing it. . . . He would always spoil everything by getting so many freakish ideas. . . . If he had given the boys a basic idea and then let them alone and let them build it and had some organization and somebody with authority. But he would have every Tom, Dick and Harry running around there with authority."[17]

Ford refused to accept or even to acknowledge the necessities of organization. "He didn't believe in administration," Galamb said. "He didn't believe in a big organization. He wanted to be the whole cheese and everything had to go through his hands first. Mr. Ford objected greatly if he wasn't informed on something."[18]

In the drastic reductions in administrative and clerical personnel which accompanied the 1920-1921 executive firings, Ford eliminated entire departments by verbal decree, with no prior thought given to the functions they served. Charles Martindale, the company's auditor after 1920, described the effects of the changes:

Mr. Ford materially reduced the non-productive personnel. I think he cut the payroll more than two million a year, just off of clerical activity. We still did work of sorts. One of the difficulties was that the accounting department eternally found themselves coming up short at the end of the year when we took physical inventory, running into millions of dollars. Well, that was something they could afford, I suppose. After all, they did know once a year where they did stand and couldn't go broke with as many liquid assets as they had, so $15 or $20 million one way or the other wouldn't make much difference.

We would write it off as inventory shortage. . . . You wouldn't believe some of the techniques I used. The one that the accountants got the biggest laugh out of was the method of pricing material requisitions. Material requisitions covering the material used, supplies and small tools ran to something like 10,000 a day. The accounting staff that was supposed to price them was cut to nothing. . . .

When I took over . . . they weren't even attempting to price them. It was physically impossible. Well, after a short time I came up with this kind of an idea. We would price them through—it would take us longer than a month to do it—and then set aside all those requisitions that were priced at less than $10, distribute them by departments and see what it looked like.

. . . We found an average cost on those requisitions of $2.43. They amounted to more than two-thirds of the requisitions but accounted for only 7 per cent of the value . . . we brought skilled men in from the factory who would just look at a requisition and know that it was more than $10. If it was less than $10, we'd just set it aside. Then instead of counting those requisitions we set aside, we had scales set up and weighed them and found that we could do a very accurate job of them just scaled to the weight of the paper. . . . Then we would multiply the number of requisitions the scales gave us by the figure we had worked out, $2.43. But that was only handling 7 per cent of the disbursements. The remainder, which involved a third of the work, we were really pricing out.

Until you were forced to think of something of that kind, it would never have occurred to a person to do it. . . .[19]

Howard Simpson, in explanation of the company's precarious position in the 1930s, said that it stemmed from "the accumulation of all this friction and confusion . . . different executives working against each other . . . a lot of thieving and the use of Ford Motor Company property for personal purposes by the executives . . . a general lack of interest in the success of the company due to the personal ambition of the executives."[20]

Simpson recognized that Ford's style of leadership had made these reactions inevitable:

I think all of this was because Mr. Ford made this into such a personal corporation that he himself was the only source of authority in it. He thought he was the only source of power, but he was manipulated so much that actually he didn't have any power at all. He was manipulated by everybody up and down the line that contacted him. These people studied Mr. Ford and knew how to handle him to get anything they wanted. It was really right for them to do it, you couldn't blame them for it, because somebody had to run the place and with no authorized general manager, different ones just had to manipulate the old man to get to do things. . . ."[21]

The sense of omnipotence, which is perhaps the clearest behavioral expression of the narcissistic style, draws sustenance from the reciprocal behavior of other men. They maintain the delusion at the level of face-to-face confrontation. But they trade submission and often personal humiliation for a power of their own—for the exercise of which they need assume no individual responsibility since what they do, they do because the leader has commanded it. The costs of submission are thus translated into profit, and the most durable subordinates of the narcissistic leader will be those who are capable of extending the pattern themselves, for there lies the profit; the submission they give to the leader, in turn they demand from their own subordinates, and in this way an organizational style is set.

The preceding chapter has attempted to trace the development of Ford's compelling need for submission from other men and the aggression which was its corollary. Freud's description of the primal leader was advanced as a model in order to clarify the fundamental symbolism that underlay the special type of relationship which Henry Ford found tolerable. Freud's primal leader was an all-powerful father figure who jealously guarded his own prerogatives, who owed nothing to the "sons," but who was at the same time a figure of the utmost importance to the "sons" since his power defined the limits of their gratifications, and through this, tied them to him in abject dependence.

It is in no way incongruous to employ this model. In their indictments of him after his death, both Sorensen and Harry Bennett have used the imagery of father and son to describe their relationship to Henry Ford. "No one retained Henry Ford's confidence longer than I," Sorensen wrote. "None, not even his son Edsel, had or exercised greater authority. . . . No two men could have been more unlike than Mr. Ford and I. We had little in common, yet I never saw two men in any business anywhere who were so close to each other as we were—in fact, we had a business relationship closer than even his family had with him, and in many ways I knew him better than did members of his family."[22]

Bennett was more explicit. The opening sentence of his book reads simply: "During the thirty years I worked for Henry Ford, I became his most intimate companion, closer to him even than his only son."[23] And in subsequent chapters the references are more detailed: "I believe that Mr. Ford thought of me as a son. He was always extremely solicitous of my health, and, I think, felt as close to me as a father might. But like many another father, he wanted me dependent on him."[24]

In their own way, both of these men later repudiated Henry Ford. Sorensen did it by insinuation:

Henry Ford was opinionated about matters about which he knew little or nothing. He could be small-minded, suspicious, jealous, and occasionally malicious and lacking in sincerity. He probably hastened the death of his only son. He came close to wrecking the great organization he had built up. . . . But when weighed against his good qualities [which Sorenson avoided citing] his sense of responsibility, [which went undemonstrated] his exemplary personal life, *these defects become microscopic.*[25]

Bennett for his part simply claimed that he did as he was told and called Sorensen in to share the blame: "Both Sorensen and I took the rap for many things that were really Mr. Ford's doings, not out of loyalty to Mr. Ford, but because we had no choice."[26]

Yet in Ford's lifetime these were the most zealous and the most brutal of his subordinates, and in so being they acquired enormous power. Their face-to-face relationships with Henry Ford maintained the fiction of the primal leader and the dependent sons—in Sorensen's case until an ill-advised spate of personal publicity (notably a *Fortune* article that described him as "The Wizard of Willow Run" in April 1942), and his assumption of an increasingly independent position led to his dismissal in March 1944. In Bennett's case the charade was played out to the end of Ford's career in the company. Bennett's rise, however, did not begin until the late 1920s. In the years following 1920–1921, it was first Liebold and then Sorensen who were closest to Henry Ford.

The power that Liebold exercised was his by default. Since Ford alone could make a decision, the channels through which a request finally reached him assumed extraordinary importance, and Liebold controlled every approach to Ford. He screened Ford's correspondence. He decided on outsiders' interviews with Ford. He handled Ford's personal finances and he kept a close watch on company affairs. He had direct control over Ford's corps of secret detectives whom he did not hesitate to use in the service of his own prejudices. An anti-Semite himself, he encouraged Ford's anti-Semitism, and the network of agents he employed in the search for anti-Semitic propaganda has already been noted.

Liebold appealed to Ford, F. L. Black said, "because he carried out orders. He was one of the persons Mr. Ford could ask to do things he wouldn't ask other people to do. Mr. Ford knew the others weren't hard enough. For this reason Liebold had tremendous power. . . . After 1921 he was riding high, wide and handsome. He told me that he expected to be General Manager. This was around '22. He was for a period Chief Executioner. . . ."[27]

To maintain his position, Liebold needed to maintain Ford's interest and his own indispensability. He did both with zeal: "He acted as a red flag in front of the bull. . . . Keep waving the flag to keep up the interest."[28] Without a structure to support him, with no logic of the job inherent in what he did, he used, and at the same time protected himself against, the relationship he established with Henry Ford. Black, who was at that time a junior member of the *Independent*'s staff, said that Liebold often told him what he should do to be a success in life: "I made it a rule not to have any friends in the company. You be in a position where you don't give a god-damn what happens to anybody. Make all of your friends on the outside. You never know when you will have to fire someone, and if you are friendly with them it makes it that much harder."[29]

It was Liebold acting as "executioner" who dismissed Klingensmith, the company's vice-president. Neither then nor later was Liebold in any way officially associated with the company, he was simply Mr. Ford's man. In his reminiscences he claimed that Klingensmith's opposition to the way in which Ford dealt with the financial problems of the 1920 depression was an outcome of his friendly relations with Jewish bankers in New York: "Klingensmith used to line up with a lot of Jewish bankers down there and that's what Mr. Ford didn't like. When Klingensmith got to advocating that we ought to borrow money, why, Mr. Ford thought that these fellows put him up to it."[30] One is left to wonder how much Liebold himself contributed to Ford's thought, since Klingensmith, as Liebold pointedly noted, was half-Jewish in any case.

The director of the company's European operations, Warren C. Anderson, was dismissed on Liebold's orders shortly after Klingensmith's departure. An article in *Automotive Industries* reported in February 1921 that Anderson had left because of Ford's anti-Semitic campaign which had resulted in a "virtual boycott" of Ford cars in Europe. Anderson, it was reported, had "made repeated entreaties, appeals, and finally demands that the Jewish attacks cease, but all of his efforts are said to have been unavailing and instead the attacks became even more bitter."[31]

Anderson's dismissal was prefaced by a cable from Liebold ordering him to return to Detroit immediately. Evidently ignorant of what impended, Anderson asked to be advised on how long he was expected to stay. Liebold ordered him simply to "manage matters so you will not be inconvenienced if you do not return to Europe." Anderson arrived in New York on January 24, 1921, and was instructed by Liebold to report to Detroit where William A. Ryan, the company's sales manager, demanded his resignation.[32] In a letter to Edsel Ford, who had been absent due to illness when his dismissal occurred, Anderson registered his disappointment:

The manner in which I was treated was anything but courteous after sixteen years of faithful service. . . . When I received the cable to report at once at the Factory in Detroit I was very much surprised to note Mr. Liebold's name at the foot of the message . . . this is the first time in my many years' service that I had ever received an order from anyone but an executive of the organization. . . . Not one time during my stay did I see Mr. Ford (appreciating your position, I feel it was impossible to see you) and I want to go on record in saying that I feel I have been treated anything but fairly in my final leave-taking. . . . I feel that I should have been at least granted an interview with Mr. Ford personally.[33]

Questioning the spate of firings within the company, a Detroit newspaper reached its own conclusions:

The answer is Sorensen and Liebold. As Mr. Ford's private secretary, Liebold has always sat close to the throne. Before they folded their tents . . . Messrs Wills and Lee predicted the early ascendancy of Sorensen. They were true prophets. It has come to pass. In the course of events Mr. Sorensen has come into the enjoyment of such power as has not already been pre-empted by Mr. Liebold. What they say goes. Which one has the most to say, we don't know, but by the way he has come to the front we would bet on Sorensen.[34]

Despite his prominence in the early 1920s, Liebold's grasp of power was fleeting. His services were tangential to Ford's sole abiding interest, and Liebold, hoping as he did to become General Manager of the company, clearly realized that he needed a more indispensable base than anti-Semitism. To this end he encouraged Ford's political ambitions. "Liebold was the main stimulation of the Ford for President boom in 1923," Black said subsequently. "He expected to be the power behind the throne in Washington, as he was then in the company."[35] But even this soon proved to be inadequate. Sorensen, on the other hand, had his feet planted firmly in the Ford factories. He was responsible, as Liebold was, for the dismissal of some of the executives who left in 1920–1921, but with the vast difference that where Liebold's actions apparently centered on men who opposed the anti-Semitic campaign, Sorensen was destroying potential rivals in the manufacturing organization. "While Mr. Sorensen was in England on the tractor deal," one employee said later, "Mr. Knudsen was in power. The early Dearborn plant was being built then, and he came out here under P. E. Martin to fill in for Sorensen. He filled the job too well. The feeling was that he became too prominent while Mr. Sorensen was gone. Immediately after Sorensen returned the battle was on."[36] It ended with Knudsen's resignation, but Sorensen's jealousy evidently remained with him all his life. In his autobiography he wrote that he could "never understand" why Knudsen had been selected for the vitally important position as head of war production under Roosevelt.[37] Elsewhere in his book he described Knudsen as widely disliked, a statement that is flatly contradicted by other executives.[38] Liebold said later:

I think Mr. Ford had occasion to regret losing Knudsen. I think Knudsen was a very capable man. . . . He had the faculty of knowing how to handle men. Of course, Sorensen used to get things done, but he used to drive hell out of a man to get it done. Knudsen . . . kind of eased in under a man's skin and said, "Now, you know, this is the way it ought to be done." . . . Fellows liked him who worked with him, they got along with him very well. . . . Knudsen could lead better than drive.[39]

The elimination of his rivals was part of Sorensen's price

for submission. Like Liebold, he did as he was told. He said himself that he never tried to change Henry Ford's ideas and the evidence is that he never did. By continually giving proof of his own unswerving loyalty, he could damn another man in Ford's eyes by the mere insinuation of disloyalty, and he used Ford's ambivalent attitude to his own son to his personal advantage.

With appropriate immodesty he described the years 1903–1913 as the Couzens period of Ford Motor Company history; 1913–1925 as the Henry Ford–Edsel Ford period; and 1925–1944 as the Sorensen period.[40] The Sorensen period was one of unalloyed organizational decadence.

Unwilling later to assume responsibility for his own complicity in the dismissal of rival executives, he passed the blame to Ford:

When [Ford] wanted to size up a man quickly, he loaded him with power. If the man took the least advantage of his new position he got some kind of warning, not from Henry Ford, but from the least expected quarter. How he accepted the warning was what Henry Ford was watching. If he went to Ford to see if the warning was really coming from him, he would be encouraged to disregard everything. That would throw him off completely, but in a few days he was out, completely mystified over what had really happened. That was the way Knudsen left the Ford organization, and probably he never knew why to his dying day.[41]

In Knudsen's case the "advantage" taken was evidently to do his job so well that Sorensen was threatened; the "warning" no doubt was Sorensen's and the "few days" after which a man would be out was clearly time enough for Sorensen to work on Henry Ford. R. T. Walker, who was assistant to W. B. Mayo, the engineer responsible for the plans for the Rouge expansion, said that Sorensen "planted his underlings" so as to

needle Mr. Mayo. . . . I don't think Sorensen's antagonisms to Mr. Mayo had any personal basis. I think he was antagonistic to any man that might become so close to Mr. Ford as to threaten Sorensen's position in the set up. . . . As Mayo grew in favor with Mr. Ford there was an increased enmity, plus the fact that at the time he came to Ford Motor [1915–1916] there was a very definite struggle for positions going on between Sorensen on the one hand and Wills on the other. Wills eventually lost on that one.[42]

Sorensen's feelings, Walker said, were further aroused when Edsel Ford showed a high regard for Mayo: "A close friendship with Edsel *could* signify that sooner or later a man would be out of the company."[43]

Mayo finally left the company in 1930. As early as 1920 his function as chief engineer had been absorbed by Sorensen. In that year the partially built Rouge plant came into operation under Sorensen. Mead Bricker, Sorensen's assistant, later gave a vivid description of the conflict that developed:

In 1920 when we first went to the Rouge, Sorenson was head man there. Martin was head man in production at Highland Park. At that time I was next to Sorensen. . . . Nobody could ever understand the dividing line of authority between Sorensen and Martin. . . . Mr. Ford had a knack of being in contact with Sorensen for a certain period and then he would stay off Sorensen and switch to Martin. He would sometimes come around to see me once in a while and that would irritate Sorensen and get him on the job. It was a balance that kept going up and down on either side. Mr. Ford was in charge of engineering and over-all manufacturing. Edsel was in charge of the business side, subject to his father's veto. Sorensen, Martin, myself and all the other production people reported through Sorensen to Mr. Ford.[44]

Despite the growing presence of two separate sites of manufacturing operations, Sorensen gradually consolidated his control over the entire production process. "He and Martin got along fairly well," Bricker said. "Martin was a little on the weaker side. Sorensen was the stronger man of the two." When Martin became vice-president in 1926 following Ernest Kanzler's resignation, it was Sorensen nonetheless who was running the plant.[45]

But in 1921 Martin was at Highland Park where Edsel Ford with Kanzler's assistance was painfully attempting to put together an organization from what remained of the company's executive personnel. In 1924, Kanzler was made a vice-president of the company.

He had a lot of new ideas [Bricker said], which I think were very good . . . a more accurate cost and production record . . . cleaner operation of the plant . . . treating the human element a little better. It was a pretty rough place up to that time. Kanzler never liked Sorensen's methods. Sorensen would go out and upset a department, turn a bench or a desk over, and it was my job or somebody else's job, to go out and straighten that all out again. When you'd go back the place was all demoralized, and everybody wanted to quit and nobody wanted to work. It was my job to go in and smooth that out, make these fellows see that they had a chance in life yet.

I have seen Sorensen grab ahold of people, but he would never kick anybody. Several times I saved him from being beaten up by these same people. He was very disliked all through the plant. Kanzler's idea was to eliminate all this. When Sorensen saw a department wasn't paying dividends he would go right in and upset the whole damn department. Kanzler had a more modern way of doing it. He wanted to make a study of what was wrong. Kanzler's method was having a line of command.[46]

As president of the company, Edsel Ford controlled the general business offices and the sales organization, managerial functions which were anathema to Henry Ford. Moving from the sales position, Kanzler's work in inventory control and production scheduling led inevitably into manufacturing operations, and through Kanzler, Bricker said, Edsel Ford "was becoming more and more in charge of manufacturing" at Highland Park.[47] But both men were in a losing position from the start. The Rouge was destined to become the company's prime manufacturing unit, and Sorensen controlled the Rouge. In 1925, in a move which clearly carried Henry Ford's sanction, Sorensen brought Martin to the Rouge and transferred Bricker to Highland Park. "When I went to Highland Park," Bricker said, "I was told to keep quiet and take it easy and see what was going on out there. That went along for about six months, then Sorensen took over again. He cut loose and started eliminating all these other fellows. . . ."[48]

The "eliminations" were effected as unit after productive unit was moved to the Rouge; if the man in charge was unamenable to Sorensen's orders, Sorensen, by virtue of his control of the rest of the plant, could make the going so difficult that either the man submitted or left.[49] Where this was not feasible, as in Kanzler's case, Sorensen worked directly on Henry Ford. "Mr. Ford never liked Kanzler," Galamb recalled. "He wanted to find out what he could do and what he knew."[50] Ford's dislike of Kanzler was rooted in his inability to accept Kanzler's closeness to his son. "Mr. Ford finally figured that he couldn't stand for two organizations in one company," Liebold said, ". . . people were more or less coalescing around Edsel. Mr. Ford thought they weren't the right influence. . . . He wanted to get rid of them."[51]

Ford's attitude to his son was in fact characterized by an ambivalence so extreme that throughout his life it laid him open to the grossest forms of manipulation: he wanted to control his son, to make him utterly dependent, and at the same time he wanted Edsel to be tough, brutal, and independent. "Henry Ford," Black said subsequently, "was constantly trying to train Edsel Ford in the way he thought the responsibilities of Edsel's job should be discharged. He felt that Edsel had to be harsher, act faster, and be turned into a personality something like Sorensen's. Mr. Ford didn't think that Edsel was tough enough."[52]

Ford's method of hardening his son played perfectly into Sorensen's strategy. "Mr. Ford would get Sorensen to do something against Edsel's will," Galamb said. "Edsel couldn't have helped to know what was going on because we knew it ourselves."[53] And to action taken by Sorensen on his father's orders, Edsel Ford had no answer:

The old man set Sorensen against Edsel a great many times, deliberately. Edsel was aware of this and I think it broke his heart. This open conflict between father and son was over business philosophies and the matter of modern design in the car. . . . The public wanted six-cylinder engines . . . semi-elliptic springs. . . . It was the old man's policy that he knew best what was good for them. You could never convince him that his transverse spring didn't have everything that the semi-elliptic spring had. Edsel on the other hand would try to give the public what they wanted. . . .[54]

Edsel Ford was in fact fighting for the company's future, and in doing so he further strengthened Sorensen's position. "Mr. Ford," said one executive later, "was unmerciful in embarrassing Edsel, in disagreeing with him, in not accepting Edsel's well-thought plans for bettering conditions within the company. . . . He was always opposed to anything that Edsel brought up that was progressive."[55] The more the son opposed his father, the more his authority was undermined and the greater was the power that devolved upon Sorensen. Sorensen's use of it was primarily in the interest of maintaining his relationship with Henry Ford and to this both the reminiscences of Ford executives and Sorensen's own autobiography attest.

T. F. Gehle described an incident at the Dearborn luncheon table which followed an agreement between Edsel, Sorensen, and Martin that Edsel Ford should raise the issue of a hydraulic brake system for the car. No sooner had Edsel begun, Gehle recalled, than Henry Ford rose, said, "Edsel, you shut up!" and walked out. Despite the prior agreement, none of the others was prepared to come to Edsel's support.

Al Esper, a test-track driver, remembered a bitter argument between father and son over the front spring suspension. Martin and Sorensen were present and Martin suggested that Sorensen should help the younger Ford: "Edsel Ford was fighting the battle for the coil spring suspension and Sorensen made the statement that he wasn't going to get mixed into any family arguments at all."[56]

The support that Kanzler gave to Edsel Ford, in contrast, came increasingly to be concerned with changes in the car. Kanzler, said Galamb, "started to come into engineering and that didn't go with Mr. Ford. I was always afraid to make any changes that Kanzler suggested, knowing how he and Mr. Ford got along. . . . All this time Sorensen was feeding Mr. Ford things about Kanzler."[57]

By the mid-twenties, with sales of the Model T slipping and those of the Chevrolet steadily advancing, Sorensen supported Ford in blaming the sales organization—for which, hardly surprisingly, Edsel Ford and Kanzler bore final responsibility. The sales organization contended that if changes were made in the cars they would be able to sell them. Sorensen's counter blast was "that the cars were all right, but that if the Sales Department was any good they could sell them . . . they used 'sales resistance' as an alibi."[58]

In this he echoed Henry Ford, who simply informed the sales organization that "most of your troubles at the present time is a question of your mental attitude."[59] When Ford was shown the annual summary of automobile registration statistics published by R. L. Polk Company, he told F. L. Black that the figures were rigged and that the Polk company had fallen under the influence of General Motors. "Sorensen," Black said, "completely backed down . . . he wasn't going to beard the lion."[60]

The executive who finally did so was Kanzler. On January 26, 1926, he submitted a seven-page memorandum to Henry Ford:

This . . . is given you so that I can feel that I have dealt honestly and squarely with the responsibility you have given me. It hurts me to write it because I am afraid it may change your feeling for me, and that you may think me unsympathetic and lacking confidence in your future plans.

Please, Mr. Ford, understand that I realize fully that you have built up this whole business, that it has been your battle and your creation and that all of the company's success day after day, regardless by whom personally conducted, are nevertheless a direct result of your conception and will really be your personal accomplishment for many years even after your lifetime.

Any powers I have are mostly due to the opportunities you have given me and have not created in me any exaggerated ideas about myself.

With skill and considerable tact Kanzler developed his argument that a new car was needed; that six-cylinder cars were increasing in popularity, and that the Ford organization could build one more efficiently and cheaply than its competitors; that a new car would lift morale within the company, and ensure that Ford employees did not suffer from the decline in sales. Even his imagery was geared to Henry Ford's: in depreciating his own achievements and ascribing every success to Ford, he wrote: "You have allowed me to play with the throttle of your engine. That's all. . . . Could we not carry out your ideas that the product must be made right, as expressed in your page of the January 16th, 1926, *Dearborn Independent*. Won't you permit the organization to develop a refined six-cylinder motor. . . . Such a power plant would never be used unless its performance satisfied you that it has real merit."

Reflecting the pass that had been reached in terms of simple communication, Kanzler wrote that the advantage of putting his thoughts on paper lay in the opportunity it offered to "write certain things I find it difficult to say to you. It is one of the handicaps of the power of your personality which you perhaps least of all realize, but most people when with you hesitate to say what they think."

In a final, if flattering, attempt to put the company's position in perspective, he wrote:

It is unique in the commercial history of the world that one man should run away with the field as you have done in the motor industry. We have had a wonderful head start because your first designs of a car were twenty years ahead of the world, as well as your methods of production and marketing. But we are losing our position because the world has learned from you, and with its combined efforts, each learning from the other, it has now developed a product that is alarmingly absorbing the public's purchasing power.

The best evidence that conditions are not right is in the fact that with most of the bigger men in the organization there is a growing uneasiness . . . they feel our position weakening and our grip slipping. We are no longer sure that when we plan increased facilities that they will be used. The buoyant spirit of confident expansion is lacking. And we know we have been defeated and licked in England. And we are being caught up in the United States. With every additional car that our competitors sell they get stronger and we get weaker.

Even on the basis of equal design value, we could still outdistance all competition because of our "from mine to finished car" ability to produce, and unified ownership. But with our competitors' volume increasing, they are rapidly approaching our formerly unique powers of producing at lowest cost. Inwardly we are alarmed to see our advantages ebbing away, knowing that the counter-measures to prevent it are not immediately at hand. . . . This feeling exists not outwardly, but I will stake my reputation it exists in every important man in the company. . . .[61]

If by this last sentence Kanzler had hoped to implicate Sorensen in the general discontent, he failed signally to do so. In the spring of 1926, with Edsel Ford en route to Europe on vacation, Kanzler was fired.[62]

At the end of the year in an extensive interview with a *New York Times* reporter, Ford said he had no intention of changing the Model T. "The Ford car will continue to be made in the same way. . . . I am not governed by anybody's figures but by my own information and observation . . . we have no intention of introducing a 'six'. We made sixes twenty years ago."[63]

By then the Ford plants were closed, the result not only of the seasonal layoff, but of a catastrophic fall in demand. A year earlier every facility had been in operation to produce 9000 cars a day; before the plant was closed only 6000 cars a day were being built, and they were selling with difficulty. In 1924 Ford had controlled two-thirds of the market, by the end of 1926 his share had fallen to one-third.[64]

The general feeling in the industry was that Ford's excess production capacity ran to nearly 40 percent; that because he had taken no step toward changing either his plants or his product a new car would take months to design, would involve scrapping millions of dollars worth of equipment and would call for a sweeping reorganization of men and methods.[65]

Ford's decision to change the car was finally made in May 1927, and what followed was prohibitively wasteful of time, money, and men. Sorensen's account of the change will be cited at length so as to permit comparisons to be drawn with the reminiscences of other executives and in order to illustrate at the same time the pattern of submission in exchange for control which was now an organizational style, moving down through the ranks of power as each emulated the man above him.

On May 26, 1927, Model T assembly lines at Highland Park and the Rouge shut down. No new cars came from the branches, and the only business done for nine more months was the sale of parts for survivors of the 15,000,000 Ford cars still on the road. Henry Ford is supposed to have taken a year to create Model A. That is not quite correct. He would not even think of tackling a new car until the last Model T came off the line. I knew instinctively that when he said "shut down" he wanted to do some serious thinking. Actually, when Mr. Ford finally decided to replace Model T, clearing the design and getting Model A into production took only ninety days. But it was six months before Henry Ford would go to work. . . . During those nine months I had my first and only disagreements with Edsel and my long-time associate and friend Ed Martin.* They felt I was not doing all I could to bring on another car, because I

* Sorensen's memory was short at this point.

would not battle it out with Mr. Ford on what they wanted. I believe that Henry Ford had built Ford Motor Company around his idea of a motorcar. He had shown by past performance that he could meet a critical situation, and I felt that he would come up with something to meet this one.* To bring out his Model T he overcame the prejudices of his partners, then moved in and took full control, and from then on saw his dream develop into the wonder plant of the world. *When his son, and those he could gather around him, started screaming at him, much like his partners used to do, I just could not join in.* As I had done in the Dodge and Couzens days, I remained neutral, *confident that Mr. Ford probably had another new idea* and we'd better let it develop. . . . I stayed with Henry Ford until I found out what he wanted. This was a repetition of my first days in Ford Motor Company. Mr. Ford did his work by intuition. Every day I would see and talk with him. I never pressed him. *I felt he must have a new idea. Any hint of what it might be would be something for me to grab and do something about, but until I could see it I would let nothing bother me.*

. . . My own feeling during all this pulling and hauling was that Henry Ford would come up again with the right product and that it was better to wait for it. I was not going to fall into a trap by avoiding him and his ideas, so I decided to wait for the storm to blow over. I suppose this must be treated as lost time, but it was no waste of time to Henry Ford. To him, it was the ideal time to give the organization a good shaking up, to trim out all unnecessary overhead. He made it clear to me that he would wait until this was all done before he would begin any new venture. Here again, Edsel and his father had differences of opinion. . . .[66]

The "lost time" which Sorensen so casually dismissed can be best assessed in sales and profit terms. New car registra-

* The only "critical situation" prior to this was the 1920–1921 financial crisis and Sorensen wrote that it was he who suggested to Ford the inventory liquidation and the overloading of dealers which gave Ford the funds he needed (Sorensen, *My Forty Years with Ford,* pp. 168–169). That he should admit his dependence on Ford so clearly perhaps explains the extraordinary brutality with which the subsequent dismissals of company personnel were carried through.

tions over the three-year period 1926–1928 for Ford and Chevrolet were:[67]

	Ford		Chevrolet	
Year	Units	As % of All Makes	Units	As % of All Makes
1926	1,129,470	36%	486,366	15.1%
1927	393,424	15%	647,810	24.7%
1928	482,012	15.4%	769,927	24.5%

In 1927 the Ford Motor Company lost $30.4 million and in 1928 $70.6 million.[68] The total costs of the shutdown and changeover were estimated at $250 million. The dealer organization suffered heavily, and many left the company to join General Motors. Others hung on by discharging their employees and economizing to the bone; still others went bankrupt.[69] Not until February 1928 was it possible to supply Ford dealers with showroom samples of the new car, the Model A, and factory cost figures for March still showed losses of $318.79 and $335.84 on every unit of the two most popular body types, the Tudor and the Phaeton.[70]

It was this extraordinary situation which Sorensen termed "the ideal time to give the organization a good shaking up," and although he attributed the responsibility to Henry Ford it was Sorensen's hand that set the shake-up in motion. In the thousands of dismissals that followed, the company lost skilled men it badly needed for the changeover to the Model A. They went because Sorensen said so, and the accounts of their going are little short of incredible.

The transfer of the last assembly lines from Highland Park to the Rouge took place in September 1927,[71] while the Model A was still on the drawing board:

We started building the cars the first part of November in 1927, [said W. C. Klann, who had been a production superintendent at Highland Park]. I took Pederson and Ed Gartha out to the Rouge plant with me to run the line.

Sorensen said, "Who are these guys?"

I said, "Sorensen, you know Pederson. You brought him in the shop yourself twelve years ago. . . . He is a Scandinavian the same as you are. You know who he is. He has had charge of the line for the last twelve years. You know who Gartha is."

He said, "Fire them."

So I did. I fired both of them. He didn't tell me why to fire them. He just said, "Fire them."

Klann was sent by Sorensen to Harry Bennett to find a replacement for the dismissed men. Bennett, as head of the Ford "Service" department, had come increasingly to Henry Ford's notice during the *Sapiro* trial in 1927, but he was still in a subordinate position to Sorensen at the Rouge. Although Klann protested—"You bring a brand new job up here and a new car and new chassis . . . and now go and get a new boss of the job"—he went to see Bennett.

I said, "Bennett, Sorensen told me to see you about getting a man for the assembly line. Who shall I get? He wants a man from the Rouge." He said, "Go get Harry Mack." I said, "Where is he located?" "In the box factory."

So I went to the box factory and I said, "Say, can anybody tell me where Harry Mack is?" "He's the fellow who has charge of making boxes."

I said to Harry Mack, "Say, did you ever assemble cars?"

He said, "No."

"Well," I said, "we've got a new job for you. You're going to have charge of the assembly line."

He said, "I heard about it."[72]

In his reminiscences Klann said that on Sorensen's orders he fired about 2000 foremen:

They didn't want the supervision from Highland Park to come to the Rouge. . . . There was a very uncertain feeling about what was going on. . . . We'd go to the Rouge plant to see Sorensen. . . . They had a big ledger up there. They'd say, "Look, Bill, here's a so-and-so." . . . We'd get four or five names and Bricker would say, "You know these men better than I do. You worked with them for the last fifteen or twenty years, so you fire them." . . . They'd have an X marked against the man's name.[73]

In a ludicrous incident Klann was compelled by Sorensen to fire a man three times; each time that the man was dismissed he was reemployed by Martin. Sorensen, under the mistaken impression that the man was Klann's brother-in-law, finally had Klann summoned by Bennett to explain what was happening. Klann took with him a fellow superintendent, John Henkel. A heated argument developed and Bennett attempted to draw a gun. Klann knocked him down, but six weeks later he was ordered to fire Henkel. The orders were given through Martin, but, Klann felt, it was Sorensen's way of getting both at Martin and at him. When Klann asked Martin what he should enter on Henkel's employment card: "He said, 'Horse shit.' So I put down horse shit."[74]

P. E. Haglund, an electrical engineer who installed and operated the electric furnaces at the Rouge, quoted Sorensen in order to describe what was happening: "Sorensen's expression at that time was 'We are [getting] rid of all the Model T sons-of-bitches.' "[75] According to Haglund, when men came to the Rouge from Highland Park they had to be "made over": "It was a hard-boiled policy at Highland Park, but it didn't compare with the intensity at the Rouge. Everybody at the Rouge plant was on edge. They ran around in circles and they didn't know what they were doing. Physically everybody was going like a steam engine but not . . . mentally. As long as their feet were on the go they were working hard. The more a man ran around the better he was."

At Highland Park, in contrast, "People worked willingly. . . . They'd tackle jobs and try to get results without any particular pressure. There was an internal desire in the man to do a good job at Highland Park. At the Rouge your job just ran from minute to minute. You didn't know when somebody was going to come along and clip you and knock your feet from under you."[76]

At one point, Haglund said, Sorensen ordered him to dismiss a group of men, whose sole offense evidently was that, as the ground crew of a locomotive on the foundry floor, they were standing in the cab while waiting for an empty ladle to be hooked up. Haglund objected that the men were not working for him. "There are no fences around this place at all," Sorensen said, "and there is no end to your power. You go on up and fire those guys."[77]

By 1928 the attempt at a structure which the managerial system at Highland Park had represented was finally shattered, and Sorensen put together his own monolithic power from the pieces. His style, the inevitable complement to Henry Ford's, was in its own turn the standard to which his subordinates adapted. "We used to call Harry Bennett Sorensen's little puppy dog," Haglund said. "Sorensen would point his finger in a direction, Bennett would go looking without thinking. . . . He pursued all the methods Sorensen advocated. He was the man who did the work. He got the fellows out of the way."[78]

Years later, in his autobiography Sorensen felt called upon to define "leadership": "Who can tell us what leadership is?" he wrote. "It is a radiant quality which some men possess which makes others swing joyously into common action. What they do is wisely conceived and eminently fair. Such leadership which is above all the characteristic of American production and the function of voluntary effort, springs from mutual understanding. The boss must know the worker and the worker must know the boss. They must respect each other."[79]

But this is little more than a series of non sequiturs, meaningless in their application to the relationships that existed at the executive level of the Ford Motor Company. They are descriptive neither of Henry Ford nor of anyone else who attained power: there was nothing wise or fair about arbitrary action, and voluntary effort was unknown in an atmosphere where men caught "Forditis" from the strain of attempting to juggle with the demands made by Sorensen, by Bennett to an increasing extent, and by their own nominal functional superior. "I don't think any of the managers caught in this would have the courage to suggest to a higher-up that some remedy be found for this split authority," said H. C. Doss, who by 1939 headed the company's sales department. "The trouble was so apparent that somebody should have thought of it and no doubt did, but no cure came."[80] In the early 1930s Doss was a branch manager, and he described the feelings with which these managers viewed a summons to Detroit: "We all came in in fear and trepidation. We tried to act nonchalant but you didn't feel it. There weren't Murads enough to go around."[81]

The organizational chaos that surrounded the changeover to the Model A was in sharp contrast to the smoothness with which in 1929 Knudsen moved from a four-cylinder Chevrolet to a six. Planning at General Motors had begun more than a year before. The wheelbase of the 1928 Chevrolet, for example, had been lengthened by four inches and the extra length disguised by a shield. In 1929 the longer wheelbase needed for the six was available without any additional delay, and the changeover in fact took 45 days.[82]

Knudsen had taken with him to Chevrolet the conviction that Ford's heavy concentration at the Rouge had been a major error. "I do not want the Chevrolet Company to become so unwieldy," he told his biographer, "that we cannot make changes to keep in step with possible demand."[83] The Chevrolet model change in fact was effected at a score of scattered plants and it was testimony to a new flexibility in the system of mass production—a flexibility made possible by new concepts of organization and control.

The primal structure at the Ford Motor Company in which the dominant figure of Henry Ford moved at will, subjecting some operational areas to incessant interference and leaving others as the prizes of executive war, had been replaced at General Motors by a system of "decentralization with coordinate control." This was Sloan's phrase and the key to it was the concept that, if there were means to review and judge the effectiveness of operations, the prosecution of those operations could safely be left to the men in charge of them. The method chosen was a system of financial control which converted the broad principle of return on investment into a yardstick for measuring the operations of divisions.[84]

In order to make the principle effective, General Motors' accounting staff was strengthened and standard accounting practices introduced throughout the corporation. As early as January 1923, a G.M. accounting manual, specifying uniform methods of procedure, was brought into use. This coincided roughly with Ford's decision drastically to reduce his own accounting staff and with the methods, already noted, to which Ford accountants were forced to resort as a consequence.[85] To Ford, accountants were nonproductive and liable to become "experts." Klingensmith was a "good bookkeeper" who became too much of "a banker's man."[86] And, as he wrote in his autobiography, "We have found it most unfortunately necessary to get rid of a man as soon as he thinks himself an expert."[87] This blithe assumption of omnipotence found its echo in Sorensen: "When one man began to fancy himself an expert, we had to get rid of him. The minute a man thinks himself an expert, he gets an expert's state of mind, and too many things become impossible."[88]

The underlying issue at work in both of these statements was put precisely by Liebold when discussing the contrast between Edsel Ford and his father:

Edsel felt that people ought to be given certain responsibilities in certain positions and their authority should be designated. Mr. Ford didn't go along with that line of thinking. He often said to me that if he wanted a real job done right that he would always pick the man that didn't know anything about it. The reason was that if he picked a man who didn't know anything about the job, the fellow never got far away from Mr. Ford. Mr. Ford in that way was able to control what was being done. . . . Of course, you couldn't get Edsel to agree to that line of thinking. If Edsel wanted a thing done, he would pick a man he thought was capable of doing it.[89]

The foremost victim of his father's conflicts—Sorensen called Ford's relationship to his son "Henry Ford's greatest failure"[90]—Edsel Ford was alternately built up and undermined in a cycle that reflected the extremes of Ford's ambivalence. According to F. L. Black, Ford would often say, "Well, you talk that over with Edsel, and do whatever he says. I'm going to turn more of these responsibilities over to him. He's got to run this company."

For a time every decision would be discussed with Edsel Ford, and then "You would find the old man back in harness reversing Edsel's decisions."[91]

With unconscious candor, Sorensen admitted to the freedom that this situation permitted the executives who sided with the father. During the 1930s relations between the two Fords

were strained almost to breaking point and it became increasingly difficult for father and son to work together on anything. Neither could settle down to plant interests; there were too many problems of their own to be concerned about. *And because I had been able to steer clear of this family discord I had a virtually free hand* to build steel mills, tire plants, press shops, glass plants, make imitation leather, and set up new plants both in this country and in Europe.[92]

It was not a question of steering clear but of taking sides and reflecting in action the issues that underlay Ford's attitude. The drive for power was as much Sorensen's as it was Ford's. At first Sorensen was able to use Bennett as Ford used him, but even as Ford had surrendered areas of power by default, so Sorensen in turn surrendered to Bennett power which it was physically impossible for him to exercise. And this is the central and paradoxical problem of the narcissistic style. The dependence and submission it demands are transformed in practice into unrestricted power within the individual's own sphere. Since men are not omnipotent, the exercise of absolute power comes to rest upon their own physical limitations, the most primitive basis of all. Those areas with which it is impossible for them to cope become in turn the fiefs of underlings who justify themselves to the leader by face-to-face submission, maintaining in this way his own delusion of omnipotence.

An example of what Sorensen accepted on a face-to-face basis from Henry Ford was given by J. L. McCloud in his reminiscences:

Mr. Ford . . . during the time he was so interested in early American dances* frequently would have a dance practice immediately after lunch. . . . He would walk back with whoever he had lunch with and gather up some of the rest of us who were out in the Engineering Department and tell us to come down to the dance hall [a section of the Engineering Laboratories building] and we would have dancing lessons during the day. I actually learned the Varsovienne by dancing with Mr. Ford and Charlie Sorensen, which bothered Mr. Sorensen terribly.[93]

But the returns on the passing discomfort were enormous. "Sorensen," said Doss, "was like a king on a throne telling you what to do."[94]

At first a loyal subject, Bennett rapidly became a rival. Sorensen's greatest strength lay in production, and Bennett, initially working under him, assumed power in the field of employee relations. In the late 1920s he hired and fired, but this was soon transformed into a far more pervasive influence. Bennett, Sheldrick said subsequently, developed a stranglehold on the organization:

The stranglehold was this. He had control of hiring and firing. He had control of the payroll department. He had

* During the late 1920s.

control of transfers. He had control of transportation and communications. He had to approve all travel vouchers.

That meant that one could not hire, fire, raise, or transfer a man. I could not make a long-distance call, I could not send a telegram if he did not wish me to do so.

You didn't send a message to anybody without him seeing it if he wanted to. And if he chose to misinterpret it he could run to Mr. Ford with a very misleading story, which he did often . . . we weren't supposed to travel unless Bennett or one of his stooges signed it.

This arrangement went all the way down. He made sure that he personally knew all the moves of the top level people. That way he could know what was going on in the entire organization. Regardless of where you were, he knew all about it. If you were in Europe, he would know whom you had dinner with. He had an actual spy system that was that thorough.[95]

In the 1930s when the UAW's drive to organize closed in on the Ford Motor Company, it was to Bennett and his "Service" department that Ford turned and Sorensen was slowly superseded even as he had himself superseded Liebold. "No one," said Black, "carried out Mr. Ford's orders quite as literally as Harry Bennett." And Ford's orders now included the destruction of the unions. The National Labor Relations Board later emphasized the active attempts on the company's part, which Bennett had led, to destroy union organization:

Since the [company's] operations and its main policy emanate from its main office, the kind of inaction on the part of employers which the act clearly contemplates could have been achieved with little effort throughout the [company's] system. But the policy makers did not choose this course. Instead, they determinedly sought to defy the law by formulating and sanctioning a highly integrated program of interference, restraint, and coercion . . . in an orbit within which the Congress has declared that employees were entitled to enjoy unhampered freedom.[96]

Nevins and Hill, in Volume III of their history, have devoted a chapter to recording the violence and dissimulation with which Bennett, encouraged by Henry Ford, fought the UAW.[97] Keith Sward, a less sympathetic biographer, gave the struggle much more prominence,[98] but the details are of less importance than the conditions that gave rise to them, and Henry Ford created those conditions.

The trade-off which Bennett made—and which Sorensen had made before him—between submission to Ford and unrestricted power in his own sphere was later put clearly by a Ford executive:

Bennett was one of those fellows who in the presence of Mr. Ford was more or less like a lamb. He would jump in the Detroit River I think, if Mr. Ford told him. He reversed that policy if it was anybody else and tried to dominate them a hundred per cent—the kind of domination you get when a man is quoting somebody else.

Sorensen knew he was a tough fellow, and many people who worked for Sorensen used *that* in handling their own people. They would say, "Damn it! You do that or else! Sorensen wants that done!" Harry Bennett was a lot like that. If he wanted something done he would use Henry Ford's name. On his own he could never get much done because he didn't know much.[99]

In this way Ford set his company against itself and in 1944 Sorensen himself fell before Bennett's ax. "Bennett's technique," Black said later, "was not to make a frontal attack . . . but to drop a remark, an off-hand remark—and a few days later another remark. That's the way he got Sorensen. It was known around the company for more than a year what he was doing . . . the conversation ran, 'Charlie sure is dumb. He can't see the handwriting on the wall.' "[100]

By then Edsel Ford was dead and Bennett had already engineered the dismissals of Wibel, the head of purchasing, Sheldrick, Doss, and Black.[101] Even Liebold, who had held no power since his eclipse in the 1920s, but whom Bennett cordially despised, was peremptorily fired.

In a letter to Henry Ford which parodied in part the letter Anderson had written to Edsel Ford so many years earlier when Liebold, acting as Chief Executioner, had fired Anderson, Liebold said:

The entire manner in which this episode was handled has proved to be a direct attack upon my personal character and a direct reflection upon my reputation for thirty-four years of diligent and loyal service to you. . . . I have hesitated to address this letter to you, but inasmuch as you have not given me the opportunity to talk with you, I am respectfully asking that you advise me of your wishes.

That you have a right to dispense with my services at will, and without cause, is indisputable; but no reason exists why our parting could not be on the same high plane which has characterized our association during the past thirty-four years. I have no thought of doing anything to cause you the slightest feeling of apprehension. . . . However, not hearing from you within a reasonable period of time, I can only reach the conclusion that the above procedure has been carried out by you as a means of ending our relations.

The letter ended with a sentence which indicated the attrition of self-respect: "With assurances of my highest esteem and respect for you and conveying the opportunity [sic] of further serving you in any way possible. . . ."[102]

Shortly after Sorensen's dismissal, Ford made Bennett a director of the company, but from Bennett's description it was a little-appreciated gesture:

Directors' meeting had no purpose other than to comply with the law. When Mr. Ford failed to show up, it was pretty funny, because all the directors dared do was conduct cut-and-dried business—putting their stamp of approval on what Mr. Ford had already done, or on what they knew he'd approve. . . . The meetings reached their peak of humor on those occasions when Mr. Ford did show up. Mr. Ford would come in, walk around, shake hands with everyone, and then say, come on Harry, let's get the hell out of here. We'll probably change everything they do anyway.[103]

By then Henry Ford was in a state of near senility. For over a year after the declaration of war in 1941 he refused to acknowledge that there *was* a war. "He often told newsmen in my office," Black said, "that there wasn't a war—it was all newspaper talk to get Americans excited and spend our money on munitions."[104]

Under severe family pressure, Ford was finally compelled to resign the presidency he had assumed upon his son's death—the first official position he had held since he had given the presidency to Edsel in 1919. In September 1945, Henry Ford II became president and in a legal deposition made in January 1950 he said that Bennett was relieved of his responsibilities "about five minutes after I was made president."[105] The rebirth of the Ford Motor Company had begun.

The approach to the issue of business leadership which has been adopted in this study has taken individual personality as its central concern. In doing so it has differed from the conventions of business history, for the attempt has been made to explain individual motivation and action rather than to rely upon a description and assessment of their tangible results. It has differed too from the generalized conclusions to which considerations of organizational structure and function customarily give rise, for the attempt has not been made to see Henry Ford solely in terms of the role he played or the function he served in the combination and allocation of resources in a complex social setting.

The approach adopted in this study examined the crucial influence of Ford's personality and its conflicts in the precipitation, definition, and attempted resolution of the problems that faced his company. This issue is implicit in the unanswered questions raised by Ford's biographers, by the company's historians, and in the incomplete evaluations reached by organizational theorists on the structure and functioning of the Ford Motor Company.

In the three volumes of their history of the company, for example, Nevins and Hill raised questions to which on the face of it there seemed no plausible answers. Why, for instance, did Ford doggedly persist in production of the Model T long after its market appeal had faded? Why did he, a self-proclaimed advocate of progress, refuse to countenance any fundamental improvement in the car from its introduction in 1908 to its withdrawal in 1927? Why did he "change" from a simple and single-minded Yankee mechanic, capable nonetheless of commanding the loyalty and best efforts of his subordinates, to an arrogant, vindictive, and deeply suspicious man, surrounded by compliant subordinates and bent on the dangerous mission of forcing external reality into the mold of his own wishes? What, at its simplest, did the Model T symbolize for Ford?

These questions have everything to do with the develop-

7
CONCLUSION

ment of the Ford Motor Company, for in attempting to answer them one is simultaneously accounting for the company's growth and its decline, for its managerial structure and for its strategy. It was Henry Ford who shaped the company and it is surely valid to examine what shaped Henry Ford.

Traditionally, historical analyses of business leadership have tended to let this issue fall where it might. Cause was held less important than effect. Schumpeter's concern with the rise of the entrepreneur, for instance, was directed toward the definition of entrepreneurial functions peculiar to particular points in time; he conceived of the individual entrepreneur as the "pivot" of the capitalist system, a strong man who for this reason could meet the demands and rise to the opportunities with which the system presented him.[1]

Schumpeter's entrepreneurs were the Vanderbilts, Rockefellers, and Carnegies, but his preoccupation with the obsolescence of the entrepreneurial function as the capitalist system "inevitably" decayed, served to obscure at least one of the directions in which his conception of the entrepreneur emphatically pointed: that of the influence of individual motivation upon the men who emerged as business leaders.

Rather than follow this lead, subsequent work concerned itself with redefinitions in which the emphasis was placed upon "entrepreneurial patterns." In this way the focus of attention shifted from the entrepreneurial functions of innovation and acceptance of risk, functions undertaken by a comparative handful of exceptional individuals, to a concern with vast numbers of small decision-makers whose actions were seen as stimulating and alternately depressing the forces of change.[2]

With this shift away from the individual a tendency to undervalue the force of individual action necessarily followed. Where circumstances demanded an explanation, the business leader might be seen as acting according to the economic ethics of the time or as inexorably conforming to functional demands. The study of the robber barons, for instance, was held to be useful inasmuch as it helped one "to understand the business process in society"—in this case the process of capital accumulation.[3]

Recent developments in economic history are now beginning to point the way back to the analysis of individual action and its underlying motivations. In discussing his study of eight important business leaders, Hughes concluded:

There is more, much more than economic motivation in the lives of men. For example, let me make a "far out" but entirely serious suggestion about these men in particular, and Entrepreneurial History in general. It seems to me that my men could have been studied most profitably indeed from a type of Freudian analysis. What were the effects upon Penn, Brigham Young, and Morgan of their all powerful fathers? Whitney was a "solitary," a bachelor into his fifties. Were these facts, together with his inventiveness, and with the secretiveness of his actions, all related in an important way? Did they have important effects? Did Harriman, the "Little Giant," act out the part in a defensive reaction to his small stature? What was the impact of strong mothers and weak fathers upon Carnegie, Harriman, Ford, and Edison? I am almost asking what was the effect of family life on American history through these men. Yet if we are seriously interested in understanding the individual entrepreneur's impact, I don't really see how we can avoid the problems of the determination of personality.[4]

This study has sought, in centering on the issue raised here, to understand what it was that impelled Henry Ford to act as he did. It has attempted to give consistency and meaning to Ford's actions and interests by examining the constant play of unconscious motivation beneath and through the rational, conscious decisions he reached. In this way it has perhaps brought into relief origins and meanings of action in a business setting which would have been lost in the glare of simpler and perhaps more appealing theories of motivation and organization.

Were one to consider, for example, March and Simon's threefold classification of the motivational assumptions upon which organizational theories are based,[5] it might appear useful to have approached Ford's introduction of the assembly line from the standpoint of the scientific management school and to have taken this as a point of departure in search of an understanding of Ford himself.

But despite the close connection between Taylor's theories and Ford's actions, a view of human motivation similar to Taylor's cannot be ascribed to Henry Ford. His firmly held opinion was that men liked to work and actively sought the opportunity to do so. Nor did he consider economic incentives particularly important. By 1919 inflation had caught up with the $5 day, and from then on Ford's wages were generally below industry levels. His executives were never as generously paid as those at General Motors, although occasionally acting as master, or feudal lord, Ford would secretly reward their efforts with cash payments. In their reminiscences both Galamb and Sheldrick referred to a gift of this kind, but the sums were not large: Sheldrick for instance received $1000.

Were the ascription to Ford of the Taylorian view compatible with the evidence, however, there would still remain a dilemma reminiscent of the "instinct" which was held to forbid incest and which was in reality only a description of the behavior observed. To make the dilemma explicit, saying that Ford viewed men as machines made to run by simple economic incentives would hardly explain why he did so. A much wider frame of reference is needed if individual behavior is to be made coherent, and it is at this point that much current theory fails to work.

Where the individual is taken as the unit of analysis, the rational, conscious nature of the motivational premises upon which action is held to be based can account neither for the ambivalences, the contradictions, the irrationalities which find expression in the actions of a man like Henry Ford nor for the adaptive outcomes of his style. And where current theory shifts its focus from the individual to the group, the results are no less unsatisfactory. Group structures and processes are analyzed to the point where the individual emerges disembodied, a function of intragroup and environmental pressures which leave little scope for the exercise of individual choice. Choice, in fact, is seen as an "organizational" function, and the individual is effectively excluded.

To distort the locus of choice in this way serves a purpose where the objective is comparative organizational analysis. Here motivational premises can be advanced as the bases for organizational choice: business organizations want to improve their rate of growth or innovation, their efficiency in the use of resources, their return on capital. Given these as the premises, judgment can then be passed on the effectiveness of an organization's choice of action.

Chandler, for example, discussed the Ford Motor Company's failure to diversify during the Depression—a policy followed by General Motors to conspicuous advantage—and concluded, "The incredibly bad management of his enormous industrial empire, which was so clearly reflected by the lack of any systematic organizational structure, not only prevented the Ford Motor Company from carrying out a strategy of diversification but also helped cause the rapid drop in Ford's profits and share of the market."[6] The assumption here is that the Ford organization would have attempted diversification (in the interests of growth, return on capital) had it not been for the poor quality of the company's management and its lack of a systematic structure. The usefulness of this approach lies in the ability it confers to compare the effectiveness of like companies on the basis of the same motivational premises; these are seen as underlying each organization's choice of action and differences in environmental pressures, strategy, or structure can then be advanced in explanation of organizational success or failure.

But because of the distortion of the locus of choice—it

is the organization, not an individual, which acts, upon motivational premises ascribed to it—this approach cannot answer the essential and less general question of why the catastrophic decline in the Ford Motor Company's fortunes should have set in at all. And yet attempts have been made to do this, and they offer striking instances of the misleading shifts in emphasis which occur when individual motivation and choice are ignored.

In *Leadership in Administration,* Selznick used this approach in discussing the structural dislocations which accompany attempts to deal with organizational crisis, and he cited the Ford Motor Company's conversion to the Model A as a case in point:

A characteristic crisis is the shift from a production orientation to an emphasis on sales and public relations. The Ford Motor Company, among others in the auto industry, went through a crisis of this sort. The organization that produced the famous "Model T" was dedicated to the goal of producing more cars per day at an ever lower cost per car. In this it was highly successful. But the organization that made this achievement possible failed to recognize or respond to changes in the market. Consumer preference was shifting to comfort, styling, and performance. By 1926, when sales were off disastrously, Ford permitted his company to engage in a national advertising campaign. He accepted this technique grudgingly, only under the pressure of a major crisis.

But much more than advertising was needed to permit sales an adequate role in the organization. Design and engineering had to be influenced as well. Finally, in 1927, production of the Model T was stopped. . . . Conversion to the Model A took eighteen months and cost $100 million. Yet even this did not bring about the changes in orientation, with attendant upward revisions in the status of sales and public relations activities, that were required. Only after World War II was a reorganization in depth completed. The Ford enterprise paid a heavy price for a policy valuable in the early stage of development, that was not abandoned in good time. Given a deep initial commitment, so often required by pioneering ventures, such adaptations are likely to require correspondingly severe shifts in personnel.[7]

To take the last statement first: it is of crucial importance that Sorensen's sweeping dismissals of production foremen, superintendents, and Model T executives be borne in mind. The "severe shift in personnel" not only took place, it deprived the company of thousands of skilled men at a time when they were vitally needed to ensure a smooth changeover to the Model A. But why did this happen? It was in no way the "organization's" choice of action in response to an organizational need; it followed a personal need on Sorensen's part to eliminate his rivals and to secure his position. Second, no matter how much it may appear so upon looking back, the Model A did not represent an organizational crisis brought about by change from a production orientation to an emphasis on sales and public relations. Henry Ford in fact intended that the Model A should last as long as the T; although the change was forced upon him by the severe decline in sales, there is not a shred of evidence that he had finally come to understand the changes in the market and was at last attempting to come to terms with them. In short, the upheaval in the company's management ranks was rooted in Sorensen's personal ambitions and the company's "production orientation" remained as dominant as before.

It is misleading in the light of this to advance in explanation of the organizational collapse a standoff between the older Model T production executives and the newer breed of sales and public relations men. When in addition, Selznick attributed resistance to the design and engineering departments, departments which Henry Ford controlled absolutely, the attempt to see the crisis in organizational terms with institutionalized groups at war with each other simply breaks down. It was not the "organization" which had produced the Model T that "failed to recognize or respond to changes in the market." It was one man, and he held the most legitimately powerful position in the company.

In this instance the attribution of a purely organizational purpose to individual action might have been taken much further. Sorensen's purge might well have been described more explicitly as an organizational necessity, ridding the company of Model T deadwood in order to give the bright, new—but nonexistent—marketing men their chance. The reality that it was a brutal, bloody struggle for power which Sorensen won might then have been forgotten as one gave serious consideration to the environmental and internal structural forces that made for or hindered organizational change.

That this is not as farfetched as it may first appear is demonstrated in a recent book by Katz and Kahn:

The organization of structure, or the initiation of structural change, is the most challenging of all organizational tasks and rarely occurs without strong pressures outside the organization. Changes in market and competition can necessitate such changes. Selznick (1957) describes well the conversion of the Ford organization from the Model T to the Model A. This organizational change was a grudging and delayed response to a disastrous decline in sales. Retooling was extensive; whole factory interiors were altered as the huge single-purpose machines of the Model T era were removed. Turnover was tremendous; the conversion required eighteen months and cost (in 1927) $100 million.* In Selznick's view, the changes in human organization continued for a decade and a half, and only during the period of World War II did the Ford Company complete a reorganization in depth.† Such changes in the formal structure of organization, the addition or elimination of major departments and the like are easily observed.[8]

* In fact it cost much more. See pp. 221–222.

† Selznick with greater accuracy said "after" World War II. The reorganization was initiated, not completed, by Henry Ford II after he had first destroyed the old structure of power. Bennett, for example, was dismissed on the same day that Henry Ford II assumed the presidency.

At the risk of still further repetition: the conversion to the Model A was not an organizational change in any accepted sense. There were no structural changes made with a view to permitting the organization to cope more effectively with its environment or to control more efficiently its own internal processes.

Chapter 6 of this study has attempted to describe and account for the structure of executive relationships which existed in the Ford Motor Company at the time. In no reasonable way can that structure be made to appear as an outcome of or a response to external pressures. On the contrary, external pressures were largely ignored as the organization rent itself from within. Power was employed and deployed in the service of highly personal, individual objectives. Ambiguity and rivalry at the executive level were encouraged by Henry Ford in ways that had nothing to do with organizational survival, maintenance, or growth. The organization provided the framework for action, but it was men who acted. And they acted under the impulse of a man whose style of leadership set the pattern, whose motives and choices of action were the strategy which molded the structure.

This study has attempted to trace the roots of Ford's style in his early history. The issue of restitution—in a dual sense, both to himself for what he had lost and to the father whom he had wronged—was advanced in explanation of Ford's fixation on the Model T, on the farmer, and in interpretation of the extraordinary symbolism with which the car became invested. The issue of retaliation, as a denial of guilt and a projection of aggression expressing itself in the assumption of an increasingly sadistic position toward other men, was advanced as the defining characteristic of Ford's interpersonal relations. Linking these issues was the idea of omnipotence, an idea upon which Ford came more and more to rely, even as the external world confirmed his ability. For confirmation stood in painful contrast to the reexperiencing of loss which came when the car was "finished" and it seemed that he had still not done enough. From the externalization of these unconscious issues there emerged a style of adaptation to reality. In the early years it centered upon the issue of restitution, upon the concrete work of his hands.

Henry Ford, during these years, was an active, creative, approachable figure. By 1907 he was the majority owner of a company clearly destined for success. He seemed touched by the gift of prophecy: his fixation, first on the car and then on the processes of production so as constantly to increase the company's capacity, was validated again and again by the market's response. He was a charismatic leader in the Weberian sense, and men worked willingly for a figure with whom their best aspirations were identified.

Ford seemed invincible, but his choices of action bore a visionary stamp which testified more to a burning need to do what he had to do than to any rational appraisal of the opportunities that lay open to him. Henry Ford deciding on the cheap car in 1905–1906 when the trend seemed so clearly in favor of the expensive cars; Henry Ford deciding to freeze the Model T's design in 1908 so that he could build it in numbers which other manufacturers felt to be a dangerous exaggeration of the market's capacity; Henry Ford deciding to lower prices and to tie his future to an expansion that he fought his more cautious shareholders to secure—and that he secured in the magical advances in mass production at Highland Park: all of these decisions bore the mark of a belief in himself and his own judgment which was independent of other men's ideas. But they were decisions that caught men's imaginations, won their willing cooperation, and the environment confirmed men's faith in Ford.

If this, then, was Ford in the early years, what were the consequences for his company? The impetus, the breathless rush of innovation and expansion had swept other men along with him. A man could make his own job, assume responsibility where he felt fit. The job, and how well it was done, formed the basis of the relationship between Ford and his executives, none of whom was a "boss" in any formal sense. They bore no titles, they were roughly equal in status. Structure was at a minimum, and its constraints were in fact less important in a situation where an identification with the leader was an internalized control, contributing to an extraordinary degree of executive motivation. Henry Ford, as a friend from his boyhood remembered, had a "magnet," and it played its part in binding others to him.

By 1915–1916, the situation was measurably different. The changes in the market were still far off when Ford appeared to lose interest. He considered selling the company but imposed conditions that could not be met. He began his series of adventures outside while rigidly insisting that the company's single-model policy and the structure of relationships which had grown up around it should continue as before. He created a power vacuum into which men like Liebold and Sorensen rapidly moved and Ford was content to let them do so. First, because they ministered to his conflicts by acknowledging his omnipotence; long afterwards a chapter title in Sorensen's autobiography would read simply, "Henry Ford's Man."[9] Second, as the market changes became steadily apparent, they made no attempt to disturb the meaning that Ford had assigned to the car. Sorensen echoed Henry Ford in blaming the company's dealers for falling sales: the Model T was a work of genius, the best car ever built. Third, Ford's refusal to change the car and the irrational meaning with which the idea of change had in fact become imbued permitted these men to consolidate their power: they accused those who supported change of disloyalty. To Henry Ford the advocates of change appeared to be challenging not only him but the car that had come to mean far more than reality conceded. His own disappointment, the reexperiencing of loss which formed the other side of the coin, he unleashed in the sadism that became the dominant feature of his interpersonal relations. He turned, in other words, to the unconscious issue of retaliation.

Playing into the hands of the men who then rose to power was the stage in its development which the company had reached. Growth was slowing, stabilization setting in. What had never been done before was now routine: the 1920–1921 executive exodus, for example, suddenly deprived the organization of the contributions of many competent and talented men, and yet the company survived with little damage done to its immediate productive effectiveness. But it is important to bear in mind that these men were dismissed not as part of a plan either to rationalize the haphazard structure that had grown up in the early years or to eliminate the costly and unnecessary duplication of effort to which the ad hoc approach to problems had given rise in the past. A man of Knudsen's ability was dismissed because he had become too dangerous a rival for Sorensen to accept, not as part of a structural shift designed to adapt the company to the new conditions.

As the years passed, Henry Ford became increasingly domineering, vindictive, rigid, and suspicious, his prescience had deserted him, and he was incapable of administering in any orderly way the vast company he had built. The point has often been made that the great innovators and empire builders, who in Chandler's phrase brought "vast numbers of men, amounts of money and materials under a single corporate roof" showed a curious lack of interest in providing for the management of those resources.[10] From his study of more than 70 of the largest industrial corporations, Chandler concluded that the reshaping of administrative structure which was vital to the period succeeding expansion "nearly always had to wait" for a change in the top command.[11]

One might well ask why. Did these men too grow as rigid as Henry Ford; did change in some way present them with the irrational threat that Ford saw in the challenges to the Model T? Did they too move out of a creative period into omnipotence and then on to a callous disregard for the men who refused to sustain their delusions? Such men decided the strategy and shaped the structure of their companies. To question why they acted as they did, as this study has attempted to ask of Henry Ford, serves to explain the work they set themselves and why and how it developed as it did.

Henry Ford built a billion-dollar company. To scant his contribution to America's progress would be to distort economic and social history. Ford's concept of mass production, his belief that lower prices and ever-widening markets would make steadily rising wages possible came some twenty years before Keynes's emphasis on consumption as the key to economic growth.

But it is insufficient to say all of this and not ask what manner of man he was. On the evidence, the force that drove Ford had little to do with economic rationality or social reality: out of his own conflicted personality there came attempts at resolution which coincided with the reality of his time. As time moved on and reality changed, he could neither move nor change with them.

CHAPTER 1

1. Hiram Percy Maxim, *Horseless Carriage Days* (New York: Harpers, 1937), p. 1.

2. *Ibid.*, pp. 3–5.

3. Theodore F. MacManus and Norman Beasley, *Men, Money and Motors* (New York: Harpers, 1930), p. 6.

4. *Ibid.*, p. 7.

5. Maxim, *Horseless Carriage Days*, pp. 7–8.

6. *Ibid.*, p. 29.

7. *Ibid.*, p. 121.

8. *Ibid.*, p. 48.

9. *Ibid.*, p. 49.

10. *Ibid.*, p. 174.

11. Allan Nevins and Frank Ernest Hill, *Ford: The Times, the Man, and the Company* (New York: Scribners, 1954), p. 187. Hereafter cited as Nevins and Hill, Vol. I.

12. Fred Strauss, *Reminiscences*, Ford Archives, pp. 79 and 82.

13. Maxim, *Horseless Carriage Days*, p. 47. See also Charles F. Kettering and Allen Orth, *The New Necessity: The Culmination of a Century of Progress in Transportation* (Baltimore: Williams and Wilkins, 1932), p. 9.

14. Alfred P. Sloan, Jr., *Adventures of a White-Collar Man* (New York: Doubleday, 1941), p. 24. See also Arthur Pound, *The Turning Wheel* (New York: Doubleday, 1934), p. 39.

15. Kettering and Orth, *New Necessity*, pp. 9–10.

16. *Ibid.*, pp. 85–86.

17. Keith Sward, *The Legend of Henry Ford* (New York: Rinehart, 1948), pp. 5–6. Sward cites other legal restrictions.

18. *Detroit Journal*, August 5, 1899.

19. Nevins and Hill, Vol. I, p. 163.

20. Sloan, *White-Collar Man*, p. 26. This was the report of Sloan's partner who went to Kokomo to take the order. See also Nevins and Hill, Vol. I, pp. 132 and 163.

21. *Horseless Age*, March 1896, p. 23. Cited in Nevins and Hill, Vol. I, p. 165.

22. "The Fad of the Automobile," in *Detroit News-Tribune*, October 28, 1900.

23. Nevins and Hill, Vol. I, p. 229.

24. Joseph B. Bishop, "Social and Economic Influence of the Bicycle," *Forum*, Vol. XXI (August 1896), p. 668.

25. Roger Burlingame, *Backgrounds of Power* (New York: Knopf, 1949), p. 272.

26. Pound, *Turning Wheel,* pp. 34–36.

27. *Ibid.,* p. 50.

28. *Ibid.,* p. 51.

29. J. C. Long, *Roy D. Chapin* (privately printed, 1941), p. 38.

30. E. D. Kennedy, *The Automobile Industry* (New York: Regnal and Hitchcock, 1941), p. 19.

31. *Detroit Journal,* May 13, 1899.

32. J. S. Corbin, "The Opinion of One of the Million," *Horseless Age,* Vol. XIII, No. 2 (January 13, 1904), pp. 41–42.

33. Benjamin Briscoe, "The Inside Story of General Motors," *Detroit Saturday Night,* Vol. 15, No. 4 (January 22, 1921), p. 7.

34. Long, *Roy D. Chapin,* pp. 23–24.

35. Kennedy, *Automobile Industry,* p. 12.

36. Nevins and Hill, Vol. I, pp. 285 and 289.

37. Sketch of R. E. Olds in *Automotive Giants of America* (New York: Forbes Publishing Company, 1926). Quoted in Pound, *Turning Wheel,* pp. 52–53.

38. Long, *Roy D. Chapin,* pp. 23–24, and Pound, *Turning Wheel,* p. 53.

39. Merrill Denison, *The Power to Go* (Garden City, New York: Doubleday, 1956), p. 111.

40. Pound, *Turning Wheel,* p. 53.

41. *Detroit Free Press,* August 19, 1899.

42. Pound, *Turning Wheel,* p. 53.

43. *Ibid.,* p. 103.

44. *Motor World,* Vol. XVII, No. 4 (October 24, 1907), p. 185.

45. *Automobile and Motor Review,* Vol. VI, No. 24 (August 16, 1902), p. 16.

46. Pound, *Turning Wheel,* p. 103.

47. David Beecroft Papers, Automotive History Collection, Detroit Public Library.

48. Nevins and Hill, Vol. I, pp. 230–232.

49. Briscoe, "Inside Story," p. 2.

50. *Ibid.,* p. 9.

51. Pound, *Turning Wheel,* p. 66; but see p. 490 for reference to the Weston-Mott Company.

52. Ralph C. Epstein, *The Automobile Industry: Its Economic and Commercial Development* (Chicago: A. W. Shaw, 1928), pp. 39–40.

53. Long, *Roy D. Chapin,* pp. 31–32.

54. Pound, *Turning Wheel,* p. 54.

55. *Ibid.,* pp. 60–61.

56. Long, *Roy D. Chapin,* p. 38.

57. *Ibid.,* Chapters 5 and 6.

58. Pound, *Turning Wheel,* p. 62.

59. Kennedy, *Automobile Industry,* p. 21.

60. Pound, *Turning Wheel,* p. 64.

61. Epstein, *Automobile Industry,* pp. 76–77.

62. *Ibid.,* p. 51.

63. *Ibid.*

64. *Detroit Free Press,* May 8, 1904.

65. Sloan, *White-Collar Man,* p. 53.

66. Nevins and Hill, Vol. I, p. 9.

67. Editorial in the *Automobile and Motor Review,* Vol. VI, No. 24 (August 16, 1902), p. 16.

68. Harry W. Perry, "Development of Buggy Type Western Cars," *Automobile,* Vol. XV, No. 5 (August 2, 1906), pp. 143–146.

69. Charles B. Duryea, letter to the editor of *Horseless Age,* Vol. XI, No. 18 (May 6, 1903), p. 554.

70. "Simplicity Apparently Not the Objective," editorial in *Motor Age,* Vol. X, No. 6 (August 9, 1906), p. 8.

71. Cited in Nevins and Hill, Vol. I, p. 324.

72. Nevins and Hill, Vol. I, p. 338.

73. *Ibid.,* pp. 644–647.

74. Pound, *Turning Wheel,* p. 56.

75. "Carriage Builders Enter the Field," editorial in *Horseless Age,* Vol. XIX, No. 26 (June 26, 1907), p. 847.

76. Epstein, *Automobile Industry,* p. 183.

77. Nevins and Hill, Vol. I, pp. 332–333.

78. Edwin Kilburn, letter to the editor of *Horseless Age,* Vol. XXI, No. 4 (January 22, 1908), p. 92.

79. Charles Coolidge Parlin and Henry Sherwood Youker, *Gasoline Pleasure Cars,* Report of Investigation. MS. The Curtis Publishing Company, Advertising Department, 1914, pp. 438–439. Copy in Ford Archives.

80. Where there is no reference given, the sources of the facts cited

are (a) Nevins and Hill, Vol. I; (b) Allan Nevins and Frank Ernest Hill, *Ford: Expansion and Challenge* (New York: Scribners, 1957). Hereafter to be cited as Nevins and Hill, Vol. II; and (c) by the same authors, *Ford: Decline and Rebirth* (New York: Scribners, 1962). Hereafter to be cited as Nevins and Hill, Vol. III.

81. Accession 903, Box 1, Ford Archives.

82. George Brown, *Reminiscences,* Ford Archives, pp. 110–111. Also, the *Reminiscences* of T. A. Mallon, p. 117; Joseph Galamb, p. 37; A. M. Wibel, p. 5. All in Ford Archives.

83. E. J. Farkas, *Reminiscences,* Ford Archives, p. 106.

84. C. E. Sorensen, *My Forty Years with Ford* (New York: Norton, 1956), pp. 5–6.

85. J. Galamb, *Reminiscences,* Ford Archives, p. 32.

86. *Ibid.*, p. 121.

87. Farkas, *Reminiscences,* pp. 97–100.

88. *Ibid.*, p. 234.

89. F. Rockelman, *Reminiscences,* Ford Archives, p. 13.

90. J. K. Smith, *Reminiscences,* Ford Archives, p. 5.

91. Galamb, *Reminiscences,* p. 22.

92. J. Wandersee, *Reminiscences,* Ford Archives, p. 26.

93. Early Ford Motor Company advertisement cited in Roger Burlingame, *Henry Ford* (New York: Knopf, 1954), pp. 48–49.

94. Allan L. Benson, *The New Henry Ford* (New York: Funk and Wagnalls, 1923), p. 9.

95. Samuel S. Marquis, *Henry Ford, An Interpretation* (Boston: Little, Brown, 1923), p. 9.

CHAPTER 2

1. W. J. Cameron, *Reminiscences,* Ford Archives, p. 95.

2. Keith Sward, *The Legend of Henry Ford* (New York: Rinehart, 1948), pp. 279–80. The Cameron quotation is taken from "Ford Sunday Evening Hour," February 14, 1937.

3. Cameron, *Reminiscences,* p. 17.

4. F. L. Black, *Reminiscences,* Ford Archives, p. 148.

5. *Chicago Examiner,* April 26, 1938.

6. Allan L. Benson, *The New Henry Ford* (New York: Funk and Wagnalls, 1923), pp. 352–353.

7. Samuel S. Marquis, *Henry Ford, An Interpretation* (Boston: Little, Brown, 1923), p. 57

8. Alfred P. Sloan, Jr., *My Years with General Motors* (Garden City, New York: Doubleday, 1964), p. 3.

9. William Greenleaf, *Monopoly on Wheels* (Detroit: Wayne State University, 1961), p. 125.

10. Allan Nevins and Frank Ernest Hill, *Ford: The Times, the Man, and the Company* (New York: Scribners, 1954), Chapters 5 and 6. Hereafter cited as Nevins and Hill, Vol. I.

11. Sidney Olson, *Young Henry Ford* (Detroit: Wayne State University, 1963), pp. 35–37; Henry Ford, *My Life and Work* (Garden City, New York: Doubleday, 1923), pp. 26–28; Nevins and Hill, Vol. I, p. 113.

12. Ford, *My Life and Work*, pp. 22, 25, 26.

13. *Ibid.*, p. 30.

14. *Ibid.*

15. Nevins and Hill, Vol. I, p. 147.

16. Charles Brady King, *Psychic Reminiscences* (Limited Edition published by the author, 1935), p. 12.

17. *Ibid.*, p. 18.

18. Nevins and Hill, Vol. I, pp. 116–117.

19. *Ibid.*, pp. 147–148.

20. Fred Strauss, *Reminiscences*, Ford Archives, pp. 16–19.

21. *Ibid.*, pp. 26–28.

22. Olson, *Young Henry Ford*, p. 91.

23. *Ibid.*, pp. 110–118.

24. Letter to William C. Maybury from E. I. Garfield, August 1, 1898. Accession 1, Box 114, Ford Archives.

25. Strauss, *Reminiscences*, pp. 53–55.

26. Olson, *Young Henry Ford*, p. 107.

27. Agreement dated July 24, 1899, between Detroit Automobile Company and Henry Ford. Accession 1, Box 114, Ford Archives.

28. Strauss, *Reminiscences*, p. 61.

29. *Ibid.*, pp. 62–64.

30. *Ibid.*, p. 36.

31. Ford, *My Life and Work*, p. 36.

32. Olson, *Young Henry Ford*, p. 107.

33. Strauss, *Reminiscences*, p. 46.

34. Accession 1, Box 92, Ford Archives.

35. Oliver Barthel, *Reminiscences*, Ford Archives, p. 28.

36. See Olson, *Young Henry Ford*, pp. 127–128, for the typical argument.

37. Ford, *My Life and Work*, p. 37.

38. Barthel, *Reminiscences*, pp. 31–32.

39. Letter to Melvin Bryant from Henry Ford, January 6, 1902. Quoted in Olson, *Young Henry Ford*, p. 153.

40. Barthel, *Reminiscences*, pp. 31–32.

41. Nevins and Hill, Vol. I, pp. 213–214.

42. Letter from Clara Ford to Melvin Bryant, October 27, 1902. Quoted in Nevins and Hill, Vol. I, p. 218.

43. Letter to Chris Sinsabaugh from Barney Oldfield, March 29, 1914; David Beecroft Papers, Automotive History Collection, Detroit Public Library. Punctuation and spelling corrected.

44. Ford, *My Life and Work*, p. 50.

45. Additional Tax Case, Transcript of Hearings, pp. 1270–1272. Quoted in Nevins and Hill, Vol. I, p. 225.

46. Agreement signed by Alexander Malcomson and Henry Ford, August 20, 1902. Accession 363, Box 1, Ford Archives.

47. Letter from Alexander Y. Malcomson to Henry Ford, October 30, 1902. Accession 572, Box 1, Ford Archives.

48. Strauss, *Reminiscences*, p. 75. There is a copy of the agreement, signed by Henry Ford and witnessed by C. Harold Wills, undated and lacking Strauss's signature in Accession 386, Ford Archives.

49. Strauss, *Reminiscences*, pp. 76 and 78.

50. Ford, *My Life and Work*, p. 36.

51. Olson, *Young Henry Ford*, p. 170.

52. *Ibid.*, pp. 176–181.

53. Benson, *New Henry Ford*, p. 129.

54. Milo M. Quaife, *The Life of John Wendell Anderson* (Detroit: Privately printed, 1950), p. 105.

55. *Ibid.*, pp. 104–105.

56. J. Wandersee, *Reminiscences*, Ford Archives, p. 40.

57. John W. Anderson interview with A. J. Lacy, June 1926. Accession 96, Box 1, Ford Archives.

58. Ford, *My Life and Work*, p. 56.

59. Strauss, *Reminiscences*, p. 78.

60. Opinion rendered by U.S. Board of Tax Appeals in the appeal of *James Couzens* v. *Commissioner of Internal Revenue*. May 5, 1928, p. 82. Accession 96, Box 1, Ford Archives.

61. Roger Burlingame, *Henry Ford* (New York: Knopf, 1955), pp. 49–51.

62. *Detroit Journal*, May 9, 1905; *Detroit Free Press*, May 10, 1905. Cited in Nevins and Hill, Vol. I, pp. 272–273.

63. *Motor Age,* Vol. 8, No. 20 (November 16, 1905), p. 11.

64. Benson, *New Henry Ford,* pp. 33–34.

65. Horace Lucien Arnold and Fay Leone Faurote, *Ford Methods and Ford Shops* (New York: The Engineering Magazine Company, 1915), p. 15.

66. Ford, *My Life and Work,* p. 58.

67. Directors Minutes, December 22, 1905. Accession 85, Ford Archives.

68. *Ibid.,* July 14, 1906.

69. *Cycle and Automobile Trade Journal,* Vol. X, No. 7 (January 1, 1906).

70. *Detroit Journal,* January 5, 1906.

71. Memorandum of Conference with P. E. Martin, Hartner and Degener, June 1926. Accession 96, Box 12, Ford Archives.

72. C. E. Sorensen, *My Forty Years with Ford* (New York: Norton, 1956), pp. 232–233.

73. J. Galamb, *Reminiscences,* Ford Archives, p. 337.

74. Nevins and Hill, Vol. I, p. 337.

75. Memorandum of Conference with Joseph Galamb, June 1926, p. 1. Accession 96, Box 11, Ford Archives.

76. Ford, *My Life and Work,* pp. 70–71.

77. Memorandum of Conference with Joseph Galamb, June 1926, pp. 2–3. Accession 96, Box 11, Ford Archives.

78. Ford, *My Life and Work,* pp. 71–72.

79. Nevins and Hill, Vol. I, pp. 646–677; Accession 84, Box 1, Ford Archives.

80. "The Wisdom of the Farmer." Editorial in *Motor World,* Vol. XVII, No. 23 (March 5, 1908), p. 959.

81. "Farmers Taking to Automobiles." *Motor World,* Vol. XX, No. 2 (April 8, 1909), p. 68.

82. "The Farmer as an Automobile Buyer." Editorial in *Motor World,* Vol. XVIII, no. 16 (July 16, 1908), p. 521; Nevins and Hill, Vol. I, pp. 646–647.

83. *Ibid.*

84. Charles Coolidge Parlin and Henry Sherwood Youker, *Gasoline Pleasure Cars,* Report of Investigation. MS. The Curtis Publishing Company, Advertising Department, 1914, pp. 1082–1148. Copy in Ford Archives.

85. *Ibid.,* p. 1069.

86. Nevins and Hill, Vol. I, p. 509.

87. Parlin and Youker, *Gasoline Pleasure Cars,* p. 1078.

88. Letter dated October 15, 1909, from the office of Henry Ford to H. B. Waldron. Accession 266, Ford Archives.

89. Galamb, *Reminiscences,* pp. 97–98.

90. *Detroit Journal,* July 16, 1909.

91. Theodore F. MacManus and Norman Beasley, *Men, Money and Motors* (New York: Harpers, 1937) p. 72.

92. Benjamin Briscoe, "The Inside Story of General Motors," *Detroit Saturday Night,* Section 2, No. 4, January 22, 1921.

93. Memorandum of Conference with Honorable W. C. Durant, November 1926. Accession 96, Box 7, Ford Archives.

94. Briscoe, "Inside Story," *Detroit Saturday Night,* Section 2, No. 6, February 5, 1921.

95. *Ibid.*

96. Letter from Thomas W. Lamont to Henry Ford, June 19, 1916. Accession 940, Box 2, Ford Archives.

97. Ford, *My Life and Work,* pp. 197–198. Emphasis added.

98. *Ibid.,* p. 199.

99. *Detroit Free Press,* January 27, 1913.

100. Nevins and Hill, Vol. I, p. 644.

101. Galamb, *Reminiscences,* pp. 43–44.

102. Norman Beasley, "Henry Ford Says," *Motor,* Vol. XLI, January 1924, pp. 71 and 312.

103. Ford, *My Life and Work,* p. 149.

104. A copy can be found in Accession 572, Box 22, Ford Archives.

105. Sloan, *My Years with General Motors,* pp. 151–152 and 302.

106. "Ford to fight it out with his old car," *New York Times,* Section VIII, December 26, 1926.

107. *Ibid.*

108. Ford, *My Life and Work,* pp. 17–18.

CHAPTER 3

1. Garet Garrett, *The Wild Wheel* (New York: Pantheon, 1952), p. 86.

2. *Ibid.,* p. 89.

3. Allan Nevins and Frank Ernest Hill, *Ford: Expansion and Challenge* (New York: Scribners, 1957), p. 673. Hereafter to be cited as Nevins and Hill, Vol. II.

4. Heinz Hartmann, *Ego Psychology and the Problem of Adaptation* (New York: International Universities Press, 1964), p.36.

5. Alfred P. Sloan, Jr., *My Years with General Motors* (Garden City, New York: Doubleday, 1964), p. 429.

6. William Greenleaf, *Monopoly on Wheels* (Detroit: Wayne State University, 1961), pp. 71–82.

7. *Ibid.*, p. 49.

8. *Ibid.*, pp. 97–100.

9. *Ibid.*, p. 112.

10. *Ibid.*, pp. 113–114.

11. *Ibid.*, p. 175.

12. Memorandum of conference with Horace H. Rackham, February 1926. Accession 96, Box 19, Ford Archives.

13. *Detroit News*, May 8, 1953.

14. *Ibid.*

15. C. H. Bennett, *Reminiscences*, Ford Archives, pp. 24–26.

16. Minutes of Stockholders Annual Meeting, October 16, 1905.

17. Memorandum of conference with Messrs David Gray and Luman Goodenough, October 1926. Accession 96, Box 11, Ford Archives.

18. "To Make It All Ford," *Motor Age*, Vol. X, No. 7 (August 16, 1906), p. 7.

19. Max Wollering, *Reminiscences*, Ford Archives, p. 15.

20. *Ibid.*, p. 34.

21. *Detroit Journal*, February 16, 1909.

22. *Ibid.*

23. *Ford Times*, Vol. II, No. 17 (June 1909), p. 10.

24. Directors Minutes, April 17, 1907.

25. *Ford Times*, Vol. III, No. 8 (January 1910), p. 3.

26. *Detroit Journal*, October 1, 1910.

27. Allan Nevins and Frank Ernest Hill, *Ford: The Times, the Man, and the Company* (New York: Scribners, 1954), pp. 458–459. Hereafter cited as Nevins and Hill, Vol. I.

28. Testimony of C. Harold Wills. *Dodge* Suit, Record on Appeal, pp. 582–660. Ford Archives.

29. Nevins and Hill, Vol. I, pp. 494–500.

30. Memorandum of conference with W. S. Knudsen, June 1926. Accession 96, Box 11, Ford Archives.

31. Nevins and Hill, Vol. I, p. 343; Memorandum of conference with J. R. Lee, June 1926. Accession 96, Box 12, Ford Archives.

32. Testimony of C. Harold Wills, *Dodge* Suit. Memorandum of conference with W. S. Knudsen. Accession 96, Ford Archives.

33. "The Story of the Ford." Speech by Norval Hawkins. Copy in Accession 96, Box 11, Ford Archives.

34. Nevins and Hill, Vol. I, pp. 644 and 648.

35. Horace Lucien Arnold and Fay Leone Faurote, *Ford Methods and Ford Shops* (New York: The Engineering Magazine Company, 1915), pp. 25–26.

36. Nevins and Hill, Vol. I, pp. 649–650.

37. W. W. Rostow, *The Stages of Economic Growth* (Cambridge, England: The University Press, 1962), p. 7.

38. This discussion and that to follow, unless otherwise cited, is based on *Couzens, et al. v. Commissioner of Internal Revenue*. Before the U.S. Board of Tax Appeals, Petitioners' Statement of Facts. April 18, 1927. Pp. 45–128. Copy in Accession 96, Box 7, Ford Archives.

39. *American Machinist,* all issues from May 8, 1913, to September 18, 1913, cited in above.

40. Memorandum of conference with Oscar C. Bornholdt, July 1926. Accession 96, Box 1, Ford Archives.

41. Alfred P. Sloan, Jr., *Adventures of a White-Collar Man* (New York: Doubleday, 1941), p. 74.

42. Reference to Petitioners' Statement of Facts as set out in note 38 ends at this point.

43. *Detroit Journal,* June 4, 1913.

44. Cited in Nevins and Hill, Vol. I, p. 504.

45. *Detroit Free Press,* March 20 and 27, 1910.

46. Maxwell Gitelson, "Therapeutic Problems in the Analysis of the 'Normal' Candidate," 1954, cited in Helen H. Tartakoff, "The Normal Personality in our Culture and the Nobel Prize Complex." Reprinted from *Psychoanalysis—A General Psychology. Essays in Honor of Heinz Hartmann,* R. M. Lowenstein, L. M. Newman, M. Schur, and A. J. Solnit, eds. (New York: International Universities Press, 1966), p. 225.

47. Interview with Henry Ford published in *Detroit News,* November 14, 1916. Emphasis added.

48. Harry Barnard, *Independent Man: The Life of Senator James Couzens* (New York: Scribners, 1958), p. 80.

49. *Automobile Topics,* Vol. XXXVIII, May 29, 1915, p. 195; June 5, 1915, pp. 283–285; June 12, 1915, pp. 381–383, 393; June 26, 1915, p. 537.

50. "Metamorphosis of the Motor Car," *Motor Age,* Vol. XXIX, March 9, 1916, pp. 5–11.

51. Quotations from Henry Ford, *My Life and Work* (Garden City, New York: Doubleday, 1923), p. 86.

52. Directors Minutes, August 21, 1913; terms of contract Secretary's Office Records, Ford Archives.

53. *Detroit News*, November 4, 1916; *Detroit Free Press*, August 17, 1913.

54. *Detroit News*, November 4, 1916. Ford estimated that the Dodges had made $10 million profit on their $27 million worth of sales to Ford Motor Company.

55. *Detroit Free Press*, August 17, 1913.

56. Nevins and Hill, Vol. II, p. 96.

57. *New York Tribune*, October 13, 1915.

58. "Whose Brains?" *Pipp's Weekly*, January 19, 1924, pp. 3–4.

59. E. G. Liebold, *Reminiscences*, Ford Archives, p. 43; R. T. Walker, *Reminiscences*, Ford Archives, p. 3.

60. *Dodge* Suit, Record on Appeal. Testimony of John F. Dodge, p. 491. Copy in Accession 572, Box 11, Ford Archives.

61. Stockholders Minutes, May 1, 1915. Ford Archives.

62. *Dodge* Suit, Testimony of Henry Ford, November 14, 1916, p. 165. P. 189 for Counsel's last comment.

63. *Detroit Journal*, June 16 and 18, 1915.

64. *Dearborn Independent*, October 22, 1915.

65. *Ibid.*, October 8, 1915.

66. *Detroit Journal*, November 20, 1915.

67. *Dearborn Independent*, November 26, 1915.

68. *Dodge* Suit, Record on Appeal. Testimony of John F. Dodge, pp. 490–492.

69. Directors Minutes, February 2, 1916; Stockholders Minutes, February 3, 1916.

70. Nevins and Hill, Vol. II, p. 93.

71. Nevins and Hill, Vol. I, pp. 644 and 647. See *Couzens* v. *Commissioner of Internal Revenue*, Petitioners' Statement of Facts, p. 89, for unfilled orders.

72. *Detroit News*, August 31, 1916.

73. *Dodge* Suit, Record on Appeal. Testimony of C. H. Wills.

74. Letter to Henry Ford from John F. Dodge and Horace E. Dodge, September 23, 1916, *Dodge* Suit Record, pp. 9–11. Copy in Accession 572, Box 11, Ford Archives.

75. Letter to John F. and Horace E. Dodge from Henry Ford, October 10, 1916. *Ibid.*, pp. 12–13; Letter from John F. and Horace E. Dodge to Henry Ford, October 11, 1916. *Ibid.*, pp. 13–14.

76. Letter to John F. and Horace E. Dodge from Henry Ford, No-

vember 2/3, 1916. *Ibid.,* pp. 331–332; Directors Minutes, October 31 and November 2, 1916. Ford Archives.

77. Bill of Complaint, *Dodge* Suit Record.

78. *Detroit News,* November 4, 1916.

79. *Ibid.*

80. *Ibid.*

81. W. J. Cameron, *Reminiscences,* Ford Archives, p. 24.

82. Nevins and Hill, Vol. II, pp. 313, 323, 351 and 618. See also Peter F. Drucker, "Henry Ford: Success and Failure," *Harper's Magazine,* Vol. 195, No. 1166 (July 1947).

83. Interviews with Mrs. Margaret Ford Ruddiman (Henry Ford's sister). November 29, 1951, p. 159; November 5, 1951, pp. 38 and 41. Ford Archives. Populism—see Andrew Sinclair, *Era of Excess* (New York: Harper, 1964), p. 91; and Richard Hofstadter, *The Age of Reform* (New York: Knopf, 1955), pp. 23–46. Keith Sward, *The Legend of Henry Ford* (New York, Rinehart, 1948), pp. 286–288.

84. John Reed, "Industry's Miracle Maker," *Metropolitan,* October 1916, p. 11.

85. *Couzens, et al.* v. *Commissioner of Internal Revenue,* Petitioners' Statement of Facts, p. 152.

86. Letter from Thomas W. Lamont to Henry Ford, June, 30, 1916. Copy in Accession 960, Box 2, Ford Archives.

87. Walker, *Reminiscences,* p. 48.

88. Nevins and Hill, Vol. II, pp. 101–104.

89. Directors Minutes, December 31, 1918. Ford Archives.

90. *Los Angeles Examiner,* March 5, 1919, reproduced in Opinion rendered by U. S. Board of Tax Appeals, *James Couzens* v. *Commissioners of Internal Revenue,* May 5, 1928, pp. 152–154.

91. *Ibid.,* p. 154.

92. *Ibid.,* pp. 161–162.

93. *Los Angeles Sunday Times,* March 16, 1919.

94. U.S. Board of Tax Appeals, *James Couzens* v. *Commissioners of Internal Revenue,* pp. 155–156.

95. Nevins and Hill, Vol. II, pp. 109–112.

96. Sward, *Legend of Henry Ford,* pp. 188–190. Nevins and Hill, Vol. II, pp. 145–147 omit Morgana's resignation.

97. Wollering, *Reminiscences,* pp. 32–33.

98. C. E. Sorensen, *My Forty Years with Ford* (New York: Norton, 1956), p. 84.

99. *Ibid.,* pp. 74–75.

100. *Ibid.,* p. 90.

101. Nevins and Hill, Vol. II, p. 152.

102. Interview with Henry Ford by James Sweinhart. *Detroit News,* July 22, 1921.

103. Nevins and Hill, Vol. II, p. 164.

104. Interview, *Detroit News,* July 22, 1921.

105. *Ibid.*

106. *Ibid.*

107. Nevins and Hill, Vol. II, p. 161.

108. Sward, *Legend of Henry Ford,* p. 192; Nevins and Hill, Vol. II, pp. 167–169.

109. Samuel S. Marquis, *Henry Ford, An Interpretation* (Boston: Little, Brown, 1923), p. 160.

110. Ford, *My Life and Work,* p. 92.

111. *Ibid.,* p. 97.

CHAPTER 4

1. Accession 1, Box 1. Notebook Number 3, Ford Archives.

2. Jonathan Hughes, *The Vital Few* (Boston: Houghton Mifflin, 1966), pp. 265–267.

3. Heinz Hartmann, *Ego Psychology and the Problem of Adaptation* (New York: International Universities Press, 1964), p. 71.

4. *Ibid.,* p. 51.

5. Harry Barnard, *Independent Man: The Life of Senator James Couzens* (New York: Scribners, 1958), p. 131.

6. Keith Sward, *The Legend of Henry Ford* (New York: Rinehart, 1948), p. 52; he is the only biographer to refer to it.

7. Anna Freud, *The Ego and the Mechanisms of Defense* (New York: International Universities Press, 1946), pp. 133 and 190.

8. Samuel S. Marquis, *Henry Ford, An Interpretation* (Boston: Little, Brown, 1923), pp. 152–153.

9. *Ibid.,* pp. 141–142. Emphasis added.

10. Henry Ford, *My Life and Work* (Garden City, New York: Doubleday, 1923), p. 220. Emphasis added.

11. 1922 edition cited by Marquis, *Henry Ford,* pp. 156–157; 1923 edition, Ford, *My Life and Work,* p. 265.

12. L. E. Briggs, *Reminiscences,* Ford Archives, p. 9.

13. "Ford's Secret Service," *Pipp's Weekly,* June 11, 1921, pp. 1–4.

14. *New York Times,* December 4, 1926.

15. W. M. Cunningham, *"J8": A Chronicle of the Neglected Truth about Henry Ford D. E. and the Ford Motor Company* (Detroit, c. 1931), pp. 60–61. Copy in Ford Archives.

16. Upton Sinclair, *The Flivver King* (Detroit & Pasadena, Cal.: The United Automobile Workers of America and the Author, 1937), p. 54.

17. Allan Nevins and Frank Ernest Hill, *Ford: The Times, the Man, and the Company* (New York: Scribners, 1954). Hereafter cited as Nevins and Hill, Vol. I, p. 581.

18. Allan Nevins and Frank Ernest Hill, *Ford: Expansion and Challenge* (New York: Scribners, 1957). Hereafter to be cited as Nevins and Hill, Vol. II, p. 130.

19. *New York World,* July 18, 1919.

20. *New York Times,* April 11, 1915; August 22, 1915; September 4 and 8, 1915; November 12, 1915.

21. Nevins and Hill, Vol. II, p. 26.

22. Louis P. Lochner, *Henry Ford: America's Don Quixote* (New York: International, 1925), pp. 8–16.

23. *Ibid.,* pp. 19–24.

24. The reminiscences of many Ford employees attest to the heavy-handedness of Ford's practical joking: Wandersee, Seaman, Galamb, and Farkas, to name a few.

25. Lochner, *Henry Ford,* p. 23.

26. *Ibid.,* p. 25.

27. Newspaper references cited by Nevins and Hill, Vol. II, pp. 30–31.

28. *Ibid.,* pp. 34–35.

29. *Ibid.*

30. Nevins and Hill, Vol. II, p. 28.

31. Henry Ford's marked copy of Emerson's *Essays* in Accession 1. Box 2, Ford Archives.

32. Accession 1, Box 1, Ford Archives.

33. Nevins and Hill, Vol. II, pp. 40–42.

34. *Ibid.,* p. 41.

35. *Ibid.,* p. 45.

36. *Ibid.,* p. 50.

37. Letter from Gaston Plantiff to Henry Ford, January 11, 1916. Accession 66, Box 1, Ford Archives; reference to Mrs. Boissevain, Nevins and Hill, Vol. II, p. 37.

38. Nevins and Hill, Vol. II, p. 51; Dr. Aked's review of the conference March 9, 1916. Accession 572, Box 9, Ford Archives.

39. Nevins and Hill, Vol. II, pp. 52 and 55.

40. Sward, *Legend of Henry Ford,* pp. 93–94.

41. Sworn statement of John Reed of *Metropolitan Magazine,* in *Henry Ford* v. *The Tribune Company et al.,* State of Michigan in the Circuit Court of the County of Macomb, Volume 9, pp. 6437–6443. Cited hereafter as *Tribune* Suit.

42. Nevins and Hill, Vol. II, pp. 129–130.

43. *Ibid.,* p. 55.

44. *Ibid.,* p. 34.

45. *Ibid.,* pp. 55–56.

46. *Ibid.,* p. 55.

47. *New York Times,* December 1, 1915.

48. Nevins and Hill, Vol. II, p. 56.

49. *Ibid.,* Chapter 3; aircraft proposal, pp. 64–65.

50. Sarah T. Bushnell, *The Truth About Henry Ford* (Chicago: Privately printed, 1922), p. 96.

51. Nevins and Hill, Vol. II, p. 85; Sward, *Legend of Henry Ford,* p. 99.

52. *New York World,* July 22, 1919.

53. *Ibid.,* July 22 and 17, 1919.

54. *Tribune* Suit, p. 5782; Sward, *Legend of Henry Ford,* pp. 103–104.

55. *Tribune* Suit, p. 5976.

56. "The Unveiling of Henry Ford," Editorial in *Nation,* July 26, 1919, p. 102.

57. Ray Stannard Baker, *Woodrow Wilson: Life and Letters* (Garden City, New York: Doubleday, 1927–1939), Volume VIII, p. 209.

58. "Why Henry Ford Wants to be Senator," *World's Work,* September 1918, p. 522.

59. F. L. Black, *Reminiscences,* Ford Archives, p. 21.

60. *World's Work,* September 1918, p. 522.

61. Nevins and Hill, Vol. II, pp. 120–123.

62. Reprinted in a full-page political advertisement for Newberry. *Detroit Saturday Night,* October 26, 1918, p. 12.

63. Nevins and Hill, Vol. II, p. 122.

64. Cited in Sward, *Legend of Henry Ford,* p. 122.

65. *Ibid.*

66. *New York Times,* November 1, 1923.

67. Nevins and Hill, Vol. II, p. 129.

68. "Henry Ford Tells Just How Happy His Great Fortune Made Him," Interview with Upton Sinclair, *Reconstruction,* Vol. I, No. 5 (May 1919).

69. Adolf Hitler, *Mein Kampf* (Boston: Houghton Mifflin, Sentry Edition, n.d.), p. 639.

70. "Henry Ford at Bay," *Forum*, August 1919, p. 141.

71. "Notes on auto-camping trip with Henry Ford, Thomas A. Edison, H. S. Firestone, and others by John Burroughs." Note for August 8, 1919. Copy in Accession 940, Box 7, Ford Archives.

72. Sward, *Legend of Henry Ford*, p. 144; Nevins and Hill, Vol. II, pp. 314–315.

73. Reprinted in the *Detroit Times*, June 9, 1920.

74. Nevins and Hill, Vol. II, pp. 314–315.

75. Letter from Dr. Leo M. Franklin to Henry Ford, June 14, 1920. Accession 572, Box 2, Ford Archives.

76. Letter from E. G. Liebold to Rabbi Leo M. Franklin, June 23, 1920. Accession 572, Box 2, Ford Archives.

77. Sward, *Legend of Henry Ford*, p. 146.

78. Letter from Constantin von Sternberg to Henry Ford, September 23, 1921. Accession 572, Box 2, Ford Archives. Italics in original.

79. Letter from E. G. Liebold to C. von Sternberg, September 28, 1921. Accession 572, Box 2, Ford Archives.

80. Reprinted in "Ford's Propaganda in Munich," *Pipp's Weekly*, March 24, 1923, p. 7.

81. There is extensive correspondence on this matter in Accession 572, Box 2. A cable to Liebold from Ford Motor Company, Delaware, confirms the shipment of photographic copies and plates of "The Protocols."

82. *New York Times*, Editorial, December 1, 1920.

83. Letter from Gaston Plantiff to E. G. Liebold, January 18, 1921. Accession 62, Box 9, Ford Archives.

84. Letter from E. G. Liebold to Gaston Plantiff, January 26, 1921. Accession 62, Box 9, Ford Archives. Italics added.

85. Letter from Lars Jacobsen to E. G. Liebold, June 11, 1921. Written from Berlin. Accession 572, Box 2, Ford Archives.

86. Nevins and Hill, Vol. II, p. 316.

87. *The International Jew*, Vol. I, pp. 145 and 90, cited by Sward, *Legend of Henry Ford*, p. 150.

88. *The International Jew*, Vol. II, p. 244, cited as in note 87.

89. *The International Jew*, Vol. IV, p. 181, cited as in note 87.

90. *New York Times*, April 20, 1924; Nevins and Hill, Vol. II, pp. 305–307.

91. *New York Times*, April 20, 1924.

92. *Ibid.*

93. *Ibid.*

94. *The Detroit News,* June 1, 1922.

95. *New York Times,* April 20, 1924.

96. *Ibid.,* February 14, 1922.

97. Nevins and Hill, Vol. II, pp. 310–311.

98. *The Ford Interview on Muscle Shoals.* A composite interview from various newspapers, printed in booklet form, and part of the Ford propaganda effort surrounding the Muscle Shoals bid. Accession 572, Box 9, Ford Archives.

99. *New York Times,* March 18, 1922.

100. *Ibid.,* March 21, 1927.

101. *Ibid.,* April 27, 1927.

102. *Ibid.,* April 22, 1927.

103. *Ibid.*

104. Sward, *Legend of Henry Ford,* pp. 153–157; Nevins and Hill, Vol. II, p. 319.

105. Sward, *Legend of Henry Ford,* p. 152; Nevins and Hill, Vol. II, p. 319, comment on Cameron's "perfect aplomb."

106. *New York Times,* July 8, 1927.

107. *Ibid.,* July 8, 1927.

108. Benjamin Stolberg, *The Story of the C.I.O.,* p. 116. Cited in Allan Nevins and Frank Ernest Hill, *Ford: Decline and Rebirth* (New York: Scribners, 1962), pp. 150–151.

109. Harry Bennett, *We Never Called Him Henry* (New York: Fawcett Publications, 1951), p. 65.

110. Norman Cohn, "The Myth of the Jewish World Conspiracy," *Commentary,* Vol. 41, No. 6 (June 1966), p. 38.

CHAPTER 5

1. Gregory Rochlin, *Griefs and Discontents* (Boston: Little, Brown, 1965), p. 184.

2. Allan L. Benson, *The New Henry Ford* (New York: Funk and Wagnalls, 1923), pp. 15–23.

3. Edward B. Litogot, *Reminiscences,* Ford Archives, p. 30.

4. Edgar A. Guest, "Henry Ford Talks About His Mother," *American Magazine,* July 1923, pp. 11–15 and 118–120.

5. William L. Stidger, "I've been helped by everybody," *True Story Magazine.* Undated but probably 1933. Clipping on file, Ford Archives.

6. Benson, *New Henry Ford*, pp. 28–30. See also William A. Simonds, *Henry Ford* (London: Michael Joseph, 1946), p. 21.

7. Margaret Ford Ruddiman, "Memories of My Brother Henry Ford," *Michigan History*, Vol. 37, No. 3, September 1953, p. 243.

8. *Ibid.*, p. 16.

9. Fred Strauss, *Reminiscences*, Ford Archives, pp. 37–38.

10. Mrs. Ruddiman, *Reminiscences*, Transcript of Interview, November 29, 1951, pp. 146–148.

11. Ruddiman, "Memories," pp. 253–254.

12. Ann Hood Manuscript, Ford Archives, p. 61. Benson, *New Henry Ford*, p. 33.

13. Ruddiman, *Reminiscences*, Transcript of Interview, November 5, 1951, p. 35.

14. Ruddiman, "Memories," p. 236. Emphasis added.

15. *Ibid.*, p. 249.

16. *Ibid.*, p. 248. Emphasis added.

17. *Ibid.*, p. 255.

18. Benson, *New Henry Ford*, p. 34.

19. Horace Lucien Arnold and Fay Leone Faurote, *Ford Methods and Ford Shops* (New York: The Engineering Magazine Company, 1915), p. 9.

20. Ruddiman, "Memories," p. 255.

21. Strauss, *Reminiscences*, p. 2.

22. *Ibid.*, pp. 3–4.

23. Benson, *New Henry Ford*, p. 35; Simonds, *Henry Ford*, p. 28; Ann Hood Manuscript, p. 61.

24. Ruddiman, "Memories," p. 255.

25. Benson, *New Henry Ford*, pp. 50–51.

26. Allan Nevins and Frank Ernest Hill, *Ford: The Times, the Man, and the Company* (New York: Scribners, 1954), p. 108.

27. Ruddiman, "Memories," pp. 257–258.

28. *Ibid.*, pp. 258–259.

29. Ruddiman, *Reminiscences*, Transcript of Interview, November 20, 1959, p. 94.

30. Benson, *New Henry Ford*, p. 25.

31. Rochlin, *Griefs and Discontents*, p. 184.

32. *Ibid.*, pp. 191–192.

33. Accession 572, Box 1. Written on three pages of 5½ x 8½ paper dated October 28, 1913. The first page bears a sketch of the farm

house, the field, and the log with the bird's nest. Punctuation has been added and spelling corrected where the original might have proved misleading.

34. Ann Hood Manuscript, p. 24.

35. Ruddiman, "Memories," p. 238.

36. Guest, "Henry Ford Talks," p. 11.

37. *Ibid.*, p. 119.

38. Ruddiman, *Reminiscences*, Transcript of Interview, November 5. 1951, p. 12.

39. *Ibid.*, p. 131.

40. Erik H. Erikson, *Young Man Luther* (New York: Norton, 1962), pp. 111–112. Emphasis added.

41. Ruddiman, *Reminiscences*, Transcript of Interview, November 21, 1951, p. 75.

42. Samuel S. Marquis, *Henry Ford, an Interpretation* (Boston: Little, Brown, 1923), p. 52.

43. *Ibid.*, pp. 136–137.

44. C. E. Sorensen, *My Forty Years with Ford* (New York: Norton, 1956), pp. 18–19.

45. *Ibid.*, p. 12.

46. J. L. McCloud, *Reminiscences,* Ford Archives, pp. 402-403.

47. Stidger, "I've been helped," p. 82. Accession 588 for gifts to Bryant family. Accession 1, Box 47, for help to William Ford. Accession 1, Box 12, for the Will.

48. *Detroit News Tribune*, October 15, 1911; clipping of Associated Press dispatched from Detroit, April 12, 1938, Ford Archives.

49. Sigmund Freud, *The Problem of Anxiety* (New York: Norton and the *Psychoanalytic Quarterly*, 1963), p. 115.

50. *New Outlook*, September 1934, p. 62.

51. *Ibid.*, pp. 62–63.

52. Gustav Munchow, *Reminiscences,* Ford Archives, pp. 76–77.

53. Ruddiman, "Memories," pp. 268–269.

54. C. T. Bush, *Reminiscences*, Interview with Orville Foster and C. T. Bush, Ford Archives, p. 27.

55. Allan Nevins and Frank Ernest Hill, *Ford: Decline and Rebirth* (New York: Scribners, 1962), p. 58; *New Outlook*, September 1934, p. 63.

56. A. M. Wibel, *Reminiscences*, Ford Archives, p. 103.

57. E. G. Liebold, *Reminiscences*, Ford Archives, p. 384.

58. Farm acreage, Accession 44, Box 18; *Ann Arbor News*, September 5, 1951.

59. J. K. Smith, *Reminiscences*, Ford Archives, p. 49.

60. *Science*, Vol. 91, No. 2368, May 17, 1940.

61. "Ford Seeks a New Balance for Industry," *New York Times Magazine*, May 29, 1932, p. 4.

62. George Brown, *Reminiscences*, Ford Archives, p. 96.

63. Marquis, *Henry Ford*, pp. 160, 164–165.

64. R. T. Walker, *Reminiscences*, Ford Archives, pp. 171–185.

65. Liebold, *Reminiscences*, pp. 365, 378–379.

66. Howard Simpson, *Reminiscences*, Ford Archives, p. 49.

67. Harold Hicks, *Reminiscences*, Ford Archives, p. 31.

68. Joseph Galamb, *Reminiscences*, Ford Archives, p. 134; McCloud, *Reminiscences*, pp. 249–251.

69. Hicks, *Reminiscences*, pp. 25–26.

70. L. S. Sheldrick, *Reminiscences*, Ford Archives, pp. 187–188.

71. Sorensen, *My Forty Years*, p. 27.

72. Sheldrick, *Reminiscences*, pp. 274–275.

73. Sorensen, *My Forty Years*, p. 27.

74. *Ibid.*, p. 28.

75. Arnold and Faurote, *Ford Methods and Ford Shops*, p. 19.

76. Sigmund Freud, *Group Psychology and the Analysis of the Ego* (New York: Bantam, 1960), p. 71.

77. Sigmund Freud, "Libidinal Types," in *Character and Culture. The Collected Papers of Sigmund Freud* (New York: Collier Books, 1963), pp. 212–213.

78. Marquis, *Henry Ford*, p. 117.

79. Barrington Moore, Jr., *Social Origins of Dictatorship and Democracy* (Boston: Beacon Press, 1966), p. 20.

80. Upton Sinclair, "Henry Ford Tells," in *Reconstruction*, Vol. 1, No. 5 (May 1919).

81. *New York Times*, October 29, 1921.

82. *Ibid.*, January 3, 1923.

83. Sinclair, "Henry Ford Tells."

84. Allan Nevins and Frank Ernest Hill, *Ford: Expansion and Challenge* (New York: Scribners, 1957), p. 342.

85. Sorensen, *My Forty Years*, p. 13.

86. Roy Schuman, *Reminiscences*, Ford Archives, pp. 34–35.

87. Norman Beasley, *Knudsen* (New York: McGraw-Hill, 1947), p. 70.

88. Liebold, *Reminiscences,* p. 1138.

89. Schuman, *Reminiscences,* p. 27.

90. Heinz Hartmann, *Ego Psychology and the Problem of Adaptation* (New York: International Universities Press, 1964), pp. 53–54.

91. *New York Times,* January 3, 1923.

CHAPTER 6

1. Allan Nevins and Frank Ernest Hill, *Ford: Expansion and Challenge* (New York: Scribners, 1957), p. 257. Hereafter to be cited as Nevins and Hill, Vol. II.

2. *Ibid.*

3. "Mr. Ford Doesn't Care," *Fortune,* December 1933, pp. 132–133.

4. Ford Motor Company, General Letter No. 1533, December 3, 1924, Accession 78, Ford Archives.

5. F. Hadas, *Reminiscences,* Nevins and Hill, Vol. II, p. 265.

6. Nevins and Hill, Vol. II, p. 267.

7. *Cram's Automotive Reports,* June 18, 1927, p. 1.

8. J. Dalton and H. Tipper, "Percentage of Ford Gain Slips Behind Other Leaders," *Automotive Industries,* March 22, 1923, p. 651.

9. Henry Ford, *My Life and Work* (Garden City, New York: Doubleday, 1923), pp. 92–93.

10. *Dodge* Suit, Record on Appeal, Testimony of C. Harold Wills, pp. 582–660.

11. H. H. Gerth and C. Wright Mills, *From Max Weber: Essays in Sociology* (New York: Oxford University Press, 1958), p. 216.

12. *Pipp's Weekly,* January 19, 1924, pp. 4–5.

13. *Ibid.,* May 15, 1920, p. 7.

14. Howard Simpson, *Reminiscences,* Ford Archives, p. 122.

15. F. L. Black, *Reminiscences,* Ford Archives, p. 128.

16. Hadas, *Reminiscences,* Nevins and Hill, Vol. II, p. 269.

17. Simpson, *Reminiscences,* p. 111.

18. J. Galamb, *Reminiscences,* Ford Archives, p. 140.

19. C. Martindale, *Reminiscences,* Ford Archives, pp. 12–13.

20. Simpson, *Reminiscences,* p. 122.

21. *Ibid.*

22. C. E. Sorensen, *My Forty Years with Ford* (New York: Norton, 1956), pp. 5–6.

23. Harry Bennett, *We Never Called Him Henry* (New York: Fawcett Publications, 1951), p. 5.

24. *Ibid.*, p. 63.

25. Sorensen, *My Forty Years*, p. 34. Emphasis added.

26. Bennett, *We Never Called Him Henry*, p. 30.

27. Black, *Reminiscences*, pp. 130–131.

28. J. L. McCloud, *Reminiscences*, Ford Archives, p. 407.

29. Black, *Reminiscences*, p. 131.

30. E. G. Liebold, *Reminiscences*, Ford Archives. He specifically mentioned the Schiff family.

31. *Automotive Industries*, February 3, 1921, p. 243.

32. Cablegrams: Liebold to Anderson, December 31, 1920. Anderson to and from Liebold, January 3, 1921; Telegrams: Anderson to and from Liebold, January 25, 1921. Accession 285, Box 9, Ford Archives.

33. Letter from W. C. Anderson to Edsel Ford, February 22, 1921. Accession 6, Box 30, Ford Archives.

34. "The Ford Riddle," *Detroit Saturday Night*, February 5, 1921, p. 1.

35. Black, *Reminiscences*, p. 134.

36. Charles Voorhees, *Reminiscences*, Ford Archives, p. 13.

37. Sorensen, *My Forty Years*, p. 296.

38. *Ibid.*, p. 46.

39. Liebold, *Reminiscences*, p. 198.

40. Sorensen, *My Forty Years*, pp. 36–37.

41. *Ibid.*, pp. 31–32.

42. R. T. Walker, *Reminiscences*, Ford Archives, pp. 113–115.

43. *Ibid.*, pp. 115 and 186.

44. M. Bricker, *Reminiscences*, Ford Archives, pp. 53–55.

45. *Ibid.*, p. 58.

46. *Ibid.*, pp. 55–56.

47. *Ibid.*, p. 56.

48. *Ibid.*

49. Ernest Kanzler, interview with Nevins and Hill, June 11, 1956. Accession 940, Box 9, Ford Archives.

50. Galamb, *Reminiscences*, p. 132.

51. Liebold, *Reminiscences*, p. 201.

52. Black, *Reminiscences*, p. 53.

53. Galamb, *Reminiscences*, p. 131.

54. L. S. Sheldrick, *Reminiscences*, Ford Archives, pp. 81-82.

55. T. F. Gehle, *Reminiscences,* Ford Archives, p. 109.

56. A. Esper, *Reminiscences,* Ford Archives, p. 70.

57. Galamb, *Reminiscences,* p. 132.

58. Black, *Reminiscences,* p. 127.

59. Nevins and Hill, Vol. II, p. 416.

60. Black, *Reminiscences,* p. 57.

61. Kanzler Memorandum dated January 26, 1926. Accession 572, Box 22, Ford Archives.

62. Black, *Reminiscences,* p. 57.

63. "Ford to Fight It Out with His Old Car," *New York Times,* Section VIII, December 26, 1926.

64. *Ibid.*

65. *Ibid.*

66. Sorensen, *My Forty Years,* pp. 219–223.

67. Compiled from figures furnished by R. L. Polk and Company, Ford Archives.

68. Nevins and Hill, Vol. II, p. 571.

69. *Ibid.,* pp. 457–458.

70. *Ibid.,* pp. 460 and 468.

71. *Ibid.,* p. 450.

72. W. C. Klann, *Reminiscences,* Ford Archives, pp. 234–235.

73. *Ibid.,* pp. 253–257.

74. *Ibid.,* pp. 262–274.

75. P. E. Haglund, *Reminiscences,* Ford Archives, p. 66.

76. *Ibid.,* pp. 70–71.

77. *Ibid.,* p. 72.

78. *Ibid.,* pp. 67–68.

79. Sorensen, *My Forty Years,* p. 51.

80. H. C. Doss, *Reminiscences,* Ford Archives, pp. 56–57.

81. *Ibid.,* pp. 68–69.

82. Norman Beasley, *Knudsen* (New York: McGraw-Hill, 1947), pp. 139 and 222.

83. *Ibid.*

84. Alfred P. Sloan, Jr., *My Years with General Motors* (Garden City, New York: Doubleday, 1964), p. 140.

85. *Ibid.*

86. Nevins and Hill, Vol. II, p. 168.

87. Ford, *My Life and Work*, p. 86.

88. Sorensen, *My Forty Years*, p. 55.

89. Liebold, *Reminiscences*, p. 2540.

90. Sorensen, *My Forty Years*, Chapter 20.

91. Black, *Reminiscences*, p. 87.

92. Sorensen, *My Forty Years*, p. 312. Emphasis added.

93. McCloud, *Reminiscences*, p. 338.

94. Doss, *Reminiscences*, p. 51.

95. Sheldrick, *Reminiscences*, pp. 87–88.

96. Cited by Allan Nevins and Frank Ernest Hill, *Ford: Decline and Rebirth* (New York: Scribners, 1962), p. 139.

97. *Ibid.*, Chapter 6.

98. Keith Sward, *The Legend of Henry Ford* (New York: Rinehart, 1948), Chapters 22–28.

99. Frank C. Riecks, *Reminiscences*, Ford Archives, p. 104.

100. Black, *Reminiscences*, p. 135.

101. Sward, *Legend of Henry Ford*, pp. 445–446.

102. Letter from E. G. Liebold to Henry Ford, May 10, 1944. Accession 587, Box 3, Ford Archives.

103. Bennett, *We Never Called Him Henry*, p. 167.

104. Black, *Reminiscences*, p. 102.

105. Deposition of Henry Ford II in *Harry Ferguson and Harry Ferguson Inc.* v. *Ford Motor Company et al.* District Court of the United States, Southern District of New York. January 1950. Accession 375, Box 2, Ford Archives.

CHAPTER 7

1. J. A. Schumpeter, *History of Economic Analysis* (New York: Oxford University, 1959), pp. 554–557, 645–647, 892–898.

2. J. E. Sawyer, "Entrepreneurial Studies," *Business History Review*, Vol. 32, No. 4 (1958).

3. T. C. Cochran, "The Legend of the Robber Barons," *Explorations in Entrepreneurial History*, May 1949, p. 2.

4. J. R. T. Hughes, "Eight Tycoons: "The Entrepreneur and American History," in R. L. Andreano, ed., *New Views on American Economic Development* (Cambridge, Mass.: Schenkman Publishing Company, Inc., 1965), p. 275.

5. J. G. March and H. A. Simon, *Organization* (New York: Wiley, 1958), pp. 34 ff.

6. Alfred D. Chandler, Jr., *Strategy and Structure* (Cambridge, Mass.: The M.I.T. Press, 1962), p. 373.

7. Philip Selznick, *Leadership in Administration* (Evanston, Illinois: Row Peterson, 1957), pp. 109–110.

8. Daniel Katz and Robert L. Kahn, *The Social Psychology of Organizations* (New York: Wiley, 1966), pp. 308–309.

9. C. E. Sorensen, *My Forty Years with Ford* (New York: Norton, 1956), Chapter 3.

10. Chandler, *Strategy and Structure,* p. 380.

11. *Ibid.*